IF IT BLEEDS, IT LEADS

That's an old piece of newspaper insider advice, and it has been transmitted to those in radio, television, video, Internet, cable news, and reality programming. Basically, the theory goes, the use of violence or the threat of violence helps news organizations sell their show, soap, and SUVs. Dan Rather said it once, quite clearly, at a speech he gave at the National Press Club in the mid 1980s: The news is all about "death."

There are the stories on the news every day: suicide bombings, war, deadly diseases, animal attacks, assassinations, car crashes, homicides, suicides, drownings, falls, murder-suicides, workplace violence, drive-by shootings, school shootings, sniper incidents, celebrity deaths, gangland killings, killings, killings, and killings, as well as near-death experiences like abductions, kidnappings, tortures, and suicide attempts. Yes, sex appears in the mix, as distraction and titillation, but death and fear of death are the dominant forces behind the news.

The media are *driven* by stories of death. . . .

THE
COPYCAT
EFFECT

How the Media and
Popular Culture
Trigger the Mayhem
in Tomorrow's Headlines

Loren Coleman, M.S.W.

PARAVIEW POCKET BOOKS
New York London Toronto Sydney

PARAVIEW
191 Seventh Avenue, New York, NY 10011

POCKET BOOKS, a division of Simon & Schuster, Inc.
1230 Avenue of the Americas, New York, NY 10020

Library of Congress Cataloging-in-Publication Data

Coleman, Loren.
    The copycat effect : how the media and popular culture trigger the
    mayhem in tomorrow's headlines / by Loren Coleman—1st Paraview
    Pocket Books trade pbk. ed.
        p. cm.
    Includes bibliographical references and index.
    ISBN 0-7434-8223-9 (alk. paper)
        1. Mass media—Social aspects. 2. Popular culture—Psychological aspects.
    3. Imitation. 4. Contagion (Social psychology) I. Title.

HM1206.C646 2004
303.6—dc22   2004050139

First Paraview Pocket Books trade paperback edition September 2004

10 9 8 7 6 5 4 3 2 1

POCKET and colophon are registered trademarks of Simon & Schuster, Inc.

Designed by Jaime Putorti

Manufactured in the United States of America

For information regarding special discounts for bulk purchases,
please contact Simon & Schuster Special Sales at 1-800-456-6798
or business@simonandschuster.com.

For
Nellie Gray,

the grandmother I never knew,
as she was shot during a murder-suicide,
and died on Valentine's Day, 1940.

Contents

Window to the World

You may vaguely remember the incident. It came over the television and radio as a "news bulletin." The dateline was Washington, D.C. The details, viewed in retrospect, are shocking.

Frank Eugene Corder, who was immediately dubbed a "lone nut" by the media, had stolen a single-engine Cessna 150L plane from an airport north of Baltimore. He then headed south to the District of Columbia, flew over the National Zoological Park and down to the Mall, and apparently used the Washington Monument as a beacon. As he closed in on that Masonic obelisk just off the Beltway, Corder banked his plane into a U-turn over the Ellipse and flew low over the White House South Lawn, clipped a hedge, knocked some branches off the magnolia tree planted by President Andrew Jackson, and crashed the plane into the White House—two stories below the presidential bedroom. This all began at 2300 hours military time, according to the White House.

There was an attack on the residence of the President and First Lady. And it happened not long ago. But few people today remember when the pilot of that Cessna launched his attack at the heart of our nation. It happened in 1994—on September 11.

Do you remember it? The incident obviously made quite an impact in the minds of some people. Coincidence? Conspiracy? Or something else?

In the wake of Frank Corder's crash and the resulting publicity, the White House was the focus of a cluster of attacks. On October 29, 1994, Francisco Martin Duran, a convicted felon, pulled a semiautomatic rifle from under his trench coat and fired at least twenty-nine shots as he ran down the south sidewalk of Pennsylvania Avenue, spraying the front of the White House with bullets. In December 1994 the White House saw five incidents. Four of them involved breaches of the mansion's grounds and ranged from fence jumping, to threats of a bomb in a car, to a homeless man waving a knife on a sidewalk outside the White House. That individual was shot by police and later died of his injuries. Then, on December 17, an unidentified person fired at least four bullets at the White House. One went through a dining room window, while others hit near the president's bedroom window on the second floor.

If you are surprised by the Corder story, you will likely be shaken by many of the other events recalled in this book. What is going on here? you wonder.

In short, we are living in times strongly influenced by "the copycat effect."

THE
COPYCAT
EFFECT

CHAPTER ONE

Beyond *The Sorrows of Young Werther*

> From the blood which flowed from the chair, it could be inferred that he had committed the rash act sitting at his bureau, and that he afterwards fell upon the floor. He was found lying on his back near the window. He was in full-dress costume.
>
> —Johann Wolfgang von Goethe,
> *The Sorrows of Young Werther*

A pattern underlies many of the events we hear about in the news every day. But the pattern is not openly discussed on your cable news network, over your twenty-four-hour news radio station, or in your newspaper. It is either overlooked or ignored.

The pattern is called the "copycat effect." It is also known as "imitation" or the "contagion effect." And what it deals with is the power of the mass communication and culture to create an epidemic of similar behaviors.

The copycat effect is the dirty little secret of the media. That doesn't prevent the media from calling the various epidemics of similar behaviors the "copycat phenomenon," often for shock impact. But, curiously, their use of the phrase seems to put a distance between the events and the reporting media, and allows them the stance that implies *they are not part of the problem.* But they are.

Sociologists studying the media and the cultural contagion of suicidal behaviors were the first to recognize the copycat effect. In 1974, University of California at San Diego sociologist David P. Phillips coined the phrase *Werther effect* to describe the copycat phenomenon. The name Werther comes from the 1774 novel *The Sorrows of Young Werther* by Johann Wolfgang von Goethe, the author of *Faust*. In the story, the youthful character Werther falls in love with a woman who is promised to another. Always melodramatic, Werther decides that his life cannot go on and that his love is lost. He then dresses in boots, a blue coat, and a yellow vest, sits at his desk with an open book, and, literally at the eleventh hour, shoots himself. In the years that followed, throughout Europe, so many young men shot themselves while dressed as Werther and seated at their writing desks with an open copy of *The Sorrows of Young Werther* in front of them that the book was banned in Italy, Germany, and Denmark.

Though an awareness of this phenomenon has been around for centuries, Phillips was the first to conduct formal studies suggesting that the Werther effect was, indeed, a reality—that massive media attention and the retelling of the specific details of a suicide (or, in some cases, untimely deaths) could increase the number of suicides.

The August 1962 suicide of Marilyn Monroe presents a classic modern-day example of the Werther effect. In the month that followed it, 197 individual suicides—mostly of young blond women— appear to have used the Hollywood star's suicide as a model for their own. The overall suicide rate in the U.S. increased by 12 percent for the month after the news of Monroe's suicide. But, as Phillips and others discovered, there was no corresponding decrease in suicides after the increase from the Marilyn Monroe–effect suicides. In other words, the star's suicide actually appeared to have caused a whole population of vulnerable individuals to complete° their own

---

°This book is careful in its use of language with regard to suicide and other events under discussion. I refrained from using the words "successful" or "failed" as these are connotations on the value of finishing the acts noted. In-deaths, over and above what would be normally expected. This is the copycat effect working with a vengeance.

Before the appearance of the Internet and cable news, the significance of stories in newspapers, on the radio, and via broadcast television news could be tracked rather well. In a 1979 study on imitation and suggestion, Phillips found an increase in the rate of automobile fatalities immediately after publicized suicides. The more publicity the suicide story received, the higher the automobile fatality rate. As might be expected, the motor vehicle fatalities were most frequent in the region where the suicide story was publicized. More surprising was the fact that younger people dying in vehicle crashes tended to follow reports of younger suicide victims, while older people dying in vehicle crashes tended to follow reports of older suicide victims. This was a striking example of peer group imitation, modeling, and suggestion.

Phillips also managed to get a handle on how long the effect lasts. In examining a two-week period beginning two days prior to the publicized suicide and ending eleven days later, he found that automobile fatalities increased by 31 percent in the three-day period after a suicide was reported in the media. The increase appears to have a lesser seven-day mirror peak as well. As we will see, this "effects period" finding extends to other types of contagious behavior, not just suicides.

Phillips is quite certain that no other variables are involved in the increase in suicides. "The increase in the suicide rate was not due to the effect of weekday or monthly fluctuations in motor vehicle fatalities, to holiday weekends, or to yearly linear trends," he reported, as his study had taken these other time variables into consideration.

---

stead, I used the word "completed." Also, as survivors of suicide object to the use of the phrase "committing suicide," I have used "die by suicide," whenever possible. Some references from old articles contain language that may be considered inappropriate today, but I have, of course, retained the original phraseology within quotations.

I became interested in the Werther effect as a university-based public policy researcher and author in the 1980s, following an explosion of copycat teen suicides throughout America at that time. In 1987, I wrote the first book on that situation, *Suicide Clusters,* to heighten awareness of the situation at a time when professionals and the media would hardly acknowledge the problem even existed. The book was dedicated to David Phillips for his groundbreaking work, which had been largely ignored by most scholars up to that time.

Suicide clusters of the 1980s would be replaced by the school shootings of the 1990s, almost all conducted by suicidal male youth. The copycat effect had merely shifted its target as the media had shifted its focus. School violence has been around for a long time, but the media-driven contagion of modern school shootings dates back to February 2, 1996, when Barry Loukaitis, a 14-year-old boy in Moses Lake, Washington, killed two students and a math teacher. He ended his rampage by saying, "This sure beats algebra, doesn't it?" Loukaitis had taken the expression directly from the Stephen King novel, *Rage,* which he had really liked and which was about a school killing. Loukaitis said his murderous loss of control was inspired by *Rage,* Pearl Jam's music video *Jeremy,* and the movies *Natural Born Killers* and *The Basketball Diaries.* Unfortunately, the explosive media attention to Loukaitis's school shooting triggered a series of similar events. Today, Stephen King says he wishes he had never written *Rage.*

As the era of school shootings, celebrity suicide copycats, cult deaths, and workplace violence was just beginning, Riaz Hassan, a sociology professor at Flinders University, Australia, essentially replicated Phillips's studies in Australia and confirmed the links between reporting of suicides and further suicides completed. He drew his data from two major metropolitan newspapers, identifying the stories that reported suicides between 1981 and 1990. He then examined the daily suicide rates between 1981 and 1990 and analyzed whether or not the newspaper stories had an effect on the number of suicides in the days following.

Hassan defined the "impact" of a suicide story by noting "the location of the newspaper story, by the size of the newspaper story and headline and by a presence or absence of photographs." Hassan found that the suicide rates of males increased significantly in the three-day period after a suicide, which included the day of publication of high-impact reports and the two subsequent days.

By early 2000, researchers Madelyn Gould of Columbia University and Steven Stack of Wayne State University would note that the contagion of the copycat effect was now a certainty in terms of suicides.

A mere twenty years ago, people did not believe the copycat effect existed. Academics and sociologists debated whether broadcasts of violence lead to other violence, and, of course, the media was quick to deny any linkage. But in the middle of the first decade of the twenty-first century, the reality has now become obvious. Few people realize that there are two to three times as many suicides as homicides in America, and that four out of five youthful suicides are young males. The copycat effect is a force to be dealt with and faced head-on.

The scope of the copycat effect is being realized. We are now seeing the impact of the copycat effect across many kinds of media-discussed violence. Even more alarming, a cross-contagion is taking place. Some school-shooting incidents are followed by workplace violence, mass killings, or other dramatic suicides or accidents. The pages that follow will illuminate these all-too-obvious patterns and reveal the covert, or twilight, information occurring in suicide clusters, workplace shootings, school violence, and the other "breaking news" that bursts onto your screen or radio every day, day in and day out, and leads directly into tomorrow's next series of violent events—all due to the copycat effect.

CHAPTER TWO

Death Sells

I f it bleeds, it leads. That's an old piece of newspaper insider advice, and it has been transmitted to those in radio, television, video, the Internet, cable news, and reality programming too. Basically, the theory goes, the use of violence or the threat of violence helps news organizations sell their shows, soap, and SUVs. Dan Rather said it once, quite clearly, in a speech he gave at the National Press Club in the mid-1980s: The news is all about death.

These are the stories on the news every day: suicide bombings, war, deadly diseases, animal attacks, assassinations, car crashes, homicides, suicides, drownings, falls, murder-suicides, workplace violence, drive-by shootings, school shootings, sniper incidents, celebrity deaths, gangland killings, killings, killings, and killings, as well as near-death experiences like abductions, kidnappings, tortures, and suicide attempts. Yes, sex appears in the mix, as distraction and titillation, but death and the fear of death are the dominant forces behind the news.

The media are driven by stories of death. In psychological terms, the mastery of this time of passage is seemingly made more manifest by practicing, thinking, and coming close to but placing some distance between death and us. What better way for the news-entertainment business to take advantage of this than to make it a major part of their programming? Happy stories don't sell, we are told, and people want their tornadoes, collapsed walkways, big-cat attacks, and crashed helicopter stories. The media is more than willing to supply them. *Death sells. If it bleeds, it leads.* The words have commercial and directional meaning to the news departments, and the mode of operation was established without anyone really thinking deeply about its implications.

Take this "death orientation" and mix it with a hint of sensationalism that disregards the facts that there are more suicides than homicides, that most of the recent epidemics discussed by the media are not based on actual statistical threats to the majority of North Americans, and shazzam!—you have the recent warm weather of "outbreak" journalism. This kind of news treatment is most apparent during the summer. The media literally goes into a feeding frenzy about what new kind of terror and death they can cover in order to hold a media-conditioned news hungry audience in rapture. The media, like a monster octopus looking for its next victim, searches around trying to figure out from what hole its next meal will come. It is this kind of media atmosphere that allows the copycat effect to thrive, even when there are no humans doing the actual copying.

Bring On the Gators

The summer of 2001 began quietly enough, with local newspapers in Florida talking about some deathly events that—before the season was over—had everyone wondering if every lagoon in the Sunshine State was crawling with man-eating alligators. At first the stories were only of local interest. On May 4, 2001, an eight-foot alligator in a Venice pond killed Samuel Wetmore, 70, near his home in Sarasota County, Florida. On June 23, 2001, little Alexandria Murphy, 2, wandered from her Winter Haven backyard, then was dragged into Lake Cannon in Polk County, Florida, by a six-and-a-half-foot gator and killed.

Then all hell broke loose, with the media engaging in epidemic reporting, taking up the thread of gators and crocs as the next big new threat on the horizon. Alligators were popping up everywhere. By the end of that month, I had accounts crossing my desk of out-of-place caimans, alligators, and crocodiles being seen and caught in downstate New Hampshire (a two-and-a-half-foot caiman), in Manhattan's Central Park (a two-foot caiman) and, on the same day, June 27, 2001, Buffalo, New York (a four-foot alligator caught), and off an island in the middle of the Rhine River in Germany (a five-foot "crocodile" sighted but not caught).

The alligator attacks concentrated in Florida, however. On Sunday, July 1, 2001, a human arm that "appeared to have been bitten" off by an alligator according to a Reuters story of July 3, 2001, was found in a canal west of Fort Lauderdale, Florida. The rest of the body could not be found. A sort of high sad comedy was reached when Reuters published on July 3, 2001, this remark from a member of the Broward County Sheriff's Department: "We're sure if they survived and they're missing a right arm, they would have come forward by now. Detectives have no idea what happened with this body part, whether it was some sort of accident and the person was eaten by an alligator and this is what's left."

During the next week in July, echoes of the Florida gators were heard in the Midwest again. Authorities were reporting the sightings of three alligators near Andrews, Indiana, in the Wabash River close to the Highway 105 bridge. No one was hurt but armed officers were trying to locate the critters.

Back in Florida, Tammy Woehle, 22, was out walking her dog before dark on Big Talbot Island, near Jacksonville, when an eight-foot-long alligator attacked her, according to a report from July 9, 2001. The gator grabbed and ripped part of the muscle out of her leg and pulled her to the ground. The news accounts almost made you feel the gator was a sneaky gremlin because it crept up to her as she stood on a sandy beach, away from the water's edge and away from high grass. She escaped with a six-inch wound on her thigh. Before the attack, the Florida Fish and Wildlife Conservation Commission had held a news conference to calm the public. They had noted that the seven alligator attacks in Florida in 2001 were slightly below average. Talk about bad public relations timing! The media would have nothing to do with it. The Woehle attack was widely reported, and it was clear to the public, from what they were hearing in the press, that this was a dangerous summer. Then drumbeats announced that a much more sinister danger was lurking just off-shore.

The Summer of the Shark

As the sun began to set over peaceful Langdon Beach at the Gulf Islands National Seashore near Pensacola, Florida, Jessie Arbogast, 8, was splashing around in the seemingly safe, shallow water. Then suddenly a seven-foot-five-inch-long bull shark attacked the innocent boy and severed his arm. Arbogast was wrestled from the shark by the heroic efforts of his uncle, Vance Flosenzier, but the boy bled out before paramedics arrived; he survived but is unable to talk to this day. The date of the attack was July 6, 2001, and on that day the media turned their attention from Florida's alligators to a more global threat, that of the shark. Of course, the case of the Arbogast lad is tragic and sad, but what the media did with it—use it as some kickoff to their reality sensationalism—only made things worse. It was *Jaws* come to life for the media.

Before you could swim a lap in 2001, most media outlets had decided to report on every shark attack incident as it occurred. Right after the near-death incident involving the Arbogast boy, a New Yorker lost his leg in a shark attack in the Bahamas. A surfer was bitten on July 15, a few miles from the Arbogast attack. On July 16, another surfer was bitten, but this time in the waters off San Diego. The tide of shark stories was coming in. A thresher shark bit a lifeguard off Long Island, New York. A tiger shark chased spear fishers swimming in the beautiful waters of Hawaii.

By August 2001, television news footage, shot from helicopters flying off Florida, showed hundreds of sharks grouping in the Gulf of Mexico. The suggestion was that they were gathering to attack humans. At one Florida beach that month, six people reported being attacked by sharks over one weekend. None of the "bites" were serious, but it didn't stop television network coverage by four news organizations reporting live from that Daytona area beach. Reporter Mark Johnson of the *Daytona Beach News-Journal* observed that as the national camera crews arrived, the tourists departed. It was like a scene out of *Jaws*, and the media did not hide the association at all.

Peter Benchley's novel *Jaws*, and the successful movie Steven Spielberg made from it in 1975, concerns a great white shark that kept attacking people trying to enjoy their summer on a New England resort island. It is a frightening movie that reaches for a primal fear in humans of sharks, and furthers the myth that sharks stalk humans and like eating them. The book and film had been the justification for widespread killing of sharks. Most shark attacks on humans, however, are cases of mistaken identity—for example, when humans swimming or on surfboards are taken for seals. In a recent interview, Benchley wishes he had never written *Jaws*: "What I now know, which wasn't known when I wrote *Jaws*," he told the *Sydney Morning Herald* of April 7, 2000, "is that there is no such thing as a rogue shark which develops a taste for human flesh."

National network news began their broadcasts on September 2, 2001, with the report of another fatality when 10-year-old David Peltier was attacked by a shark at Virginia Beach, Virginia, and died in the local hospital the following day. Sergei Zaloukaev, 26, died in an attack off Cape Hatteras, North Carolina, the next day, and his girlfriend, Natalia Slobodskaya, 23, lost a leg. Then on September 4, 2001, *Time* magazine ran a cover issue that designated this outbreak of 2001 the "Summer of the Shark." But suddenly it seemed as if all the shark attacks had stopped at once. Of course, the only reason the shark attack coverage seemed to come to an abrupt end was that the events of September 11, 2001, took all the media's attention away from the beaches.

The media has rarely acknowledged the fact that the summer of the shark attacks was media-driven, however. The total of seventy-six unprovoked attacks worldwide in 2001 was less than the eighty-five recorded in 2000. The actual fatalities were down from twelve to five in the same period, according to George Burgess, director of the University of Florida's International Shark Attack File. The "Summer of the Shark" was all hype. "Last year was anything but an average year, but that's because it was more like the summer of the media feeding frenzy," Burgess told the Associated Press in 2002.

And how about those swarms of sharks filmed off the southwest coast of Florida? Audiences around the globe were treated to repeat broadcasts of those hundred or more sharks swimming in a huge school up the coast. Television news people characterized it as a major scare for life and limb, but shark migrations occur annually and are as natural as birds flying south for the winter. But that, of course, was too boring a story—and, well, yes, less life-threatening.

Abducted by the Media

On September 16, 2002, after another summer in which the media had demonstrated a remarkable ability for overstatement, *The Christian Science Monitor (CSM)* editorialized using the brilliant headline "Abducted by the Media."

Noting that the recent summers had produced, through "many headlines and news broadcasts, a parade of ongoing, out-of-proportion crises," the *CSM* commented that the media was revealing "a penchant for the bizarre rather than the factual. Most bizarre is a media tendency to speculate about a 'trend' when there is none."

It was becoming clear to media observers that, just as alligators and shark attacks had been exaggerated beyond the dimensions of the actual problem in 2001, we were seeing something similar happen with child abductions in 2002. Child kidnappings, Amber alerts, and Elizabeth Smart aside, missing and exploited children are certainly a national problem, but it was not one that in 2002 was on the increase. As the *CSM* observed, "Child abductions are not up, they're down. Without trivializing the seriousness of the crime, about 300 children are abducted annually in the US by strangers."

Likewise, in the summer of 2002, the West Nile virus was declared a great danger to Americans. As it developed, however, only a small number of people died (fifty-four), but as the *CSM* noted, "One would think from media reports that Americans are suffering the plague."

During the spring and summer of 2003, severe acute respiratory syndrome, the "SARS epidemic," replaced the hysteria of the West Nile virus. SARS first emerged in November 2002, in China's Guangdong Province, but by the first warm months of 2003 you would think it was spreading like wildfire all over the world. On April 23, 2003, *USA Today* was warning that health officials were saying that "if SARS is not contained, it could cause millions of deaths worldwide—and some of those deaths would almost certainly occur in the USA." The death drumbeat of the media was very clear. *USA Today* continued: "In terms of sheer numbers, the SARS epidemic so far pales in comparison to other worldwide epidemics. The Spanish flu of 1918–1919 killed roughly 30 million people, including about 675,000 Americans. Over the past 20 years, the slow-motion funeral march of AIDS has carried off 20 million people; 40 million more are poised to die in the next decade. Yet SARS is just beginning. The death toll could rise dramatically."

On June 24, 2003, the newspaper that publishes "All the News That's Fit to Print" did a special sciences spread on the "SARS Epidemic." *The New York Times* had proclaimed it the "Summer of SARS," just as surely as *Time* had crowned 2001 the "Summer of the Shark." The source of the disease was unknown and serious, but a look at the known death tolls in June 2003, when the "epidemic" peaked, reveals that worldwide there were 812 deaths, of which 348 were in China, 298 in Hong Kong, 84 in Taiwan, 32 in Singapore, and 38 in Canada.

For all the talk of wild animal attacks and deadly viruses sweeping the world, it is obvious the media misses the bigger picture daily, instead going for the melodramatic, the dramatic, and the sensational. If news organizations were really interested in talking about the most deadly animal around, for example, they would be doing more reports on mosquitoes, which, according to the World Health Organization, are responsible for two million deaths annually from encephalitis, dengue fever, malaria, and the West Nile virus, or the tsetse fly, which wipes out another 66,000 people every year. But news story about a mosquito just doesn't have the "bite" of a shark story, obviously.

The media loves melodrama. Sensationalism now rules the news. In the human realm, the media reinforces the events it covers. Otherwise it blows subjects out of all proportion to reality. The unjustified amount of attention it devotes to shark attacks and SARS, for example, demonstrates that the level of media coverage has no relation to the real impact these topics have on most people. As conservative commentator and friend of Newt Gingrich, historian William R. Forstchen, said to me in January 2004: "I have a higher chance of being struck by lightning than getting mad cow disease, but you won't know that by listening to the media." And while the media has no ability to increase or decrease the behaviors of alligators attacking Floridians or sharks biting swimmers worldwide or the spread of viruses, the contrivance of the media's feeding frenzies adds fuel to the fire that is the copycat effect.

CHAPTER THREE

Snipers Fall

The Washington, D.C., sniper stories followed the pattern of the most deadly seasonal items of interest to the media—with one big difference. In the case of these attacks by humans, these individuals were in control of the situation, and other humans began copycatting them.

The events of the fall of 2002, when the area around the nation's capital was held in the crosshairs of an unknown sniper's scope, are well known and need not be retold here in depth. The terror from a .223-caliber rifle lasted for twenty-three days, beginning September 14, 2002. The shooting spree resulted in what initially was thought to be at least thirteen people shot, supposedly at random, and ten of those victims killed. (By late 2003 the death toll would be said to be eleven, with five other people wounded.) Eventually, on October 22, 2002, after twists and turns in the case in which Montgomery County Police Chief Charles Moose's face became the most famous to come out of all the news conferences, two suspects, John Allen Muhammad, 41, and John Lee Malvo, 17, were arrested for the crimes. Their capture wasn't a matter of great detective work so much as the suspects making phone calls, leaving messages, and revealing themselves to the authorities in bizarre fashion. It became the media event of the fall of 2002, but buried in the "search for the sniper" (no one knew it involved two people until they were arrested) were copycats around the country, historic events that appeared to presage the 2002 sniper incidents, and hidden backstories of intrigue and possibility.

On the very day the D.C. snipers were caught, October 22, 2002, an editorial published in *The University Journal* of Southern Utah University commented: "Once this sniper is caught or stops shooting for some other reason, there could be copycat snipers all over the nation, just as there were school shootings." Little known to most Americans, and underreported by the press, the Beltway Sniper events had already spawned copycat sniper incidents throughout the nation—and abroad.

On the weekend of October 11–13, 2002, three random sniper incidents occurred near Christopher Morley Park, just off the Long Island Expressway. On October 15, two vehicles were hit by shots on I-71 near Ohio 95, in Morrow County, about fifty miles north of Columbus; no one was hurt. On October 11, 2002, in Lake Worth, Florida, someone took three shots in a quiet neighborhood and hit 5-year-old Wilson Calvert in the muscle near the spine. A suspect was never caught. Around the same time, according to KTLA-TV, Los Angeles County sheriff's detectives investigated a copycat sniper shooting at the Marshall Canyon Golf Course, in La Verne, California. A shot was fired and hit a tree on the eighth tee; no one was injured. Golfers said they saw a man with a rifle in a nearby parking lot.

Late in October, a British copycat sniper injured six people in London. One was a Labor member of Parliament. Police in London said the four-day shooting spree had "an eerie resemblance" to the Washington sniper series. All the attacks took place between October 12 and 16. The last victim, Bradford North MP Terry Rooney, was shot in the face in south London on October 16. Scotland Yard investigated and finally caught a suspect. A year later Jason Kemp, then 17, "began his campaign after watching TV news reports of the shootings carried out in the US in October last year, a court heard," according to the *South London News,* which called the sniper "a warped teenager." The story saw limited coverage in the U.K.

"He had been following the attacks of the Washington sniper and he glorified that sniper's actions. Like the sniper, he said he would avoid capture," said Simon Sandford, prosecuting at the Old Bailey. Kemp admitted firing his rifle at three people during a five-day period, which coincided with the D.C. sniper attacks. Kemp pleaded guilty to two charges of having the firearm with intent to commit an offense, two charges of assault occasioning actual bodily harm, and assault and beating, between October 12 and 16, 2002.

On Friday, October 18, 2002, a copycat sniper event occurred in Ankara, Turkey. A mysterious man shot and wounded seven people—six of them women—in a shooting spree the local authorities believed directly "imitates recent sniper attacks in the United States," according to the Canadian Press. The man, using a pellet gun, first shot an 18-year-old student on a busy street in the capital Ankara around noon on October 18. The individual escaped on foot and struck again in other nearby districts in the afternoon and late evening, shooting at a teacher, a nurse, three students, and another woman, most in their late teens. The police never caught the gunman.

Copycat sniper events continued after the capture of the D.C. snipers. Pittsburgh police were looking for a possible copycat sniper who shot and wounded a 9-year-old boy who was playing football at the McKinley Park field on October 23, 2002. The shots were fired from a wooded area overlooking the field. The injury was minor and no suspect was caught.

Meanwhile, on Halloween 2002, two teens were being charged in Memphis, Tennessee, for an alleged sniper plot planned for November in which they intended "to kill as many people as the DC sniper did in one day," local law enforcement said. Inspector J. D. King of the Memphis Police Department told reporter Giovanna Drpic of WREG Channel 3 TV news: "These individuals obviously had taken note of what happened there and wanted to do something spectacular."

The news of these sniper events was not covered widely; in fact, the local media was the only source of these the copycat sniper reports. In Cary, near Fayetteville, North Carolina, police were investigating five shootings during the third week in November that left bullet holes in an Embassy Suites, the Cary High School, Christ the King Lutheran Church, Saint Paul's Episcopal Church, and the windows of a parked car.

By the end of November 2002, police were concerned that a sniper might have shot twice at people in moving vehicles along State Road 33, near Lakeland, Florida. State troopers were investigating a link between the sniper incidents of October 26 and November 21 that took place in western Polk County. The police told the local newspaper that they had not ruled out the possibility that the two shootings were the work of someone inspired by the serial shootings in the Washington, D.C., area. "We have no evidence that the shootings are connected, but we have to consider the possibility," Florida Highway Patrol trooper Larry Coggins told the Lakeland *Ledger.* "And we have to ask, 'Do we have a copycat here shooting at vehicles?' " On October 26, two days after the two suspected snipers in the Washington area were arrested, a shot fired at about 9:05 P.M. from or near the Memorial Boulevard overpass of I-4 struck a 1995 Airstream on the interstate, just missing Wayne R. Haynes, 43, and the passenger, his 4-year-old daughter. The shooting sites were about fifteen miles apart. On November 21, at about 5 A.M., a bullet hit a 1999 tractor-trailer owned by Florida Food Tankers of Lake Wales and driven by Terry R. Miller of Winter Haven. Miller was driving north on State Road 33 near Deen Still Road.

A year after the sniper incidents in the D.C. area, a little known series of sniper killings popped up on the media radar and then disappeared. They were so similar in style and method that they could hardly be ignored for what they were, clear copycats of the Beltway snipers. In August 2003, three fatal "sniper-style" shootings took place outside convenience stores in Kanawha County, West Virginia, within a four-day period. At about 10:20 P.M. on Thursday, August 7, a woman was shot while pumping gas into her red Pontiac Firebird at a SuperAmerica store in Campbells Creek. The second fatal sniper shooting happened a little more than an hour later and ten miles away outside a Go-Mart in Cedar Grove, on U.S. Route 60, when Okey Meadows Jr., 26, was shot in the neck and killed. Then on Sunday night, August 10, George Carrier Jr., 34, of South Charleston, was shot in the head and killed while using a pay telephone outside a Charleston Go-Mart. Police acknowledged that the bullets in all three attacks were fired from the same caliber and class of weapon, all from more than thirty yards away. The *Charleston Gazette* noted that the shootings were "an eerie reminder of Washington, D.C., sniper shootings last year."

When the Associated Press decided to write up the story on August 17, they led with the obvious connection: "When a sniper preyed on the Washington, D.C., suburbs last year, Jeanie Patton feared she could be next, though she lived hundreds of miles away. She said, 'Mom, I'm almost afraid to go out. Something like that could happen here in West Virginia,' her mother, Joyce Patton, recalled. Jeanie Patton, 31, was shot in the head Thursday while pumping gasoline at a Speedway convenience store about five miles from her home."

While the story received little attention outside West Virginia and the D.C. area, it was reported widely in the United Kingdom. The Glasgow *Evening Times* of August 18, 2003, for example, noted that the FBI had joined the West Virginia sniper hunt and had quoted them as saying that a serial sniper appeared to be copying the killings of the previous year's Washington snipers. By November 2003, CNN and other news resources would occasionally mention that the West Virginia sniper incidents were still open cases and that local authorities were looking into a drug angle for the killings—although the families of the victims were outraged by this attempt to sweep the lack of arrests under the rug.

Meanwhile, also late in 2003, Ohio investigators were beginning to connect the copycat dots after 62-year-old Gail Knisley was killed by a sniper on November 25 as she was being driven to a doctor's appointment. Federal investigators now looked back into the eighteen shootings that had occurred along Interstate 270 in southern Franklin County, Ohio, in 2003. The new Ohio activity appeared concurrently with the media reports about the trials of the D.C.-area snipers. By early 2004, authorities linked twenty-four shooting incidents to an Ohio copycat sniper, with a few copycats of that uncaught shooter. During the last week of February 2004, reports of eight sniper incidents surfaced on highways near San Francisco.

Revealing the Truth

As it does for so many events, the media boiled the facts of the very complex D.C. sniper story down to the common denominators of death, fear of death, the randomness of death, and the alleged "lone nuts" that, underneath it all, are out there to get you. A few reporters did, however, note the historically cyclical nature of such events.

Before the Beltway pair worked their way into history, no multiple sniping incidents impacted the United States like the one committed by Charles Whitman, who was born in Lake Worth, Florida, in 1941. Early on the morning of August 1, 1966, Whitman killed his mother in her apartment and his wife at their home. At about 11:30 A.M., Whitman then climbed up to reach the University of Texas Tower (elevation of 231 feet), bringing along six guns, a shotgun, ammunition, a footlocker, knives, food, and water. On his way up, he clubbed the receptionist (who died later) on the twenty-eighth floor and killed two persons and wounded two others who were coming up the stairs from the twenty-seventh floor. From the observation deck of the tower, Whitman then opened fire on persons crossing the UT campus and on side streets, killing another ten people and wounding thirty-one more (one of whom died a week later). For ninety-six minutes he held the campus hostage. Finally, at 1:24 P.M., after several attempts, police and deputized private citizen Allan Crum reached the observation deck, where police officers Ramiro Martinez and Houston McCoy shot and killed Whitman. Altogether, seventeen persons were killed, including Whitman, and thirty-one were wounded in what is still regarded as one of the worst sniper events in modern American history.

Little known today is that this event encouraged police departments across the United States to develop what came to be special weapons and tactics (SWAT) teams, as Gary M. Lavergne points out in his excellent reference work on this subject, *A Sniper in the Tower: The Charles Whitman Murders*. The tower itself became a site of tragedy remembered and deaths produced. A series of suicides from the tower, along with the horror of Whitman's act, convinced the University of Texas Board of Regents to close the observation deck of the tower in 1975. Not until 1998 was a vote taken to reopen the tower, but only after the introduction of metal detectors and the building of protective fencing around the deck to discourage suicidal jumpers. With those changes in place, Whitman's sniper nest was reopened to the public in 1999.

The cultural influence of the Whitman event lives on in our society to such an extent that it colors how we look at any sniper event, the D.C. sniper incident included. From songs to movies, there are hints of Charles Whitman all around us. Singer Harry

Chapin wrote a long 1970's folk tune titled "Sniper," and Texan Kinky Friedman's facetious "The Ballad of Charles Whitman" carried on the tradition. Kurt Russell starred in *The Deadly Tower* (1975), later renamed *Sniper*, which was set at the Louisiana State Capitol because Texas officials would not allow UT Tower's use by the filmmakers. References to Whitman continue in Stanley Kubrick's *Full Metal Jacket*, Oliver Stone's *Natural Born Killers*, Rick Linklater's *Slacker*, and even in Ron Howard's *Parenthood*. Whitman is even credited with having an impact on the works of writer Stephen King and Unabomber Ted Kaczynski, as both have admitted. As the D.C. sniper horror unfolded, one lone sniper, Charles Whitman, was brought up, over and over again, from such diverse publications as the *Workers World* to the *Right Wing News*, from New Age tracts to less-than-mainstream Internet sites, demonstrating the widespread effect that this person's story was having on the D.C. sniper tale.

Oddly, the media never seemed to mention the more obvious sniper precursor to these D.C. incidents. As Peter Hernon recalls in his book *A Terrible Thunder: The Story of the New Orleans Sniper*, on December 31, 1972, in New Orleans, Mark James Essex began one of the most violent and deadly sniper attacks that any American city had ever seen. Mark Essex was a quiet African-American man who grew to hate whites in the Navy. Then he went to New York City's Harlem and aligned himself with the Eldridge Cleaver faction of the Black Panther party. In August 1972 he moved to New Orleans and began studying African culture, attempting to learn Swahili and Zulu. Hernon says that the killing of two black Southern University students at Baton Rouge during a standoff with sheriff's deputies motivated Essex. Essex had taken up the call of the Black Panther urban guerrilla faction, the Black Liberation Army, to kill police. Essex would do that and much more. Before Essex's sniper attacks were through, six hundred police officers and a helicopter gunship had been deployed to stop him. *The*

New York Times reported on January 8, 1973, "After a day of terror . . . New Orleans policemen, in a borrowed Marine helicopter . . . swooped out of rain and darkness to provide a mobile platform for police sharpshooters to hunt down snipers on the roof of the Downtown Howard Johnson's Motor Lodge. The dead sniper, who was dressed in green, was reported to have been riddled by tracer bullets." Ten would die (including Essex and four police officers) and thirteen were wounded (including one firefighter and four police officers).

The Washington, D.C., sniper case demonstrates the many facets of the copycat effect. The media promotes a huge story, which they understand only in terms of death and mayhem. It assumes a dominant place in the headlines, cable news, and nightly overviews of what is happening in our world. While the actual danger to the majority of media's audience is slight, it becomes an overwhelming focus. The mainstream media generally fails to examine the precursor events that foreshadowed or created an atmosphere in which this could occur. Copycat events do occur but are little known by most people because they are only reported on a local or regional basis. The media fails to examine its own role in these copycat events and merely goes about its business of finding the next hot death story. Then, when another death or breaking story comes along, yesterday's story is forgotten—until the next copycat event occurs. . . .

CHAPTER FOUR

Planes into Buildings

On November 20, 2003, the White House was briefly evacuated after a warning sounded that a small plane was flying within five miles of the restricted airspace around the presidential residence. Official sources later revealed that a "false blip" had appeared on radar and nothing had actually come close to the White House. Normal activities resumed about an hour after the scare.

It was a nervous month for government officials: Earlier, on November 10, Air Force fighter jets scrambled to intercept a private plane flying too close to the White House. The plane was later determined to be off course and not a threat. All reports of unauthorized planes around the White House have been taken seriously since the presidential residence was the target of Flight 93 on September 11, 2001; the passengers themselves forced this plane down in Pennsylvania in an apparent struggle with the terrorists. But few people remember that a small plane, in fact, was stolen for the express purpose of crashing it into the White House seven years before to the very day, on September 11, 1994. The events of September 11 are all too genuine.

Ellen Stele, 81, heard the screams of her 81-year-old husband Robert on September 11, 2001, and couldn't do anything to save him. But most people never heard about Robert and how an eleven-foot-long alligator near Sanibel, Florida, fatally attacked him as he walked his dog that day. There was something much larger on the media horizon that day. On September 11, 2001, four jet airliners, with Flight 11 being the first, were involved in the largest single homicidal-suicidal effort in history to bring bloodshed, death, and terror to the core of American society.

But several factors converged to prevent any immediate copycat effect after 9/11. To begin with, air travel in the United States was canceled for several days and resumed only slowly after that. Private planes were not allowed back into the air until after September 14, 2001; crop dusters were grounded for a longer period of time. Though sociologist David Phillips noted in 1978 that airplane accident fatalities normally increase just after newspaper stories about murder and suicide, a reverse effect was actually in play at the time. Historical studies conducted by sociologist Steven Stack and others have discovered a noticeable dip in suicides and related violent events when there is society-wide anguish, for example, in times of massive grieving in periods of wars and during economic depressions.

Though more subtle, the copycat effect from 9/11 is nevertheless in evidence. Soon after 5:00 P.M. on Saturday, January 5, 2002, a 15-year-old named Charles J. Bishop crashed the Cessna plane he had stolen into Tampa, Florida's forty-two-story Bank of America building. Bishop had clearly modeled his action on the September 11 terrorists' suicide plane crashes. Bishop left a suicide note behind saying as much, though most of the media merely paraphrased him as saying that he had "admired Osama bin Laden."

On February 6, 2002, Tampa authorities released actual copies of the note. Here is the transcription of what Bishop wrote, which was not widely reported:

I have prepared this statement in regards to the acts I am about to commit. First of all, Osama bin Laden is absolutely justified in the terror he has caused on 9-11. He has brought a mighty nation to its knees! God blesses him and the others who helped make September 11th happen.

The U.S. will have to face the consequences for its horrific actions against the Palestinian people and Iraqis by its allegiance with the monstrous Israelis—who want nothing short of world domination!

You will pay—God help you—and I will make you pay!

There will be more coming!

Al Qaeda and other organizations have met with me several times to discuss the option of me joining. I didn't.

This is an operation done by me only. I had no other help, although, I am acting on their behalf.

Osama bin Laden is planning on blowing up the Super Bowl with an antiquated nuclear bomb left over from the 1967 Israeli-Syrian war.

Don't look in *Time* or *Newsweek* for this note; they did not publish it. You will only find the copies of this note at such sites as *The Smoking Gun*, now owned by Court TV.

Why would a young man named Bishop be influenced by the 9/11 attacks or the 1967 war in the Mideast? Early stories about Bishop told of him being the "good boy next door" and even of his patriotism. The mass media never delved too deeply into who this young man was, instead noting that his mother wanted to sue an acne cream company for causing her son to die by suicide. Test results would later show that Charles Bishop's body did not contain any foreign substances—no alcohol, drugs, or even acne cream chemicals. Instead, Charles Bishop seems to have been more of a perfect candidate for the copycat effect that anyone realized.

Bishop identified more strongly than originally thought with the young Arab men on the planes that crashed on September 11. A good place to start looking for some understanding of young Bishop's real heritage is in his birth name. He was not exactly the ordinary "kid next door." A few newspapers mentioned the fact that Charles Bishop's real family name was Bishara, not Bishop. Reportedly, during the first Gulf War his mother did not like their Arab-sounding name and changed it to Bishop. It turns out the teenager's father is the half-Sicilian, half-Syrian Charles J. Bishara, a petty criminal in the Boston area with a penthouse condominium at the new Ritz-Carlton Golf Resort in Naples, Florida.

Thus, the youthful Charles Bishara Bishop, suicide plane pilot, was a complex adolescent who once thanked one of his school's teachers for defusing anti-Muslim feelings among her students. He was part Arab and he knew it. It was somewhat ironic that right after Bishop flew the plane into the Tampa Bank of America, Fox News featured Arab Muslim civil-rights advocates pointing to the youth as an example of non-Arab terrorism.

Bishara . . . Bishara? Where have we heard that name before? Oh, yes, Sirhan Bishara Sirhan. Sirhan Sirhan, of course, is the convicted assassin of Robert F. Kennedy. On June 5, 1968, Sirhan, 24, who is generally described in quick historical overviews as a "Jordanian Arab," shot RFK in the Hotel Ambassador in Los Angeles. RFK died the following day, but the actual day he was shot—and this is a significant fact overlooked time and time again—was the first anniversary of the first day of the Six Day War between Israel and its Arab neighbors that began on June 5, 1967 (or, as Bishop labeled it, "the 1967 Israeli-Syrian war"). Sirhan Sirhan's shooting down of a successful presidential candidate is often characterized as one of the first acts of Palestinian terrorism to take place on American soil, with 9/11 being the most recent example. Sirhan Bishara Sirhan saw himself as a Palestinian militant. In a diary police found at Sirhan's home, he allegedly wrote: "My determination to eliminate RFK is becoming more the more [sic] of an unshakable obsession. RFK must die. RFK must be killed. Robert F. Kennedy must be assassinated . . . Robert F. Kennedy must be assassinated before 5 June, 1968." Sirhan and his family had been uprooted from their home in Jordan by the Arab-Israeli war in 1948, and prosecutors at his trial claimed Sirhan, who was a Christian Arab, was vehemently anti-Israel. Charles Bishara Bishop, whose suicide note clearly indicated he was a student of the 1967 Israeli-Arab conflict, may have also read what another Bishara, as America's first Palestinian assassin, had done because of it.

The overlapping similarities between the threads of Charles Bishara Bishop's family background and Sirhan Bishara Sirhan's are difficult to ignore. Sirhan Sirhan was born March 19, 1944, in Jerusalem, Palestine, the fifth son of Bishara Sirhan and Mary Muzher. The family practiced Christianity but belonged to the Arab-based society in the divided region. When Sirhan was 12, in 1956, his family obtained U.S. visas as Palestinian refugees and they relocated first briefly to New York City and then to California. Sirhan Bishara Sirhan's father could not feel comfortable in his new country and soon returned to Jordan, leaving Sirhan's mother to raise him. Charles Bishara Bishop's father, who would divorce Charles's mother, traces his roots back to the Arab Christian clans of Lebanon—some say Syria, too—and would move away from the boy at a young age. Sirhan Bishara Bishop worked at the Santa Anita racetrack, which was controlled by well-known mobster Mickey Cohen.

The cultural and ethnic legacy between Bishop and Sirhan

cannot be brushed aside as coincidence. In the copycat effect, the greatest influence occurs on those that identify with the ones being made manifest in the media. Charles Bishara Bishop, who may have known more about the Arab links between himself and Sirhan Bishara Sirhan than we shall ever know, certainly modeled his suicide by plane after the young men of al-Qaida. Modeling, timing, and imitation are all strong factors in the copycat effect, and Bishop's plane's final act seems a classic case. This Tampa suicide event was not about acne but a mirroring of an event that became pivotal in his own personal view of his life. In the measure of these times and the copycat effect, the cycle did not end with Charles Bishop.

The story of Bishop's spectacular death became the spark for others who received less media attention. The incidents were like ripples on a pond after the pebble is dropped in. What we began to see after Charles Bishop's suicide is what we see from other well-publicized suicides in the media: the Werther effect. There was an increase in single-engine aircraft crashes and more recorded suicides in the wake of Bishop's very obvious suicide. The repeating nature of the phenomenon included an abnormally high incidence of Cessnas, the kind of plane Bishop had flown into the Bank of America building on January 5, 2002. His suicide in a stolen Cessna 172R happened on a weekend in which seventeen other small plane crashes occurred, seven of which were Cessnas. Seven of the seventeen involved fatalities. Four of the crashes occurring on the day after Bishop's suicide, January 6, were of Cessnas. This is an unusually high number of small-plane crashes. Some of these included apparent and overt suicides; others were more hidden. Certainly, the death of another "C.B.," a Charles who was a former British special forces veteran named Charles Bruce, author of *Freefall,* was a clear suicide: He jumped from a Cessna without a parachute over the English countryside on January 8.

On April 18, 2002, after five P.M. local time, another unmistakable example of a copycat plane suicide occurred. On that day a man apparently acting deliberately flew at top speed into Milan's (and Italy's) tallest skyscraper, hitting the twenty-fifth and twenty-sixth floors of the thirty-story Pirelli Tower. The skyscraper dominates the skyline of Italy's financial capital, as did the Twin Towers of New York City. Milan's stock exchange suspended share trading after the incident. Charles Bishara Bishop's plane hit almost at the same height, the twenty-eighth and twenty-ninth floors of the forty-two-story Bank of America building, at about the same local time. Italian Transport Minister Pietro Lunardi and Roberto Formigoni, the president of the region of Lombardy, both said they were convinced that Luigi Fasulo, the pilot of his powerful Rockwell Commander 112TC, had purposely died by suicide. Fasulo's son and others also felt it was a suicidal act. Besides the pilot, two women who worked in the Pirelli Tower were killed.

A rash of related incidents continued through the end of 2002. On the Fourth of July 2002, an Egyptian immigrant, Hesham Mohamed Hadayet, opened fire at the El Al ticket counter at Los Angeles Airport, killing two people before he was shot dead by an airline security guard. It perhaps is not a coincidence that this was Hadayet's birthday—as well as that of the United States, of course. The next attempted plane suicide would involve the same airline. On November 17, 2002, an Israeli Arab was accused of trying to hijack an El Al Airlines flight because he wanted to copy the September 11 attacks and fly the aircraft into an undisclosed "official building" in Tel Aviv, according to Turkish police officials. Tawfiq Fuqara, 23, armed with a small knife, attacked a flight attendant and tried to rush into the cockpit, saying he wanted "to make heard the voice of the Palestinian people." Two Israeli security guards on board the plane quickly subdued him. Fuqara was not linked to any known political or militant groups, police said.

Exactly ten days later, on November 27, 2002, a hijacker threatened to take and then blow up an Alitalia flight from Bologna to Paris. It was the third time that Stefano Savorani, 29, a former Italian police officer, had attempted a hijacking. Previously he tried to seize an Air France Marseilles-Paris plane and a Rome-Milan train. He told the pilots that he had hidden a bomb on the plane and was acting "against Osama bin Laden" but also claimed to be a member of bin Laden's al-Qaida network. "He did not have all his faculties," said Gerard Laurent, the Paris police spokesperson. When the plane was finally forced to land in Lyons, police arrested the suspect but found no explosives.

And still the copycat plane incidents continued, with clues to its propagation scattered in such places as anniversary dates along the way. On January 6, 2003, almost exactly on the first anniversary of the Charles Bishop–Bank of America incident, a Frankfurt, Germany, pilot stole a plane and threatened to crash into the European Central Bank. He told authorities he was trying to finally meet his idol, the late *Challenger* astronaut Judith Resnik. Military jets scrambled after the single-engine plane began flying slowly over the center of the city. "I am circling here above Frankfurt and will finish my life today and go to meet Judith," said the pilot to the airport tower controllers. He identified himself as Franz Strambach but asked to be called Steven. Strambach finally agreed to land his plane at 5:11 P.M. local time and he was arrested.

Planes targeting buildings in murder-suicides, of course, are merely another form of hijacking, which have been with us since the hijackings from Cuba in the 1950s. Studies of the contagious nature of hijackings have appeared in the sociological and psychological literature. As long ago as 1972, social scientists talked about a "skyjack virus" that was transmitted through the media. In 1973, David Phillips did one of his Werther effect studies that specifically looked at media imitation in relation to the wave of hijackings occurring at that time. Richard Holden of Indiana University, in his review of similar studies, noted that in 1975 some were considering a "hijacking as fad" hypothesis, while others looked at it as another variation on the idea of contagion and discussed hijacking in terms of the diffusion and modification of a basic invention, claiming in effect that each hijacker is attempting to outdo previous hijackers by inventing a better hijacking. Holden's survey and analyses of aircraft hijackings in the United States between 1968 and 1972 showed that completed hijackings in the United States did generate additional hijacking attempts.

Some people have taken David Phillips's observations on suicide and the Werther effect to heart. "Professor Phillips's findings have persuaded me of a distressing tendency for suicide publicity to motivate certain people who are similar to the victim to kill themselves," writes Robert B. Cialdini in his *Influence: The Psychology of Persuasion,*

> because they now find the idea of suicide more legitimate. Truly frightening are the data indicating that many innocent people die in the bargain. A glance at the graphs documenting the undeniable increase in traffic and air fatalities following publicized suicides, especially those involving murder, is enough to cause concern for one's own safety. I have been sufficiently affected by these statistics to begin to take note of front-page suicide stories and to change my behavior in the period after their appearance. I try to be especially cautious behind the wheel of my car. I am reluctant to take extended trips requiring a lot of air travel. If I must fly during such a period, I purchase substantially more flight insurance than I normally would. Dr. Phillips has done us a service by demonstrating that the odds for survival when we travel change measurably for a time following the publication of certain kinds of

front-page suicide stories. It would seem only prudent to play those odds.

Though our awareness—and acceptance—of the copycat effect in suicides is relatively recent, these events have a long historical pedigree.

CHAPTER FIVE

In Search
of Ancient Clusters

It is fear that first brought gods into the world.
—Petronius, first century A.D.

When the phrase *suicide clusters* was first used to describe the series of teen suicide events in the United States in the 1980s, people had only a foggy idea of what the words meant. Obviously they referred, in an elementary way, to a number of suicides close together in some way. But what number? And how close together? Today we understand suicide clusters to mean at least three or more completed suicides closely related in time and space. One suicide becomes a model for others in the community at risk. The 1980's clusters appear to reflect the possibility that suicide was like a contagious disease and that it could spread quickly. Exposure to the idea, the event, the act, appeared to trigger similar events later on—an excellent illustration of the copycat effect. The history of that idea is now more than two thousand years old.

The Greeks

The first documented suicide clusters occurred during the fourth century B.C., in Miletus, the mother city of the Euxine

Sea. Occupying a very favorable place at the end of the rich valley of Asia Minor's Maeander River, Miletus was a natural outlet for trade. Its four harbors were world renowned, and its influence extended far inland as well as east across the Black Sea and south to Egypt. Miletus was also the seat of great literary and religious activities. Thales, Anaximander, Anaximenes, and Hecataeus all lived and wrote in Miletus. One place they certainly visited was the chief temple of the city, that of Apollo Delphinius.

The record of this early suicide cluster comes down to us by way of the writings of Plutarch, the Greek biographer, historian, and writer. His accounts on the cluster of Miletus were written many years after the incidents, but his authority on the matter is deeply respected. Later scholars date the Miletus cluster sometime between 400 and 301 B.C. According to Plutarch:

A strange and terrible affliction came upon the maidens of Milethos, from some obscure cause—mostly it was conjectured that some poisonous and ecstatic temperament of the atmosphere produced in them a mental upset and frenzy. For there fell suddenly upon all of them a desire for death and a mad impulse towards hanging. Many hanged themselves before they could be prevented. The words and the tears of their parents, the persuasions of their friends, had no effect. In spite of all the ingenuity and cleverness of those who watched them, they succeeded in making away with themselves. The plague seemed to be of an unearthly character and beyond human remedy, until on the motion of a wise man a resolution was proposed that women who hanged themselves should be carried out to burial through the market-place. The ratification of this resolution not only checked the evil but altogether put an end to the passion for death. A great evidence of the high character and virtue of the women was this shrinking from dishonor and the fact that they who were fearless in face of the two most awful things in the world—death and pain—could not support the appearance of disgrace nor bear the thought of shame after death.

In another comment on this cluster, Plutarch noted that the decree stated the virgins were to be carried *naked* through the marketplace, and "the passage of this law not only inhibited but quashed their desire of killing themselves." Why would Greek virgins begin to kill themselves in such great numbers that it would be noted as extraordinary? Mass-suicide researcher J. A. M. Meerloo described these suicides as a "mass epidemic of the satyr delusion occurring in Miletus. Young girls began to indulge in all kinds of ecstatic and orgiastic bodily movements which eventually led to epileptic convulsions and suicide." This is clearly one of the earliest instances of the copycat effect, spread through word of mouth and songs of the poets, as the case may be.

Miletus seems to have been the site of more than one wave of suicides among its young women. From the third century B.C., we find Tegea recording this epitaph from a gravestone: "We leave you, Miletus, dear homeland, because we refused unlawful sex to impious Gauls. We were three maidens, your citizens. Violent war with the Celts brought us to this fate. We did not wait for unholy union or marriage, but we found ourselves a protector in Death."

Another Greek location, Leucadia, was famous for its suicides in pagan times during the fourth and fifth centuries B.C. On a broken white cliff at the extreme southwestern end of that island stood a temple to Apollo. Nearby was a spot for lover-suicides named Lover's Leap. From this promontory a series of notables died by suicide, including the poet Sappho of Lesbos and Queen Artemisia of Caria, who ended their pangs of unrequited love and sorrow by jumping into the sea. These suicides were often witnessed by large crowds, and later celebrated in poetry and history. (The copycat effect can be evidenced by suicides that are often repeated at favored locations, such as the Golden Gate Bridge in San Francisco today: See Chapter 15.)

A common theme running through these early Greek suicide clusters was that of passion, intimacy, and sexual feelings. Interestingly, if we look closely at the Greek mythic character Pan, we discover a personification of some of the feelings hidden beneath the surface of these suicides. Pan, the goat-footed, manlike god, was supposed to preside over shepherds and flocks and to delight in rural music. He was the giver of fertility, and thus he was shown as phallic, vigorous, and lustful. Representations of Pan often show him frolicking with virgins in the hillsides.

Pan, however, was also regarded as the creator of sudden and groundless terror: panic. The word *panic,* which appeared in the English language as an adjective about A.D. 1600, symbolizes the contagious emotion that was attributed to the influence of Pan, a sudden and excessive feeling of alarm or fear, usually leading to extravagant or injudicious efforts to secure safety. Literally, Pan made humans stampede in terror. Suicide waves and the copycat effect illustrate two important underlying elements of the clustering phenomenon: the combined elements of satyrism (with its essential component of companionship and/or loss of it) and panic. In Pan, and through his effect, panic, we see the personification of behavioral contagion, the spreading of one form of conduct or action from person to person. This is the element linking all the stories.

The Romans

Records exist as well of copycat effect clusters in the early days of the Roman Empire. Many of the soldiers who fought under

Tarquin the Proud (534–510 B.C.) were forced to work in the sewers of Rome and, because of this distasteful labor, took to killing themselves. Tarquin stopped this suicide epidemic, however, when he ordered the body of every suicide be nailed to a cross and publicly exposed.

The poet Horace, who lived from 65 B.C. to 8 B.C., noted in his day that many suicides were occurring from the Fabrician Bridge into the Tiber River. His view of suicide gives some insight into its place during his time. His most famous quotation is: "He who saves a man against his will as good as murders him." During the first century B.C., Pliny the Elder expressed a similar notion when he wrote: "Amid the sufferings of life on earth, suicide is God's best gift to man."

In the reign of Claudius I (A.D. 41 to 54), quite a few men took their own lives. Seneca the Younger, famed Roman rhetorician, who was later also to die by suicide in A.D. 65, wrote Lucilius and told of the many people of all ages and ranks who were killing themselves. He further observed that the epidemic had reached even circus performers, at the time regarded on a par with Roman civil war heroes.

The Vikings

The Viking concept of death as a concrete, positive place to go to speaks to the reasoning behind some of this culture's suicide clusters. Valhalla, the abode of Odin in Asgard, was seen as a warrior's paradise to which only those who died violently could move on to after death. The roof of Valhalla was made of polished shields upheld by spears. Troops of heroes issued daily from its 540 doors to delight themselves in battle and return to drink and feast and hear tales into the night. The Valkyries, Odin's beautiful handmaidens, served at the banquets but were best known as the "choosers of the slain" who were sent forth by

Odin to every battle and to every suicide location: They rode through the air and with their spears designated who shall die, afterward leading the slain back to Valhalla. In Sweden, where death and a trip to Valhalla were highly regarded, people frequently flung themselves from lofty rocks rather than die in some other more mundane fashion. Several of these rocks in Sweden are termed *allestenar,* or "family rocks." One is located on the shore of a lake in Blekinge Province. Two found in West Gotland are named Valhal, because they supposedly stand at the entrance of Valhalla. The rocks named Stafva Hall was by tradition the location in ancient times of wholesale suicides by Odin's worshippers.

In Iceland, one such rock exists from which many "afflicted and unhappy ones" killed themselves by leaping to "depart unto Odin." Anthropologist Paul H. Mallet, in his 1873 book *Northern Antiquities,* quotes an ancient saga: "It is useless to give ourselves up to groans and complaints, or to put our relations to needless expenses, since we can easily follow the example of our fathers, who have all gone by the way of this rock." Oral traditions were the cable news networks of their day, and this media passed on the models of copycat behavior for how people should deal with the troubles of their times.

The Norsemen's suicide clusters, like many of today's, were enhanced by a specific and positive view of death. We see it reflected, for example, in all that was written in 2001 about the seventy-two private virgin maidens waiting in the afterlife for the 9/11 hijackers. The elaborate Viking mythology about the place a victim would travel to after a leap from the rocks made suicide a good second choice if one could not die in battle. In a parallel fashion, modern suicidologists have discovered that a twenty-first-century teenager's concept of death is often filled with complex myths about how the young person will be able to come to his or her own funeral, watch the parents' and friends' reactions, and spend death in a pleasant, wondrous paradise. Death imagined in such terms has apparently triggered some youthful suicide clusters as well as Mideast-inspired suicide bombers.

The Jewish Legacy

A mass suicide is a form of a suicide cluster in a very specific location and narrow time frame. Some of the most intense episodes of mass suicide are found in Jewish history. Many suicide clusters can be found in the chronicles of Flavius Josephus from the time of the Jewish-Roman conflicts.

Josephus wrote that in 63 B.C., when Jerusalem fell to Pompey, "countless numbers" of citizens burned their homes and jumped from cliffs. In 20 B.C., after an unsuccessful revolt against Herod, the Gadarens killed themselves en masse by sword in their homes or by jumping from cliffs and drowning in rivers. That suicide spread throughout the community, from person to person, is significant.

Josephus noted that in A.D. 67 the army of Vespasian overran the citizens of Jotapata after a forty-seven-day siege; seeing that "they could kill none of the Romans, they resolved to prevent being killed by the Romans, and got together in great numbers, in the utmost parts of the city, and killed themselves." Indeed, Josephus had been deeply involved in one of the first mass suicides to be recorded, that of thirty-nine eminent men of Jotapata holed up in a cave with Josephus. After the Romans discovered the cave, Josephus and the men discussed a suicide pact as an alternative to capture. The Jotapata citizens were determined to carry out the act, despite Josephus's pleas to the contrary. Finally they drew lots, and Josephus and another were scheduled to be last. When Josephus talked the other man out of the plan, they surrendered to the Romans, and Josephus began his career as an adviser and friend of the Romans.

Other mass suicides of A.D. 67, according to Josephus, occurred among some Jotapata soldiers who killed themselves by sword rather than surrender to the Romans, and among a group of Joppa sailors who also decided to die by sword instead of drowning when their ship began to sink in a storm. In an incident that may be the largest mass suicide event in history, Josephus detailed the siege of Gamala, near Mount Tabor, by Vespasian's army. As the end was at hand, many Gamalans retreated to the city's citadel. Then, in Josephus's words:

> The Romans got up and surrounded them, and some they slew before they could defend themselves, and others as they were delivering up themselves; and the remembrance of those that were slain at their former entrance into the city increased their rage against them now; a great number also of those that were surrounded on every side, and despaired of escaping, threw their children and their wives, and themselves also, down the precipices, into the valley beneath, which, near the citadel, had been dug hollow to a vast depth . . . while the Romans slew but four thousand, whereas the number of those that had thrown themselves down was found to be five thousand.

Suicidologists such as L. D. Hankoff have examined the event and do not dispute that five thousand died in this mass suicide. We can only ponder why more has not been written on the Gamalans' deaths. One clue, of course, is that the source of this account, Josephus's *Wars of the Jews*, Book IV, Chapter 1, is a relatively short passage, compared to the space he and others have devoted to the mass suicide at Masada.

Masada is the most famous mass suicide of ancient times. In A.D. 73, with the Romans winning battle after battle in Judea, the last Jewish stronghold was the mountaintop fortress founded by the Maccabees and made nearly impregnable by Herod the Great. Masada played a great part during the war, holding out for some time after the fall of Jerusalem. In the end, however, the defenders of the huge rocky mesa three hundred yards wide, six hundred yards long, and a sheer twelve hundred feet above the Dead Sea found themselves in a hopeless battle against the Roman Tenth Legion's fifteen thousand soldiers. As the siege of Masada was coming to a close, the Jews' commander and leader, Eleazar Ben Yair, gave a lengthy speech persuading his followers, consisting of nearly a thousand Zealots, to set an "example, which shall at once cause their astonishment at our death, and their admiration of our hardiness therein." When Masada had to surrender its garrison, the men first killed their wives and children, then themselves. As the Romans made their final assault, they were greeted by a "terrible solitude on every side" and "a perfect silence" but no enemy. Instead they found 960 dead men, women, and children.

Early Christians

The impact of the early Christian church was great; the dramatic deaths of the first Christian leaders had a profound influence on their followers. The martyrs of early Christianity sometimes left clusters of suicides in their wake. In about A.D. 107 or 116 (authors disagree on the proper year), as his captors led Saint Ignatius of Antioch to the Roman amphitheater, he requested the right to secure his crown of martyrdom. He stated that, if necessary, he would himself provoke the wild beasts to kill him. "I bid all men know that of my own free will I die for God, unless ye shall hinder me. . . . Let me be given to the wild beasts. . . . Entice the wild beasts that they become my sepulchre . . . come fire and cross and grapplings with wild beasts, wrenching of bones, hacking of limbs, crushings of my whole body; only be it mine to attain unto Jesus Christ."

As suicide researcher James O'Dea noted, "the contagion of this feeling spread to the general body of Christians." Many did provoke wild animals to kill them; others leapt into fires with "exclamations of joy," still others jumped from their tall homes. Saint Perpetua, according to Saint Cyprian, helped raise the trembling right hand of the young gladiator who was to slit her throat and slay her.

After martyrdom, the preservation of chastity was the second most frequent reason for suicide in the early Christian church. One noteworthy cluster has been related to this form of suicide. When the German Visigoth king Alaric invaded and plundered Rome on the twenty-fourth of August, A.D. 410, many Christian virgins of the city died by suicide to avoid being raped by the conquerors. How many killed themselves is open to debate. Edward Gibbon in his *The Decline and Fall of the Roman Empire* noted:

> Augustine intimates that some virgins or matrons actually killed themselves to escape violation; and though he admires their spirit, he is obliged, by his theology, to condemn their rash presumption. Perhaps the good bishop of Hippo was too easy in the belief, as well as too rigid in the censure, of this act of female heroism. The twenty maidens (if they ever existed) who threw themselves into the Elbe when Magdeburg was taken by storm, have been multiplied to the number of twelve hundred.

Saint Augustine also discussed an epidemic of suicide among the sect of Donatists, especially the party named the Circumcelliones of North Africa, in the fourth century A.D. They viewed themselves as the apostles of death, and thus would daily try to kill themselves by jumping from rocks, burning themselves alive, or by forcing others to kill them. Often they would stop travelers on highways and, through bribes or threats, try to induce these individuals to kill them. And they completed their objective, succeeded, killing themselves in great numbers.

The tradition of suicide clusters among early Christian sects is a long one, and has been carried into more recent times. For example, during the thirteenth century, the Albigenses, a Christian sect living in the south of France, often died in mass suicides through fasting and self-bleeding.

Europeans of the Middle Ages

The pestilence and illness that swept through the population during the Middle Ages turned many disease-stricken European lands into sites of suicide clusters. In seventh-century England a pestilence, probably the bubonic plague, devastated the land, and led many people to suicide. As one contemporary, Roger Wendor, wrote: "In the year of Grace 665, there was such an excessive mortality in England, that the people crowded to the seaside, and threw themselves from the cliffs into the sea, choosing rather to be cut off by a speedy death than to die by the lingering torments of the pestilence."

Many more died by suicide throughout Europe in 1027, 1237, 1278, and 1418, as epidemics of Saint Vitus's dance gripped the people. Similarly, Saint John's dancing mania, beginning on June 24, 1374, caused suicides all over Europe. Sweating sickness, something like influenza with a high fever, turned up in epidemic waves in Europe in 1485, 1517, and 1551; in London in 1506; and in England and Germany in 1528. The horror of the sweating sickness led great numbers of people to take their own lives while attempting to escape the suffering. Between the fifteenth and sixteenth centuries, many people, especially in Italy, were overcome by tarantula mania—or tarantism, as it is more commonly known today—a dancing mania similar to Saint Vitus's, and drowned themselves at sea.

At the beginning of the eleventh century, a major suicide cluster of women occurred because of a major change in their status within the Catholic Church. Between the years of 1074 and 1078, Pope Gregory VII issued various decrees imposing celibacy on the clergy of the Catholic Church. Few people realize that before Gregory VII, priests in the Roman Catholic Church had wives. Gregory's decrees against married priests caused a wave of suicides among discarded wives throughout Europe.

Suicide epidemics were frequent among Jews during the Middle Ages, as they were often the targets of persecution. In France, in 1095, a large number killed themselves to escape torture. In 1190, anti-Jewish riots broke out in the walled city of York, and the Jews were allowed by the sheriff to take refuge in the royal castle. Soon the castle was besieged, and York's Jews were given the choice of renouncing their religion or killing themselves. On March 16 and 17, 1190, six hundred Jews died by suicide, jumping from the walls of the castle that still sits on a mound in the middle of York. Today a simple plaque in their memory stands by the castle.

In 1320, another five hundred Jews came to the same end during the siege of the Castle of Verdun on the Garonne in France. During the Black Death of 1348 to 1350, Jews were accused of poisoning wells throughout Europe, and many burned themselves to death in their synagogues or killed themselves in their homes to avoid the fury of the masses.

The Middle Ages was a time of many group suicides that are only footnotes in the available records. These include the suicide clusters of women in Marseille and Lyons, during the reign of France's Hugh Capet from 987 to 996, and the massive suicide waves of Christian soldiers who put on the mantles of fallen Knights Templar and were martyred after the Battle of Hitten during the Crusades.

The Russians

Frequent outbreaks of suicide clusters in Russia have been recorded down through the years. For example, historian James O'Dea wrote that during one epidemic in 1666, whole communities were said to have killed themselves during a revival of religious fanaticism. After the Jonestown mass suicide, *Time* magazine noted: "In the 17th century, Russian Orthodox dissenters called the Old Believers refused to accept liturgical reforms. Over a period of years some 20,000 peasants in protest abandoned their fields and burned themselves."

Certainly, Russia has a significant history of secret religious sects, some of which have taken suicide as one of their major tenets. Among these, one was the *soshigateli,* or self-burners, who picked voluntary death by fire as the only means of purification from the sins and pollution of the world. They abounded in Siberia in the 1850s. Between 1855 and 1875, groups of *soshigateli* numbering fifteen to one hundred burned themselves in large pits or dry buildings filled with brushwood. In about 1867, seven hundred were reported to have voluntarily chosen death by fire at Tumen, in the Eastern Urals. Another sect with similar tendencies, the *morestschiki,* or self-sacrificers, preferred iron to fire. In 1868, a massive mystical sacrifice took place on the Gurieff Estate on the Volga, where forty-seven men and women killed themselves with swords.

A religious suicide cluster occurred in 1897, at Tiraspol, in what is now Moldova, when twenty-eight individuals buried themselves alive to escape a census enumeration that they apparently believed was sinful. Social scientist Lucy Davidson reports a cluster of children's suicides occurred between 1908 and 1910 in Moscow.

Old records confirm that the copycat effect occurred longer ago than is generally believed. And modern news stories show that the copycat effect continues unabated.

CHAPTER SIX

Fiery Copycats

Dear Master, I have only my feeble body to offer to
further the cause of the people living in Vietnam,
and pray that my wishes will be fulfilled one day.
—Thich Chan Hy, December 24, 2003

Historically, suicides by fire—often termed self-incinerations, self-immolations or simply immolations—have led to widespread imitation, copying, and clustering. Perhaps no other type of modern suicide produced by the copycat effect has been as dramatically and extremely political—and therefore so strikingly justified as newsworthy. The media has played a central role in the spreading awareness of these incidents.

Without making value judgments about what is right or wrong, it's clear that some of these fire suicides are based on a deeply felt sense of persecution, and may be culturally understood to be an altruistic or an "unselfish" and "worthy" form of suicide. Those that are reported as "mere copycats" by the press are usually not politically motivated. Just because someone dies by fire suicide does not mean that the person is a political martyr.

But most fire suicides do have some things in common. The death is so ghastly and painful that the copycat effect has to play a major role in subsequent suicides selecting this method of death. Once the decision to die has been made, the fire suicide is often viewed as an attractive option based on the media coverage and perceived results and benefits.

Social scientists, journalists, historians, and suicidologists generally classify the contemporary fiery immolations according to the country of origin and the political source or situation of the protest. For many Americans, the most memorable immolations took place during the era of the Vietnam War.

The Burning Monks

In the early days of 1963, the ongoing Indochinese war was made more complex by the dictatorial policies of the Ngo Dinh Diem regime of South Vietnam. The country's Buddhists felt that the members of the Diem family, all Roman Catholics who led the American-backed government, were extremely repressive. In Hue, South Vietnam, on May 8, 1963, during a demonstration against the Diem policies, government troops fired into the crowd, killing nine Buddhists. In a country that was 70 percent Buddhist, the resulting protests were frequent and widespread. A month later the protests would take a form that would influence political suicides for decades to come.

On June 11, 1963, the Buddhist monk Thich Quang Duc doused his yellow robes with gasoline in the public square of Saigon and set himself on fire. Thousands watched, and Buddhist nuns and monks carried banners demanding religious freedom and social justice. The media had been forewarned that a demonstration was to take place, but they had not known that a monk would burn himself alive. The next day photographs and films of the event were published and broadcast worldwide. Thich Quang Duc's dramatic declaration of dissent was headlined around the world.

During the summer of 1963, others in Vietnam chose to kill themselves in protest of the Diem regime. On July 7, Vietnam's famous writer Nguyen Tuong Tam, a Buddhist, killed himself in prison by taking poison. But Thich Quang Duc's act was viewed as more dramatic and was quickly imitated by others. On August 4, a Buddhist monk, in his twenties, Le, burned himself to death in the center of the seacoast town of Phan Thiet. Government troops removed his charred body before his fellow monks could reach it.

The self-immolations spread quickly. On August 13, 1963, a 70-year-old novice monk burned himself to death. Two days later a Buddhist nun named Dieu Quang set herself on fire in the coastal town of Ninh Hoa and died shortly thereafter. The next day a 71-year-old monk took his own life by burning in Hue's biggest pagoda. Three Buddhists had died by fire in one week. The South Vietnamese government declared martial law in Hue and searched for ways to stop the suicides. But the political repression caused a renewed sense of outrage on the part of the Buddhists, and protests continued.

By the end of the year, at least four other monks had burned themselves to death. In 1964 and 1965, five more Buddhist monks incinerated themselves in South Vietnam.

The fire suicides then spread to India, which has a tradition (the sacrifice of suttee, now outlawed) of widows immolating themselves on the funeral pyre of their husbands. In 1965 political self-immolations were used in widespread protests in India. As the villagers of Kizhapazhuvur in Tamil Nadu state's Tiruchi district looked on in shock, Chinnasamy, a poor farmer, set fire to his gasoline-saturated body on the eve of Republic Day (January 26) in 1965 for the preservation of the Tamil language. After his death, the Tamil Nadu became the scene of a new, fiery form of Indian political protest: self-immolation. The next night, T. M. Sivalingam of Kodambakkam, in Chennai, immolated himself, protesting the government's imposition of Hindi on Dravidian land. And the next day Aranganathan of Virugam-bakkam in Chennai took the same route to death for the same cause. The spate of suicides over the imposition of Hindi continued for a week that year, leaving as many as nine people dead, and Tamil Nadu came to be labeled the land of self-immolation. In the months that followed, the government withdrew its call to outlaw the Tamil language. (Today, self-immolations in India are said to be caused by the "Chinnasamy effect.") The copycat nature of the Vietnamese monk's act in 1963 was considerable and its literal and political impact quickly understood by an increasingly media-influenced world.

Burning American Protestors

The Vietnam-era American self-immolations began with Alice Herz, an 82-year-old Quaker and librarian. She poured cleaning fluid over herself and set herself afire on Saint Patrick's Day, March 17, 1965, on a street corner in Detroit. As she was rushed to the hospital covered with second-degree and third-degree burns, she told a firefighter: "I did it to protest the arms race all over the world. I wanted to burn myself like the monks in Vietnam did." In her purse, police found a note stating Herz was protesting "the use of his high office by our President, L.B.J., in trying to wipe out small nations. . . . I wanted to call attention to this problem by choosing the illuminating death of a Buddhist."

Norman Morrison, 32, also a Quaker, burned himself to death on November 2, 1965, in front of the Pentagon in Washington, D.C., because of the Vietnam conflict. Eight days later, 22-year-old Catholic Worker Movement member Roger Allen LaPorte calmly went to the wide avenue in front of the United Nations, doused himself with gasoline from a gallon can, stepped off the curb, and sat cross-legged in the fashion of the Buddhist monks. He struck a match and was engulfed in flames.

As he was rushed away, between asking for water repeatedly, La-Porte told the ambulance attendants: "I'm a Catholic Worker. I'm against war, all wars. I did this as a religious action." LaPorte had always wanted to become a Trappist monk, and he had attended the St. John Vianney Seminary in Barre, Vermont, for a year in 1963. As LaPorte lay dying on a hospital-operating table, two psychiatrists asked him if he wanted to live. He nodded affirmatively but died the next day.

The highly visible protest suicides of Herz, Morrison, and LaPorte appear to have directly influenced the method of suicides carried out by other Americans not so politically motivated during this same time period. For example, the day that LaPorte died, a South Bend, Indiana, woman attempted to use fire for her suicide. Despondent over the October death of her 3-month-old baby and the casualty reports from Vietnam, Celene Jankowski, 24, set herself ablaze in front of her home. A police spokesperson noted that one of Jankowski's brothers had been killed in the Korean War, and she had been deeply disturbed by the Vietnam situation, although she was not a member of any formal protest organization.

The wave of political immolations continued in 1966 and 1967. Thirteen Buddhists in Vietnam, one Soviet citizen, and one American student received widespread publicity during 1966 for their acts. In 1967, five Buddhists in Southeast Asia and five Americans in the U.S. died in fiery political protests. Three other Americans died by immolation between 1966 and 1967, but apparently not for political reasons. Still the contagion effect is deemed important in these suicides.

Indeed, throughout the early 1970s, immolations related to the Vietnam War continued in Southeast Asia and America. Times Square in New York City was the scene of a dramatic immolation when Hin Chi Yeung poured two cans of gasoline on himself and struck a match at two P.M. on Saturday, July 18, 1970. On August 24, 1971, a 37-year-old Vietnam veteran and father of six, Nguyen Minh Dang, set himself afire in Saigon's central market, praying for another veteran who burned himself to death on August 16 in a peace protest. A 58-year-old laborer at Vietnam's Tan Son Nhut Air Base burned himself to death "for the cause of national peace" on September 6, 1974.

The moving death of the Buddhist monk Thich Quang Duc forever changed the face of recent political protest. As researchers Kevin Crosby, Joonh-Oh Rhee, and J. Holland noted in their analysis of suicides by fire from 1790 to 1972, 71 percent of the reported immolations occurred in the final ten-year period of their survey. The rise and actual clustering of this form of suicide began after the death of Thich Quang Duc in 1963. These researchers attempted "to explain the clusters of protest immolations in South Vietnam" by pointing to the "high level of tension among the opposing factions" and the "intense emotional atmosphere" it produced. They felt that similar suicides by fire are likely to recur when times are "unsettled, emotions inflamed and when no appropriate outlet exists for the expression of commonly shared emotions." It is also quite clear that the swift, electronic distribution of the strikingly graphic pictures and written descriptions of the immolations presented potential suicide victims with a collective method and model for behavior.

Remembering Jan Palach and "Torch No. 2"

The explosive nature of strained emotional times has produced other fire immolations. During August 1968, the invasion of Czechoslovakia by the Soviet Union was met by a wave of international protest. But the outrage did not really come to a head until Jan Palach, a student at Charles University in Prague, startled passersby by pouring a liquid over his body at about three

P.M. on January 16, 1969, and then setting himself ablaze. The 21-year-old student chose the statue of Wenceslas, the Czech hero saint, as the site of his protest in Prague. Palach had left a note declaring that he belonged to a group whose members planned to self-incinerate themselves, one every ten days, until the Soviet troops departed. Palach's protest and death three days later got worldwide media coverage, with others following his lead.

On January 20, 1969, crowds of people waving the Czecho-slovakian state flag, black flags and enlarged photographs of Jan Palach, gathered at the spot of Palach's suicide. In the philoso-phy faculty building, the clocks were stopped so they showed the exact time of Palach's death (3:15 P.M.). Josef Hlavaty then self-immolated himself just as Palach had. Two days later, on January 22, Miroslav Malinka killed himself through suicide by fire, and Blanka Nachazelova suffocated herself with coal gas. On the day of the Palach funeral, Hlavaty died.

In the next well-publicized suicide, Jan Zajic, an 18-year-old student at a vocational school in Sumperk, set himself on fire on February 25, 1969. Before his death, he gave his friends a poem about Palach and four letters in which he described himself as "Torch no. 2." He did it in Prague in the passageway of a build-ing on Wenceslas Square as he was trying to run to the saint's statue, but he fell in flames and died there. He said he decided to immolate himself after seeing that life was returning to its old routine despite Palach's action.

On April 4, 1969, in another square, this time in the south-eastern Bohemian city of Jihlava, Evzen Plocek, 40, set himself on fire. At least twenty-six people attempted suicide between January 20 and the end of April 1969, with at least seven of these dying by fire in Czechoslovakia, Scotland, and Hungary after Palach's death. Reports of seven other fatal self-immola-tions came from India, Pakistan, England, and the United States. Meanwhile, in France, Palach's suicide would have an anniversary copycat effect. Although the political motivation was different, the method was pure copy.

Biafra Thoughts in France

Late in the 1960s, children were starving to death in the small African territory of Biafra. When television and newspapers showed disturbing pictures from the area, schoolchildren throughout the world expressed concern for these victims of war and famine. In France young people took up suicide by fire as the appropriate form of protest that might end the suffering.

In January 1970, exactly one year to the day after Jan Palach had burned himself to death, a 16-year-old boy in the northern French city of Lille doused himself with gasoline and set himself ablaze in his high school playground. On a piece of notepaper he had written: "I offer myself to atone for the wrongs committed in Biafra, against war, violence and the folly of men." Four days later a 19-year-old boy burned himself to death in his schoolyard in Lille. He left a note that read: "I did it because I cannot adapt myself to this world. I did it as a sign of protest against violence, to see love again." In various parts of France, two days later, two men died by fiery suicides, and another made an attempt. Then, on January 24, a 17-year-old girl set herself on fire at a Paris Roman Catholic high school, and then jumped to her death from the fourth story.

Five immolations took place in one week. In the two weeks after the first youth's death, six other youths died by fiery suicides. For the entire year of 1970, sixteen cases of suicide by fire occurred in France, with ten of them clustering during the month of January.

The English-Welsh Epidemic

Between October 1978 and October 1979, eighty-two people, mostly young single men and older married women, died by burning themselves in England and Wales. Researchers John Ashton and Stuart Donnan did not view these suicides by fire as primarily political protests but as an epidemic stimulated and copied widely from one well-publicized fiery death.

Late in September 1978, Lynette Phillips, a 24-year-old Australian heiress, was arrested in London and deported after she said she was going to kill herself in Parliament Square. Phillips was a member of PROUT, the Progressive Utilization Theory, an Asian-based religious sect. PROUT had developed out of a political and religious conflict with the Indira Gandhi leadership of India. They had staged demonstrations in India and at Indian consulates in Australia and England to protest against the Indian government's outlawing of PROUT. By the time Phillips was deported, seven PROUT members had burned themselves to death.

On October 2, 1978, Phillips set herself afire in front of the Palais des Nations in Geneva, Switzerland. Her statement made it clear she had died by suicide in the hopes of changing the world order.

Three days after the Phillips suicide, Pamela Evans Cooper followed suit on the banks of the Thames at Windsor. By the end of the month, England and Wales were in the midst of a full-scale immolation cluster. Ten people had died by burning. Reports in the English media noted six similar suicides throughout the Commonwealth: three in New Zealand, two in Australia, and one in India.

Soon after the start of this cluster, suicide researchers Ashton and Donnan took notice of the growing epidemic and began obtaining death certificates and coroners' reports, which revealed the full extent of the self-burnings. After analyzing the data, they wrote: "What we have called an epidemic is, we think, an example of the phenomenon of imitation. . . . There can be little doubt that the spread of this specific epidemic must have been mediated by news coverage; deaths occurring in this manner tend to be widely reported."

The English and Welsh suicides by fire decreased as 1979 came to an end. (It should be noted that during 1979, the Indian government went through a housecleaning, and the PROUT-led fire suicides came to a halt.)

Eastern Europe Again

Fire suicides would become increasingly significant in the protests leading up to the disintegration of the communist regimes in Eastern Europe.

For Lithuanians, the model and traditional method of resistance, suicides by fire, has been part of their culture since 1972. Few in Lithuania have forgotten the so-called Young People's Rebellion that occurred that year, and all modern Lithuanian history is keyed to whether it happened before 1972 or after. The pivotal event for Lithuania occurred on May 14, 1972. That day, a Lithuanian student and Roman Catholic, Romas Kalanta, 19, poured nearly a gallon of gasoline over his body and set himself on fire in front of the Music Theater in the central Lithuanian city of Kaunas. The Soviets underestimated the spread of the news of Kalanta's immolation. Three fatal immolations and one near-fatal attempt followed.

When mourners arrived for Kalanta's funeral, they discovered that the Soviets had secretly buried Kalanta. Riots ensued. On May 18 and 19, 1972, several thousand youths battled Soviet policemen and soldiers, first in Kaunas, then in other cities, ending in fatalities for the Soviets. Troops arrested reportedly as many as five hundred Lithuanians. Kalanta's suicide remained a symbol of Lithuanian resistance throughout the 1970s and 1980s.

Kalanta's immolation served as the model of new protests in Lithuania as the nation struggled from under Soviet rule and declared its independence. On April 26, 1990, Stanislovas Jamaitis, a 52-year-old Lithuanian, threw gasoline on his clothes and set himself on fire in front of Moscow's Bolshoi Theater. He died a short time later. According to his suicide note, he was protesting the Soviet reaction to Lithuania's declaration of freedom. Tass, the Soviet news agency, did not mention any political motives in its story of the suicide and just reported that Jamaitis had written of an "impossible family life and a desire to commit suicide."

Then on May 11, 1990, a Lithuanian identified as Rimantas Daugintis, a resident of Vilnius, doused his body with alcohol and set himself on fire at a border crossing near Zahoney between the Soviet Union and Hungary. Suffering serious injuries, he was placed in a hospital with burns over 80 percent of his body. On May 27, 1990, a Romanian, Miroi Dimitru, 31, set himself on fire in front of the U.S. embassy in Budapest, Hungary.

These events did not go unnoticed in America. The elder George Bush had sent U.S. forces against Iraqis, and the first Gulf War was stirring up war protests. Fire suicides soon followed. Gregory Levey understood the power of the media and symbolism; after all, it was in his blood. On February 18, 1991, Levey, 30, son of newspaper reporter Bob Levey and stepson of *Boston Globe* columnist Ellen Goodman, set himself on fire in protest of the Gulf War in the university community of Amherst, Massachusetts. Levey identified with Buddhist beliefs and left clear symbols of his intentions at his side, a placard with the word *Peace* on it, and a statue of the Buddha. Three days later, in nearby Springfield, Massachusetts, Raymond Moules followed suit.

In 2002, Amherst remembered Levey on the day before the

anniversary of his death, with a walk to "wake up peace." Starting at the Leverett Peace Pagoda, the walk went to the Amherst Town Common where a memorial to Greg Levey was held. The service lasted an hour, and people brought candles, poems, and flowers. It was a flashback to the Vietnam-era protests, and the link between Greg Levey and Buddhist monk Thich Quang Duc was not lost on the crowd. In March 2003, about a hundred people protesting the second Gulf War made pilgrimages to the spot of Levey's self-immolation, while hundreds more marched in Amherst and surrounding communities.

A Sacrificial Light in Tajrish Square

By the 1990s, fire by suicide was being widely employed in support of many causes. The method proved extraordinarily effective in spreading, via contagion, the news of a protest across a society.

In Iran during the fall of 1994, many educated women took up self-immolation as an act of protest against the Iranian Islamic Republic's treatment of their gender. One of the most spectacular examples of this occurred on the tenth day of Ramadan, February 21, 1994, with the act of a fervent nationalist Homa Darabi, M.D., who had formerly supported the revolution. In a haunting essay in *On the Issues* entitled "A Sacrificial Light: Self-Immolation in Tajrish Square, Tehran," journalist Martha Shelley writes:

Dr. Darabi . . . put on her ropoosh, a long overcoat considered an acceptable substitute for the chado. She tied her headscarf, tucking every strand of her hair out of sight, and got into her car. On that day, especially, she was apparently determined not to be stopped by the pasdaran (revolutionary guards) before reaching her destination. Dr. Darabi drove to the local gas station and asked the attendants to fill her tank and a spare can. Then she drove to northern Tehran, to a plaza in an upper-class neighborhood. . . . Dr. Darabi stopped her car and walked to the center of the plaza. It was 3:00 p.m. Passersby stopped, frozen, as she tore off her head-scarf and emptied the gasoline can on her head. She began to shout at the top of her lungs, and her voice rang out over the noise of the traffic, over the wailing of the loudspeakers. 'Death to oppression! Long live liberty!' Then she lit a match. Homa Darabi died at 1 a.m. the next day, leaving one less physician to tend to the needs of the Iranian people. About 10,000 people attended her funeral, according to her sister.

When Homa Darabi's sister, Parvin, heard the news of her sister's fiery death, she sent a press release to the U.S. television news shows, but there was no coverage of the event. "When I called them," Parvin said, "they told me that this story wasn't sensational because I didn't have a picture of my sister burning in fire. I was really shocked and humiliated."

Frequent accounts of self-immolations by women in Iran and surrounding regions have taken place since 1994. Only after America's war to bring the fall of the Taliban did the West learn of the local reports of young Afghan women in villages near the Iranian border killing themselves by lighting gasoline thrown on their bodies. In one string of self-immolation cases in Herāt, a city of 330,000, four women killed themselves and nine others attempted self-immolations in the first six months of 2002. Whether the reasons for their actions involved a loveless husband or a difficult family conflict, the method was the same: by fire.

New Freedoms, Old Problems, More Fires

Once the communist regimes crumbled in 1991, troubles surfaced in old Soviet Bloc countries and people turned to suicide by fire yet again as both a way of ending their pain and as a way to get media attention for their protests.

On March 12, 2002, V. Goncharova of Feodosiya, Ukraine, poured fluid over herself and set herself on fire before a crowd of a hundred in Kiev's main square and the cameras of the *People's Platform* television program. She demanded from the government justice for her son, a fireman who almost lost his legs while on duty. She survived. On March 26, 2002, in the Russian republic of Mordvinia, Alexandra Prokhorova, a 52-year-old nurse, set fire to herself in the bathhouse because she had not been paid in months. She died.

The following year, in the Czech Republic, a wave of fire suicides occurred. In November 2003, the Czech media reported that young countrymen were setting themselves ablaze, with five dying and eleven surviving. One of these incidents occurred in March 2003, when teenager Zdenek Adamec doused himself with gasoline and lit a match in Prague's central Wenceslas Square—just a few steps from the spot where Jan Palach had set himself on fire. He died forty minutes later in an ambulance. In a letter he had written that communism had been replaced by a democracy that amounted to nothing more than "the rule of officials, money, and treading on people." He could no longer live, he said, in a world filled with violence, pollution and apathy.

In a harsh and unrealistic analysis of the situation, Prague psychologist Karel Humhal refused to link the recent fire suicides to the deaths under Communist rule. "In a way, Palach's act was appropriate for that era . . ." he said. "These others express nothing." Nevertheless, Humhal would not discount the powerful effect of Palach's communist-era suicide on those considering taking their own lives today.

Law enforcement officials told the Czech media that Adamec's suicide might have triggered a copycat phenomenon. Five days after his death, a mentally unstable 21-year-old man was critically injured after setting himself on fire. Police spokesman Stanislav Dobes told Czech media that, according to the victim's father, the young man had seen a newspaper account of Adamec's suicide, "which could have inspired him to do what he did."

Modern Self-immolations Visit the Far East

The Chinese view self-immolation as an extreme form of protest. Though the act has been rare in the past, recent times have seen an increase in fire suicides.

On April 27, 1998, as Indian police broke up a marathon hunger strike in New Delhi, Tibetans took direct action against China's occupation of their Himalayan homeland and confronted the police. Thupten Ngodub, a 50-year-old supporter of the hunger strikers, then set himself on fire at the scene during the police crackdown. He suffered 100-percent burns and died of cardiac arrest two days later. It was the first self-immolation of a Tibetan since 1951, when China occupied Tibet. Strong statements from the Dalai Lama in support of nonviolent struggle put a stop to further immolations.

But in China other suicides were occurring, including some of the most dramatic by fire. On Tuesday, January 23, 2001, five people set themselves on fire in China's Tiananmen Square. Two of them died, though the reasons for their act would get lost in a series of debates between the Chinese government and members of the Falun Gong spiritual movement. Who these people were and what they were doing continues to be the source of political disagreements. Initial reports noted that the self-immolations, which cable news television captured on a tape later confiscated by Chinese police, were protests against the Chinese government. China's state media accused followers of dying by suicide at the instigation of sect leader Li Hongzhi.

The "dramatic and disturbing" event was broadcast and printed by the Western media. A CNN producer and camera operator were at Tiananmen Square on the Chinese New Year's Eve, a place where Falun Gong members had already protested at the beginning of the lunar New Year. Outlets such as *The Washington Post* and *The Boston Globe* reported that the crew watched as a man sat down on the pavement just northeast of the Peoples' Heroes Monument at the center of the square. After pouring gasoline on his clothes, he set himself on fire. Police ran to the man and extinguished the flames. Moments later four more people immolated themselves; a woman and her 12-year-old daughter died.

Spokespeople for the anti-Chinese sect said that accounts that the five were members of Falun Gong were part of a smear effort against the group by the Chinese government. "Don't you see what the PRC (People's Republic of China) is doing?

An interview with Falun Gong survivor Chen Guo that appeared in the Chinese *People's Daily* of April 9, 2002, detailed how she recalled the events that led her to set herself on fire in Beijing's Tiananmen Square more than a year earlier. "Falun Gong is indeed an evil cult and it led me to this," said Chen Guo, according to the Chinese paper. Falun Gong denounced the interview as lies.

Whatever the truth was behind the causes of the Tiananmen Square immolations of 2001, fire suicides were taken up as a form of protest throughout China. For example, on August 22, 2003, Weng Biao, 39, of the eastern Chinese city of Nanjing, charged into an office responsible for demolitions and relocations and killed himself by setting fire to his gasoline-doused body. Then on September 15, 2003, a disgruntled Chinese farmer upset at a government plan to relocate his family attempted to set himself on fire in Tiananmen Square. At about 8:40 A.M., Zhu Zhengliang, 45, from eastern Anhui Province, tried to ignite himself on the Golden Water Bridge that leads to the Tiananmen Rostrum, just under the famous portrait of late revolutionary Mao Zedong. He survived with burns on his hands and arms. The incident came as workers prepared the square for the October 1 National Day holiday, when hundreds of thousands of Chinese visit Beijing's vast esplanade, which is decked out with flower arrangements, banners, and exhibits trumpeting China's successes.

On January 13, 2004, the Chinese state media reported that two elderly people had set themselves on fire close to the Zhongnanhai area of Beijing, where China's top leaders live. The couple lit a bonfire along the wall that surrounds Zhongnanhai before being transformed into "fireballs," the *Xin Jing Bao* said, citing witnesses. One of them died on the way to the hospital while the other was in critical condition. They gave no reason for the self-immolations.

Vietnam Again

Coming full circle, Buddhist monks in protests are once again using fire, and media attention to their acts appears to have stimulated copycats. In September 2001 a member of a dissident Buddhist sect, the Unified Buddhist Church of Vietnam, immolated himself on Vietnam's national day to protest repression of religion in the country, according to the Paris-based Buddhist Information Bureau.

Then just before daybreak on Christmas Eve 2003, Thich Chan Hy, 74, a Vietnamese monk, set himself afire in a Buddhist temple in the United States to protest the lack of religious freedom and demand democracy in his communist homeland. He killed himself in front of a fifteen-foot tall statue of Avalokita Bodhisattva, a figure of compassion, at the Lien Ha temple in east

Charlotte, North Carolina. "He left a letter to his master on a scroll . . . with three wishes that he had given up his life for," Phuong Huynh, a leader of youth programs at the Buddhist temple, told Reuters. "The three reasons were I wish that all the people living in Vietnam be entitled to freedom of religion and belief, I wish that all the people in Vietnam be entitled to human rights and democracy, and I wish that Vietnam will preserve its sovereignty of its lands and sea borders." Hanoi recognizes six religions and permits only a single official representative group of each to operate. One of the groups that Vietnam has cracked down on is the outlawed Unified Buddhist Church of Vietnam.

With news coverage of these events and a reminder published by the Associated Press that the "most famous act of self-immolation by a Vietnamese Buddhist" had taken place in 1963, it is not surprising that other attempts at self-immolations occurred. Two days after the North Carolina monk's fiery death received global notice, a young man attempted self-immolation in front of Norway's Parliament building on the afternoon of Friday, December 26, 2003. He first appeared outside the Parliament (Stortinget) around midday. There were few people around, because it was a public holiday in Norway known as "Second Christmas Day." Vidar Hjulstad of the Oslo police said the man, in his late twenties, poured gasoline from a can over himself and lit a match. Police said they did not know why the man had tried to set himself on fire. He survived, according to the newspaper *Aftenposten*.

Meanwhile, back in the United States, Fayette County, Kentucky, experienced a fire-immolation on December 30, 2003. Stephen Stumph, 33, of Harrodsburg, doused himself with gasoline and set himself on fire at his home. Although his family found him alive, he was pronounced dead at the burn unit of the University of Kentucky Medical Center in Lexington, just before two A.M. on New Year's Eve 2003. No reason was given for his suicide.

The next day, with American, South Vietnamese, and Buddhist flags fluttering, Thich Chan Hy's funeral took place in North Carolina. With the smell of incense filling the temple where he set himself on fire, Hy was remembered with compassion. His body was carried through Charlotte in a coffin for later cremation.

Self-immolations Worldwide in the Twenty-first Century

The copycat effect of fire suicides is a powerful phenomenon. Dr. Jaroslava Moserova, a Czech senator and a burns specialist who treated Jan Palach, reflected on the fire suicides wave in his country in 2003: "People who find themselves in situations without a solution . . . opt for this form because it is so dramatic and attracts attention." He then added: "It's very atypical for our country. After all, it's more of a tradition in India."

The "Chinnasamy effect" continues today with as many as 1,451 committing self-immolations in 2000 and another 1,584 people in 2001, possibly the highest in southern India. Fire self-immolations are so common in the news media of India today that a soccer team threatened to immolate themselves en masse unless they received better pay, a human rights protester burned himself alive in front of a United Nations building in New Delhi, and an unemployed worker poured gasoline and set himself on fire outside Bombay House because he could not find work—all of which happened during November 2003. The model for these suicides, self-immolation, is the widespread first choice for many Indians seeking a solution for their problems, no matter how petty.

Could this frightening situation spread to the rest of the world? Could a better understanding of the underlying impact of the copycat effect prevent such a situation from occurring?

CHAPTER SEVEN

Cultic Copycats

The deaths of cult members, whether by suicide or murder-suicide, demonstrate the internal and external forces, the micro and macro elements, of the copycat effect. These cultic waves of mass mortality emerge from a component of the human personality that emulates and duplicates behaviors, especially those portrayed and transmitted by strong charismatic individuals, their peers, and the media. When all of these elements are mixed together in the pressure cookers that are cults, the results are sometimes horrible beyond belief.

Jonestown

One of the most discussed modern mass suicides occurred in the unique setting of Jonestown, Guyana. Jonestown in the early 1970s was little more than a nine-hundred-acre island cut out of the thick South American rainforest. It was there that the Reverend James Warren "Jim" Jones relocated his People's Temple from the San Francisco area. Allegations were first published in the *Guyana Daily Mirror* that Jonestown was a "concentration camp" in which Jones's flock were given psychotropic drugs, sexually abused, sleep deprived, and forced to work eighteen-hour days. Former members told of drills, called "white nights," in which middle-of-the-night sirens called members to a lineup where they were told they were going to have to take a poison. Jonestown residents became preconditioned into expecting a coming invasion of the camp by Russians, the CIA, or other imagined "enemies" by the delusional Jones. In the wake of these claims, the pressure mounted for San Francisco officials to look into the Jonestown "cult."

On July 26, 1977, San Francisco mayor George Moscone announced that he would not hold an investigation of Jones. In a letter to President Jimmy Carter, San Francisco supervisor Harvey Milk defended Jones as a friend to minority communities. But soon San Francisco family members asked their congressional representative to fly to Jonestown to look into the situation and hopefully rescue their relatives. This finally occurred with a one-day delegation headed by Congressman Leo Ryan. On November 18, 1978, supposedly frightened by the investigative visit of Ryan, cult leader Jim Jones ordered Larry Schacht, a medical school graduate and designated camp doctor, to prepare a huge cyanide-laced vat of grape Flavor Aid. At the Guyanese airstrip near Jonestown, Jones sent gunmen to ambush Ryan and about thirty newsmen, government aides, and relatives of People's Temple members before they could board their plane to return to the United States. Ryan, three reporters, and a Jonestown defector were killed, and among the wounded were the area's alleged CIA Chief of Station Richard Dwyer and Ryan aide Jackie Speier. Later Jones, with armed guards at his side, had his followers drink the potion and kill themselves. Those who refused to take the poison were machine-gunned to death by guards who apparently escaped. Thus some of the Jonestown deaths were indeed murders.

By most counts, the death toll was 913. Initially the general public could not believe that the news accounts were true, despite widespread press and broadcast attention bringing the details into American living rooms. Media reports about the People's Temple suicides would drag on for years. It was not until 1986 that one of Jim Jones's assistants, Larry Layton, the only person prosecuted for any of the events in and around Jonestown, was convicted for his involvement in the Jonestown incidents and Ryan's death. Layton was released from custody in April 2002 on parole after eighteen years in prison. Many believed he was an innocent scapegoat.

As often happens after well-publicized suicides and mass suicides, the copycat effect took the form of follow-up murders. This happened quickly and in spectacular fashion in San Francisco. Nine days after the Jonestown events, on November 27, 1978, San Francisco Bay Area residents would learn of the assassinations of Mayor Moscone and Supervisor Milk. Law enforcement officials repeated the local rumors that some Bay Area residents believed that Moscone and Milk were murdered by the hauntingly named "White Night" hit squads said to have been sent by the People's Temple to avenge Jim Jones. As *San Francisco Chronicle* reporter Richard Rapaport observed, "When authorities went through the personal effects left behind in San Francisco by Jones, they found a hit list with the names of erstwhile political friends and allies like George Moscone and Willie Brown."

The Moscone-Milk murders were carried out by a disgruntled former supervisor, Dan White, and were not directly linked to Jim Jones. White had impulsively retired from his position one year after his election and a mere two days after the Jonestown event. A former Vietnam veteran, former police officer, and former firefighter, White would often go into trances during supervisors' meetings and then impulsively goose-step around the room. His past was filled with mystery, including an enigmatic "missing year" of 1972. White's murderous instability appeared to have been set off by the Jonestown murder-suicides and their link to San Francisco. The *Chronicle's* Rapaport noted in 2003: "Part of the connection between the events came through media coverage. Each day between Saturday, Nov. 18, and Monday, Nov. 27, new and terrible video, photos and revelations emanated from the jungle retreat where many former San Franciscans had chosen, been coerced or programmed to join the man they called 'Father.'"

In 1979, Dan White was found guilty of "manslaughter by diminished capacity," despite opening arguments by attorney Doug Schmidt that linked Jonestown to the assassinations. Many still believe that the reason White was not convicted of first-degree murder was because of what most of the media reported as the "Twinkie defense"—a phrase coined by well-known satirist Paul Krassner—that junk food had made White commit the crime. While it was in reality Ho-Hos and Ding Dongs, White's defense claimed that his love of junk food was the result of his depression, not the cause of it. The night the verdict was handed down, on May 21, 1979, the streets around San Francisco, especially near City Hall, erupted in violent protests. They became known, ironically, as the "White Night Riots." Dan White would only serve five years of his seven-year sentence. He was paroled in January 1984. He tried self-exile in Ireland, and then returned to San Francisco despite requests from Mayor Dianne Feinstein (who had succeeded Moscone) not to do so.

On the morning of October 21, 1985, Dan White attached a garden hose to the exhaust pipe of his car, ran the other end to his yellow 1970 Buick Le Sabre's interior, and died by suicide at his San Francisco home. Tom, his brother, discovered the body just before two P.M. White had died as an Irish ballad, "The Town I Loved So Well," played from a cassette player inside the car as it filled with deadly carbon monoxide.

Milk's less-than-a-month-old will requested that his body be cremated and his ashes enshrined with a mixture of bubble bath (to denote his gay lifestyle) and Kool-Aid (to signify the People's Temple victims). On the twenty-fifth anniversary of the assassinations, Milk was remembered as the world's first openly gay politician to hold office, the subject of the Oscar-winning film *The Life and Times of Harvey Milk,* and the focus of operas, plays, and museum exhibits. An elementary school, a civic plaza, a restaurant, a gay cultural institute, and a library in San Francisco bear his name, as does a one-of-a-kind high school in New York for gay students who have been tormented in mainstream schools.

Milk and Moscone were not the only persons killed in the wake of the People's Temple suicides and murder-suicides. In 1980, news accounts told of an alleged People's Temple "hit squad" that was suspected of killing, on February 26, a family of three who had defected in 1975 and testified against the cult. Elmer Mertle (identified in early news accounts under the alias Al Mills), was found shot in the head and lying facedown in his bedroom in the family's Berkeley home. The body of his 40-year-old wife, Deanna Mertle (also known as Jeannie Mills, author of *Six Years with God*), also shot in the head with a small-caliber weapon, was discovered on her back in an adjacent bathroom. The couple's 15-year-old daughter, Daphene, was taken to Alta Bates Hospital with two gunshots in the head, and died there later. The Mertles were the founders of Concerned Relatives and the principal organizers of Ryan's attempt to intervene in the Jonestown cult. Jones called them "white devils."

Less than a month later the ripples from the San Francisco murders reached civil rights worker Dennis Sweeney. On March 14, 1980, Sweeney shot seven bullets point-blank into his former friend, Congressman Allard K. Lowenstein, at Lowenstein's New York City law offices. Activist Lowenstein had marched in the 1964 Freedom Summer in Mississippi, campaigned for Robert F. Kennedy, authored the "Dump Johnson" movement, and ran the National Student Association, which was later revealed to be CIA-subsidized. After the shooting, Sweeney sat down, smoked a cigarette, seemed to be in a trance state, and calmly waited for the police to arrive. During his trial, Sweeny testified that the CIA (with Lowenstein's help) had implanted a chip in his head fifteen years earlier and that he could hear voices transmitted through his dental work. Sweeney blamed CIA "controllers" for his uncle's heart attack and the assassination of San Francisco mayor George Moscone. Sweeney was found not guilty by reason of insanity, and in 2000 he was released from a mental hospital in upstate New York. (The media loved the Sweeney-Lowenstein story. Teresa Carpenter even won a Pulitzer prize for her *Village Voice* exclusive in which Sweeney was quoted as saying that the shooting was a gay lovers' quarrel. The only trouble was that Carpenter never interviewed Sweeney: She had made the whole thing up.)

Other deaths followed. Joe Mazor, the private detective hired by the Concerned Relatives to persuade people to leave Jonestown, was shot dead a few years after the Mertles-Mills deaths. Walter Rodney, an intellectual and renowned Caribbean scholar born and raised in Guyana, was assassinated there on December 13, 1980, via a bomb-implanted walkie-talkie. Paula Neustel Adams, Jim Jones's top liaison in the upper echelons of the Guyanese government, was murdered in suburban Bethesda, Maryland, in October 1983. Her longtime companion, Laurence Mann, Guyana's ambassador to the United States from 1975 to 1981, apparently killed her, their child, and then himself in a murder-suicide. Members of the Jonestown Institute and author Garrett Lambrev have written that many questions remain unanswered about the true extent of all the copycat suicides, murder-suicides, and murders that have occurred since the Jonestown massacre.

The specter of Jonestown filled the newspapers for years and produced a made-for-television movie called *Guyana Tragedy: The Story of Jim Jones* (1980), starring the then-new and unknown actor Powers Boothe in a highly acclaimed performance as Jones. But the Jonestown event had other broad cultural outcomes besides creating a model for mass suicides. For example, despite the actual use of Flavor Aid, the media had quickly mislabeled what was used as Kool-Aid, and worldwide sales of Kool-Aid crashed. Another lasting linguistic legacy of the People's Temple tragedy is the expression "Don't drink the Kool-Aid." This has come to mean "Don't trust any group you find to be a little on the fanatical side."

Jonestown Copycats

The island of Mindanao lies six hundred miles southeast of Manila in the Philippines. Hidden deep in its jungles is the village of Gunitan, which can be reached only by hiking up rugged trails through thick forests. The village is at the base of the 9,540-foot Mount Apo, the highest mountain in the Philippines.

Living in Gunitan are the Ata, a "very peaceful" mountain people who wear loincloths, eat roots, and hunt animals with bows and arrows. In September 1985, the Atas' high priestess, Mangayanon Butaos, like Jim Jones of the People's Temple, convinced members of her mountain tribe to kill themselves. She promised them they would see God if they ate the poisoned food she offered them, and sixty died soon after eating it. Survivors said they were forced to eat the porridge that was laced with insecticide. Butaos reportedly stabbed herself to death after her followers ate the food.

Civilian officials trying to reach the scene on September 14 turned back, overwhelmed by the stench of decaying flesh. Only later did a team of militiamen manage to reach the scene. They found that many of the dead had been ripped apart by wild boars and dogs.

Other cult mass suicides were in the news after Jonestown as well. On November 1, 1986, the charred corpses of seven women were found on a beach in Wakayama Prefecture, in western Japan. They were members of the Church of the Friends of Truth who decided to create fiery suicides after the death of their leader, Kiyoharu Miyamoto. On August 29, 1987, in Yongin, South Korea, the bodies of thirty-two people were found in a factory attic after they took drugs and apparently strangled each other. Another report noted that several of them had had their throats cut after absorbing a nonfatal dose of poison. Authorities said factory owner Park Soon-ja, who died with the group, was called "Benevolent Mother." She claimed God told her to become a priestess and seek disciples. Her sect preached that the world was coming to an end.

The Jonestown-like mass murder-suicides continued into the 1990s. On December 13, 1990, a dozen people died near Tijuana, Mexico, after drinking a sacrament, a punch poisoned by industrial alcohol, in a religious ritual. A year later, also in Mexico, Minister Morales Almazan and twenty-nine followers suffocated after he told them to keep praying and ignore the toxic fumes filling their San Luis Potosí church. The minister reportedly told his dying congregation that God was drawing near and that he could feel the presence of the Lord.

On April 19, 1993, eighty-one Branch Davidian cult members and four U.S. government officials died in fire and gunfire when police and federal agents ended a fifty-one-day siege of the group's compound near Waco, Texas. Sect leader David Koresh died of a gunshot wound to the head sometime during the blaze. In October 1993, fifty-three Vietnamese hill tribe villagers died by mass suicide using flintlocks and other archaic weapons in the belief that they would go straight to heaven. Nineteen children were among the villagers who died in the hamlet of Ta He, about two hundred miles northwest of Hanoi. A blind man named Ca Van Liem, who had proclaimed himself king, inspired the mass suicide. On March 20, 1995, members of Aum Shinrikyo, founded by Shoko Asahara, released sarin gas on Tokyo subway trains, injuring over five thousand people and killing twelve. Reportedly, Aum members previously had committed a variety of murders and attempted to commit more murders after the Tokyo subway attack.

Comet Copycats

At the end of the twentieth century, with the media attuned to the newsworthiness of cult suicides, I became one of the talking heads—an "expert" for the evening television broadcasts—on suicide clusters and mass suicides. Requests for phone interviews started coming in immediately after the news broke on March 22, 1997, of a cult's mass suicide in California. The cult death cluster story we all know as Heaven's Gate would soon swamp the media. In the first few hours after the discovery of thirty-nine bodies in a Rancho Santa Fe mansion, the television and radio networks began covering the story "wall-to-wall," as they say.

The media was in a fog about the cult and were looking for simple answers about how the deaths could have happened. But there were no simple solutions to Heaven's Gate.

Heaven's Gate began to tie its future to the Hale-Bopp comet after the comet's appearance became a frequent topic of conversation on the overnight Art Bell radio talk show and then the Internet. One of the guests who talked about Hale-Bopp was Richard Hoagland, most famous for his "Face on Mars" commentaries. Art Bell also had on his program astronomer Chuck Sharamek, who discussed an object that he had observed near the comet. Remote viewer Courtney Brown decided this object was a sphere inhabited by aliens. Cult leader Marshall Applewhite regarded this as the signal he had been waiting for: that Hale-Bopp was hiding a spaceship that would take his followers from this plane of existence to the next.

Others also saw the remarkable appearance of the "comet of the century," Hale-Bopp, as a heavenly sign of doom and gloom. While Heaven's Gate will certainly be a defining moment in the rush to the end of the second millennium, there is in fact a long history of such comet lore. The bond between comets and disasters, like copycat suicides, goes back to antiquity. Comets were originally regarded as evil stars, and the Latin word for *evil star* is *dis-aster,* or disaster.

One ancient record on the Ipuwer Papyrus, a chronicle called "Admonitions of a Sage," states that in 1369 B.C. a huge comet and catastrophic events visited Egypt simultaneously. As the astronomers Victor Clube and Bill Napier noted in *The Cosmic Serpent* (1982), this comet's appearance drove many people to suicide. This tendency to publicize or remark on this connection has continued down throughout history.

Between 1347 and 1348, two comets blazed over Europe. During their visit, the Black Death appeared and eventually killed 25 million people, a third of Europe's population. Mass suicides occurred throughout Europe. Earthquakes took place in Cyprus, Greece, and Italy. Mass suicides and comets are also linked in the years 1506, 1528–29, 1582, and 1666.

In 1927 comet Skjellerup appeared, followed by Germany's "Black Friday." The collapsed economy was the beginning of a worldwide depression. Many related suicides occurred. Other disasters included the death of Ferdinand I, king of Romania; an earthquake in central Japan, leaving thousands dead; and floods in India, Siberia, Romania, New England, and Algeria, killing hundreds. All these disasters, in the public and *media's* mind, were somehow related to the appearance of the comet.

The frequent return of Halley's comet has been tied in folklore and the media to deaths and suicides. It has often been remarked that Mark Twain "came in" (was born) with Halley's comet and "went out" (died) with it. Other people have used Halley's as their final marker as well. In A.D. 66, as Halley's comet hung over Jerusalem "like a sword," the Romans warred against the city and many suicide clusters occurred throughout the land.

Even Edmund Halley, the discoverer of the comet that carries his name, was star-crossed by this weird synchronicity. On March 5, 1684, his father, Edmund Halley Sr., walked out of the family house and never returned. His body was found in a river at Temple Farm, near Rochester, Great Britain. In 1932, examining the evidence carefully, the distinguished Halley scholar Eugene Fairfield MacPike declared the death of the elder Halley a suicide.

When Halley's comet made its closest approach to the earth in 1910, several people killed themselves out of contagious fear and panic. Spurious connections between an astronomical event and human phenomenon must be guarded against, but there is clear evidence of a media-driven connection between suicides and Halley's comet in 1910. People the world over were scared to death of the impending close encounter with the comet. They honestly wondered if the earth would survive its passage. "May 18, 1910, was a day of dread," historian Jerred Metz noted in his 1985 book *Halley's Comet,* addressing the astrosociology of the event. That was the day the earth was to have passed through the supposed poisonous tail of the comet. The anxiety led many to suicide. Suicide clusters occurred in Japan, Italy, and Spain. "Comets kill people by self-fulfilling superstition," noted Nigel Calder in *The Comet is Coming!,* "when those who read them as telegrams from the gods or the Devil turn in panic to homicide or suicide."

In the United States the attempted and completed suicides clustered around that fateful day in May. Fearing no escape from the comet, Blanche Covington of Chicago locked herself in her room and turned on the gas. Her death is one of the most widely mentioned suicides said to be "caused" by Halley's comet. But there were other, less well-known American copycat comet suicides. Sophie Houge, also of Chicago, killed herself by the same method as Blanche Covington, through the use of illuminating gas. Viola Gastenum of Anaheim, California, gave lye to her two children and swallowed some herself. This attempted murder-suicide left three traumatized survivors. Jeanette Niebert of Denver swallowed morphine on May 18 and died. Her last words, according to the *Rocky Mountain News,* were "I think—the comet." Bessie Bradley, 25, became so disturbed by all the various predictions that when the comet did not appear on May 19, she turned on the gas and killed herself. On May 21, W. J. Lord of Cottonwood, Alabama, was recovering from four attempts he had made on his own life. First he shot himself, then jumped off a roof, then tried to cut his own throat, and finally jumped into a well.

"Suicidal mania," as Metz labeled it, was so widespread in 1910 that newspapers like the *Seattle Post-Intelligencer* carried the headline: "Fear of Annihilation Leads Weak-Minded to Suicide and Crime." *The New York Times* for May 19, 1910, put it this way: "Some Driven to Suicide, Others Become Temporarily Insane from Brooding over Comet." There is no doubt that newspaper reports caused panic in some individuals in 1910.

Another epidemic of suicides occurred among teenagers in 1910. Adolescent suicide was such an extraordinary problem that year that the world's first youth suicide prevention conference was organized by none other than Sigmund Freud. He opened the conference "On Suicide, Particularly among Children" on April 20, 1910, in Vienna, Austria, and also gave the closing remarks. He noted that "youthful suicides" were occurring "not only among pupils in secondary schools but also among apprentices and others."

When Halley's comet returned in 1985–86, with its closest approach on February 10–11, the United States found itself in the midst of another teen suicide epidemic, and once again, newspaper headlines proclaimed a connection. The *Press-*

Herald of Minden, Louisiana, asked, "Comets—Are They Linked to Suicides?" and the *Las Vegas Sun* ran two-inch-high headlines with the question answered: "Teen Suicide? Blame Halley."

Timing Is Everything

Comet Hale Bopp had a devastating effect at the end of the twentieth century. Within hours of the Hale-Bopp–inspired Heaven's Gate suicide episode, researcher Brad Steiger, I, and others were on the air speculating that the cult, led by Marshall Applewhite, had it origins in "The Two," the original "Bo and Beep" UFO cult of the 1970s.

The bizarre story of Heaven's Gate begins in 1972 when Marshall Applewhite met a psychiatric nurse named Bonnie Lu Nettles. She introduced him to astrology, mysticism, and mediation. Over time and in various guises, they took on different names: as "Brother Sun" and "Sister Moon" in 1973, as "Guinea" and "Pig" in 1974, then later that year as "Bo" and "Peep," and finally as "The Two" in 1975. Before long they had gathered a cult around them but, fearing assassination, split up the group and went "underground" in 1976. That year Brad Steiger's book about "The Two," *UFO Missionaries Extraordinary,* was published. In 1982 an NBC-TV movie was broadcast about Bo and Peep entitled *The Mysterious Two,* starring John Forsythe and Priscilla Pointer. Nettles died of cancer in 1985, and five years later Applewhite began to rebuild his group into what would become known as Heaven's Gate. By the mid-1980s he was using the name "Do" and, if he had not already, would soon become a eunuch. A half-dozen of his male followers would follow his lead and get castrated. By 1993, Applewhite (as "Do" or "Doe") used the media again to gather his flock, placing ads in *USA Today.* In February 1997, once Hale-Bopp was clearly "speaking" to Applewhite, he and several members of his group showed up at a book signing for Lee Shargel. Applewhite conveyed to Shargel, the author would later tell ABC-TV, that Applewhite thought Shargel's science fiction novel *Voice in the Mirror* contained messages from aliens to Applewhite for his group.

On March 22, 1997, thirty-nine members of Heaven's Gate (twenty-one women, eighteen men) consumed phenobarbital, some suffocating with plastic bags, and all dying by suicide. All were dressed exactly alike in black clothing, down to their black shoes with their identical white Nike check-mark logo. The thirty-nine had packed tote bags and each had one five-dollar bill and seventy-five cents in quarters in his or her pocket. The deaths occurred in shifts, so those who remained could correctly arrange the bodies and place the purple triangular shrouds on the bodies. The police found the corpses at their Rancho Santa Fe, California, compound on March 26, after being alerted by Richard Ford, an ex-member who had received a Federal Express package of two videotapes from Applewhite.

Reporters jumped from one factoid to another rumor without regard to the complexity of the story or how its various elements tied together. They shied away from the twilight language of dates and astrological connections related to the event that were key to deciphering the clues as to why the suicides were committed and when. While many of these little twilight details were conscious on the part of the cult members, others were known only to the leaders, and still a few more seemed to work on a purely subconscious level. More attention to the twilight language involved in such episodes may provide advance warning of future mass suicides and murders.

The Heaven's Gate cult watched closely for subtle signs from the cosmos. But the moment their suicides occurred was extremely important in Marshall Applewhite's delusional system. The Hale-Bopp comet's closest approach occurred on Saturday, March 22, 1997. For the Heaven's Gate cult, this was the "marker" they were waiting for. They believed a spaceship was following behind the comet, a speculation that had begun to circulate earlier via the Art Bell show and on the Internet. (It would later turn out that the controversy had begun with photographs that had been faked; there was no "companion" with the comet.)

Heaven's Gate was not just concerned with spaceships and comets: They were also very attuned to the calendar, and March 1997 was a very hot month. There was a solar eclipse on March 9. March 20 was the spring equinox. March 22 was the closest approach of Hale-Bopp. Then there was a lunar eclipse on March 24, March 23 was Palm Sunday, March 28 was Good Friday, and March 30 was Easter Sunday.

One of the Heaven's Gate relatives explained the timing issue. Suzanne Sylvia Cooke was one of the thirty-nine people who died by suicide on March 22. Her husband, Wayne, told CBS's *60 Minutes* that he wished he had had the courage to follow the other members of Heaven's Gate. He said, "They left when a comet came. A comet has significance, historically. They left in the Easter Week. That has significance historically. They left by laying down their bodies; that has enormous impact. Obviously a stage is being set by the next level for this world, for others, to examine this."

Wayne Cooke's network broadcast interview was a suicide note to the world, but few understood that. On May 6, 1997, Cooke and another ex-member of Heaven's Gate tried to "exit their vehicles" in an Encinitas Holiday Inn Express four miles from the cult's Rancho Santa Fe mausoleum. Cooke was found dead with a plastic bag on his head. The other former member, Chuck Humphrey of Denver, was found unconscious but alive and was taken in critical condition to Scripps Memorial Hospital in Encinitas. Both men had been found with small tote bags next to them, dressed in the same black outfits as their Heaven's Gate mates, wearing black Nikes, with purple shrouds next to them, and a five-dollar bill and three quarters in their pockets. Like those who went before, they both had ingested phenobarbital washed down with vodka. Cooke said in his videotaped "exit statement" sent to family members and CNN that he wanted "very much to join my classmates and my teachers . . . I've never doubted my connection with them." He concluded his comments by saying good-bye with a smile eerily similar to the expression Applewhite had on his face in a video repeatedly shown by the media after the Heaven's Gate bodies were found.

At a San Diego news conference after the March mass suicide, Humphrey, 56, said, "I left the group because it had been fifteen years, because many of the things we were told were going to happen didn't . . . I got tired of waiting." In his "exit statement" he erroneously states: "By now you should be aware that I . . . too have exited my vehicle . . . I do not pretend to have accomplished my task of overcoming this human vehicle and gaining the degree of control I would have liked, but nonetheless, I know who I am and that I must go back with them whether I am ready or not . . . I'd rather gamble on missing the bus this time than staying on this planet and risk losing my soul." Humphrey felt like a failure because his exit plan had misfired.

Humphrey and Cooke were not alone. A week after the Heaven's Gate episode, Yuba County deputies checking out a trailer in a remote canyon near Marysville, California (population 9,900), discovered the remains of a man who had gassed himself to death. The victim was identified as Robert Leon Nichols, 58, a former roadie with the rock band Grateful Dead. Nichols was last seen alive on Saint Patrick's Day. Nichols was lying on his back in bed with a clear plastic bag over his head and had hung a model spacecraft, made of silver foil, from his ceiling. A hose ran under the bag to a propane tank, and a three-by-three-foot purple shroud covered his upper torso. Nichols reportedly left a suicide note that said, in part, "I'm going on the spaceship with Hale-Bopp to be with those who have gone before me." The *New York Post* pointed out that the Nichols note was dated ten A.M., Thursday, March 28, 1997, two days after the thirty-nine Heaven's Gate bodies were discovered but several hours before the public was told how the cultists died and that their bodies were covered with purple shrouds.

On May 7, 1997, as researcher Antonio Mendoza quotes Dick Joslyn of Tampa, a former member of the Heaven's Gate cult, at least six other cultists might also have been interested in trying suicide. Joslyn, who had been in contact with Chuck Humphrey, the cultist who survived the latest passage to the "next level," said his friend had grown frustrated by the lack of attention given to the group's ideas. "He was a little discouraged by the inability to get the word out. He made it clear to me that when his work was done, he would go too." Another former member who goes by the name of Sawyer said that Humphrey, one of the brains behind the Higher Source Web design team, "was supposed to spread information about the 'next level' and maintain the Internet site." When someone "commandeered" the site and Humphrey could no longer work on it, he tried to kill himself.

The New York Times, meanwhile, was whipping up anxieties by quoting Aaron Greenberg, a former Heaven's Gate member from Oregon, who said that he knew of sixty to eighty members who might be ready to die by suicide, and that about one thousand people had passed through the cult. The media alleged, through Greenberg and others, that two groups of surviving Heaven's Gate followers—one from Canada and the other from New York state—were converging on a secret site in the Southwest. Greenberg claimed: "This is not a good thing. Remember what they say in the videotapes: 'Come join us, the time is now, the window is small.' "

On May 16, 1997, Charles Humphrey, fully recovered from his suicide attempt, persuaded a judge to release him from a psychiatric facility so he could write a book and go on the speaking circuit. But Humphrey failed to get the media to pay attention, so on February 20, 1998, Humphrey, who saw himself as one of the remaining Heaven's Gate members on spaceship Earth, died by suicide in a tent in the Arizona desert. The cultist was found with his head sealed in a plastic bag and pipes running to a car's exhaust pipe and a tank marked Carbon Dioxide. He was dressed in black sweatpants and a black T-shirt with a patch on the sleeve that read Heaven's Gate Away Team. Like those who went before him, he wore a pair of brand-new black Nike sneakers, kept a purple shroud next to him, and carried a five-dollar bill plus three quarters in his pocket.

Order of the Solar Temple

On March 22, 1997, just as the Heaven's Gate thirty-nine were dying by suicide, a documentary film about the Order of the Solar Temple cult aired on French television, and, in what was probably not a coincidence, five members of the Order of the Solar Temple killed themselves that day in a "Christic Fire." The Order of the Solar Temple, founded in 1986, keyed their suicides to the equinoxes and solstices of the year. The Solar Temple suicides were supposed to take place on the spring equinox, March 20, 1997, but delays meant that the big event could not happen until the following Saturday, March 22. The cult members believed that a fiery exit led to rebirth on an invisible planet circling Sirius. The Order's membership spoke of these "voyages" as "departures" rather than death.

At its peak in January 1989, the Order of the Solar Temple had 442 members. Ninety were in Switzerland, 187 in France, 86 in Canada, 53 in Martinique, 16 in the United States, and 10 in Spain. Members included celebrities such as Patrick Vuarnet, son of the president of an international fashion company; former

Olympic champion Jean Vuarnet; Robert Ostiguy, mayor of Richelieu, Quebec: and Camille Pilet, a former director and international sales manager for the Swiss multinational watch company Piaget.

The group began to unravel in 1993 when Solar Temple members were arrested for buying handguns, and a few members began to question the group's leadership. The two leaders were Luc Jouret, a Belgian medical doctor and homeopath, and Joseph Di Mambro, a Canadian whose background as a con man and fake psychologist was apparently unknown to the Solar Temple's membership. One former associate of the group, Tony Dutoit, spoke out against Di Mambro, admitting that he, Dutoit, had installed the electronic equipment that projected the spiritual appearances that Di Mambro would proclaim as supernatural.

According to London *Sunday Times* investigative reporter Russell Miller, Di Mambro picked out two members of his "golden circle" to carry out Dutoit's ritual murder, sending one from Switzerland to Quebec for the task. On October 4, 1994, Tony Dutoit was stabbed fifty times, his wife Nicky Dutoit eight times in the back and four times in the throat (where conception was believed by the group to occur), and once in each breast. Their infant son, Emmanuel, was stabbed six times. (The Dutoits had named their baby Christopher Emmanuel, even though Di Mambro had "reserved" the name Emmanuelle for his "cosmic" daughter.) Once the two assassins left, two other devout members came to make final arrangements at the crime scene. They wrapped the infant in a black plastic bag and left a wooden stake on his chest before meticulously preparing for their own suicide and the incineration of all the bodies. Meanwhile, the assassins made their way back to Switzerland to rejoin their comrades, Jouret and Di Mambro, who had left Quebec just months previously under increasing scrutiny.

A half-day later Swiss locals found a chalet burning on the

edge of their tiny village of Cheiry. As the firefighters forced their way "into what they thought was a basement garage, they found themselves in a mirrored chapel draped with crimson fabric and with a Christ-like painting on one wall. On the floor, arranged in a sun-shaped circle with their feet pointing inwards, were 22 bodies: nine men, 12 women and a 12-year-old boy . . . Some of the dead were wearing the coloured ceremonial robes [of the Order of the Solar Temple]," wrote the *Sunday Times's* Miller. Nineteen had been shot in the head and nine were hooded with black plastic bags. Among the dead would be the Dutoits' assassins as well as Luc Jouret, Joseph Di Mambro, and his "cosmic child" Emmanuelle, age 12. In another town, Granges-sur-Salvan, Switzerland, another fire was burning.

By dawn on October 5, 1994, more people were found dead in Quebec, a result of a mass suicide mixed with more than a little murder. The victims, many of them well known, included the former Richelieu mayor Ostiguy, a Quebec City journalist, and a Hydro Quebec vice president. On his last day of life, Di Mambro gave Patrick Vuarnet a short note that said, "Following the tragic Transit at Cheiry, we insist on specifying, in the name of the Rose+Cross, that we deplore and totally disassociate ourselves from the barbarous, incompetent and aberrant conduct of Doctor Luc Jouret. He is the cause of veritable carnage."

On December 23, 1995, three children and thirteen adult members of the Order of the Solar Temple were found dead in a burned home in Grenoble in the French Alps. They appeared to have been killed or killed themselves on December 22, the winter solstice. Laid out in a star-shaped pattern, like the bodies that had been found in Switzerland a year earlier, most had been drugged and had plastic bags pulled over their heads. Each body had at least one bullet wound in it and had been doused with flammable liquid before being burned.

In June of 1996, during the summer solstice, police kept Solar Temple members under surveillance after rumors surfaced of another possible ritual killing. But nothing happened, and police then concluded that the cult was no longer an active movement. That proved not to be the case.

As firemen fought a fire at one of the group's homes at St.-Casimir near Quebec City on March 22, 1997, three teenagers, two males, 13 and 16, and a 14-year-old female, emerged from a nearby woodshed. According to Reuters, Pierre Robichaud, a provincial police officer from Sûreté du Quebec, said the youths told him that "The voyage was set for Thursday, for the spring equinox, a voyage for eight people, and the children were included without their knowledge. What happened is that the lighting mechanism did not work Thursday night, so when the parents woke up Friday morning, they were surprised to still be alive. The children understood what was happening and they told their parents that they did not want to go, and on Saturday, the parents gave them a choice. The children voluntarily took medication, sleeping pills, and went to sleep in the shed knowing that when they woke up, their parents and grandmother would be dead."

At the end of 1997, the Solar Temple number of dead stood at seventy-four: October 4, 1994, Morin Heights, Quebec—five victims; October 5, 1994, Granges-sur-Salvan, Switzerland—twenty-five victims; October 5, 1994, Cheiry, Switzerland—twenty-three victims; December 15, 1995, Vercors, France—sixteen victims; and March 22, 1997, St.-Casimir, Quebec—five victims.

Today, French and Canadian authorities feel that mass suicides could occur again at any time with this cult. Remarkably, the group has gone largely unnoticed by the American media.

More Tomorrow?

When the media did pay attention to the Solar Temple deaths, they tended to see Solar Temple copycats everywhere.

On January 8, 1998, according to Canary Island police, German psychologist Heide Fittkau-Garthe, 57, was charged with attempted murder and inducement to suicide for her role in a suspected mass suicide plot on the Spanish resort island of Tenerife. Spanish police officials foiled the suicide plot during what they described as a "last supper" at her chalet. Police found poisonous chemicals, which they believe were to be used in a mass suicide by her thirty-two followers. Police spokesman Juan Antonio Perez said Fittkau-Garthe had brainwashed her disciples into poisoning themselves, Reuters reported. The group's members had planned to kill themselves at the top of Tenerife's Pico de Teide volcano, from which they believed a spaceship would pick up their souls, officials said.

Founder of the Center for the Studies on New Religions Massimo Introvigne wrote on the watch group's website: "Another Solar Temple hoax concerns Dr. Heide Fittkau-Garthe . . . The information published by many newspapers on January 9 that Dr. Fittkau-Garthe was the leader of 'a branch of the Solar Temple' is inaccurate. She was never a member of the Solar Temple. A prominent leader of the German branch of the Brahma Kumaris, she left the Indian movement (or was excluded from it) and eventually became one of the most prominent self-help motivational speakers in Germany. She lectured on behalf of a number of German large corporations and was hailed as a 'star psychologist.' The esoteric doctrines of her core group of followers involved references to both Western and Eastern occult lore. Her name—like Princess Grace's—has never surfaced in any document on the Solar Temple."

Another scare occurred on September 5, 2002, when the guru of a tiny French doomsday cult under police suicide watch in Nantes, France, said his group was looking forward to voyagers from Venus collecting them before the world ended on October 24, 2002. Arnaud Mussy, 36, denied any plans for a mass suicide, dismissing parallels that police and the media had made between his New Lighthouse sect and the Order of the Solar Temple cult.

The farther away the cults are from America, the less the American media tends to talk about them, regardless of the horror involved. At least 530 members of the Ugandan cult Movement for the Restoration of the Ten Commandments of God were burned to death on Saint Patrick's Day, March 17, 2000, in their church after controversy arose from the failure of the world to end on December 31, 1999. Most were Roman Catholics who had grown dissatisfied with the Church or were simply drawn to the movement by blood ties. They found their way to a little patch of the western jungle, where the cult site in Swese and its ominous secrets stood unwatched. Investigators uncovered five mass graves that indicated that more than a thousand people were murdered on the orders of cult leaders Joseph Kibwetere, Dominic Kataribabo, and Gredonia Mwerinda. Deborah Layton, who fled Jonestown just before the killings, was asked by the British media to comment on the mysterious movement: "Nobody joins a cult. You join a self-help group, a religious movement, a political organization. They change so gradually, by the time you realize you're entrapped—and almost everybody does—you can't figure a safe way back out."

The Copycat Effect in Cult Persuasion

What we now know about the psychology of mass suicides and cultic relationships can help us better understand these events. The work of Margaret Thaler Singer, who wrote *Cults in Our Midst* with Janja Lalich, provides a "road map" to the anthropology of these groups. I have worked with cults and former cult members since the 1960s and I found Singer's work to be the most organized and logical attempt to understand cults yet written. Singer identified a process of persuasion/coercion/fear at work that is very similar to what occurs in some dysfunctional marriages. This is a good starting point for our general understanding of the psychological processes involved because, while most people do not have direct knowledge of any cults, almost everyone knows someone who has been in a relationship with a person they talk about "loving" yet with whom they are unable to feel safe with or from whom they cannot separate. The mechanics of a harmful marriage resemble those in a cult with an abusive leader or regime.

Anyone who has watched videotapes of Marshall Applewhite, Charles Manson, or Jim Jones can see these men were legends in their own minds and held a charismatic power over their groups. Margaret Singer explains the influence of such cult leaders:

• *Cult leaders are self-appointed, persuasive persons who claim to have a special mission in life or to have special knowledge.*

The fact that everyone in Heaven's Gate bought into Applewhite's belief that comet Hale-Bopp was the signal to begin their transition clearly shows the extent to which his delusions could influence the whole group. Jim Jones's sense that the CIA or others were going to invade their camp is another example of their "special knowledge."

• *Cult leaders tend to be determined and domineering and often described as charismatic.*

The energy and sexuality of the charming and seductive David Koresh and others are channeled into ultimate control and decision-making. Nettles and Applegate convinced their followers to drop contact with their families, to hand over their financial resources, and in some cases to give up their lives.

- *Cult leaders center veneration on themselves.*

   Genuinely altruistic leaders—be they religious, political, or other—refocus adoration and idolization on God, a principle, or the masses. In contrast, cult leaders make certain that they receive this adoration directly. Applewhite, for example, even as he was leaving his "container," had the biggest, most elegant bedroom.

   We can add that even the sexuality of the leader is reflected in the group, whether this takes the form of a "complex marriage," as John Noyes, founder of the Oneida community, called their practice of open group sex; the sexual assaults by David Koresh on children he called his "teen brides"; or the asexuality and castration of Heaven's Gate males inspired by Marshall Applewhite's own long history of confused sexuality. Jim Jones received the sexual favors of the people he wanted. Before every Order of the Solar Temple ritual, Luc Jouret would have sex with one of the group's women to give him "spiritual strength" for the ceremony. Di Mambro would instruct a female chevalier *to perform a sex act, and she obeyed without question.*

How a cult is controlled depends upon its structure; in most cases, all power, decisions and ideas come down from the leaders. Singer states the obvious but often overlooked when she wrote: "Cults are authoritarian in structure." The members of Heaven's Gate did almost everything based on Applewhite's decrees—including what *Star Trek* episodes they watched, where they went, what jobs they had, and how they dressed. To many people, the members' apparent intelligence and seemingly peaceful deaths implied that they made the decision to kill themselves voluntarily.

Unfortunately, this view does not take account of the subtle coercion that we know goes on in such groups. Applewhite was very aware that the mass deaths would attract a great deal of media attention; he made certain that the deaths were conducted in shifts so that the bodies, when found, would appear orderly. We know from Robert Ford—"the one he left behind to tell his story"—that Applewhite wanted the faces of the dead to be covered by the purple shrouds because he knew their video images would be flashed around the world by the media. The message, as much as the act, was important to Applewhite. Cults use the media. And the media spreads the virus.

Clearly, the Heaven's Gate cult followed a top-down structure in planning. The media compared this event to the "mass suicide" of the People's Temple in Jonestown, and the similarities are there, of course, in forced actions and the behavior contagion between members to do as the leader wished. Applewhite, Koresh, Jones, and all these cult leaders are psychological cousins.

Exploitative brainwashing, mind control, persuasion, or thought reform—no matter what you call it—does exist and is used by strong-willed leaders and individuals to recruit and keep members and, in the end, sometimes coerce them, albeit sometimes subtly, into killing themselves. Singer points out two critical factors in this regard: first, that "cults tend to be totalistic, or all-encompassing, in controlling their members' behavior and also ideologically totalistic, exhibiting zealotry and extremism in their worldview." Nettles and Applewhite would pair the members—"classmates," as they were called (giving the idea they were always learning something from Applewhite)—who would then have to tell each other everything they knew about themselves. Luc Jouret and Joseph Di Mambro had their "golden circle." With these very effective mind-control techniques, members begin to lose all sense of self. Once the sense of individuality is destroyed, it is replaced with a group self. Persuasiveness and the ability to manipulate followers are the real tools of cult leaders.

Suicidologists now recognize that one of the major underlying risk factors for suicide is a sense of being isolated, which is directly akin to the feelings of loneliness, sadness, neediness, and despondency that are known to drive people toward cult membership. Once inside the group, members are enmeshed and brainwashed into feeling that they are part of the whole, and fears of separation from the group compel them to obey the leader's commands. This situation also reinforces the group or herd mentality that is conducive to copycat behavior.

This is also the process that so often leads to tragedy. It is why, when asked to make the choice between going back to outside-world "isolation" or going on to "the next level" through group suicide, the choice is so often so very clear to the members of a cult. At this stage the choice is not made freely: Each member is completely enmeshed in an unsafe, dysfunctional, and deceptive world of the leader's creation.

The guns owned by the Branch Davidians and those found in Heaven's Gate storage room indicate the extent to which these groups were prepared to defend their belief systems. They feared that their lives and their spiritual progress were in jeopardy from, or under siege by, the outsiders, whether they called themselves Luciferians or the FBI.

Massive cult deaths will continue to happen. The question is: Can we decipher their messages and put it all in context before more tragedies occur?

CHAPTER EIGHT

Teen Clusters

The phenomenon of youth suicide clusters is nothing new, but not until the 1980s did the extent of the youthful suicide clusters come to public attention. If one followed the unfolding of the drama in the media, young people were killing themselves in groups of threes and fives throughout North America.

The increase in teen suicide clusters seemed to be the latest manifestation of the pressures of our times. As Susan and Daniel Cohen pointed out in 1984 in their book *Teenage Stress,* the tensions for contemporary adolescents came from a variety of sources: competition in school, fights at home, changes in physical appearance, drugs, sex, and dating. The suicide clusters that resulted occurred in places familiar and unfamiliar, in Plano, Clear Lake, Peekskill, Wind River, Leominster, Omaha, and Mankato. The timing of these clusters pointed to a hidden pattern in these stories.

Suicide Months

According to most records kept since the beginning of the twentieth century, the peak time for suicides among the general American population is May. The number of suicides then decreases through the summer and into autumn and early winter until they reach a low point in December. Then the climb begins anew in January until reaching a peak in May. But in a 1983 study of 1970's data, researcher Kenneth Bollen showed that among 15- to 29-year-olds, November was the peak and January the trough.

But when I examined closely the teen suicide clusters of the mid-1980s in particular, I discovered something unique. Neither May nor November stood out as peak months for limited-time-frame, small-geographic-area suicide clusters. Instead, the month of recurring importance was February. During February 1983, two teens in the space of seven days killed themselves in Plano, Texas, at the beginning of that cluster. Throughout the month of February 1984, southeastern New York experienced six teen suicides that signaled the start of that area's cluster, and Plano, Texas, registered another suicide, which may have demonstrated the repeating anniversary syndrome. In February 1985 a teen-suicide television movie aired, and more teen suicides occurred in New York and Colorado. Finally, during February 1986, clusters of adolescent suicides and attempts broke out in Nebraska, Massachusetts, Minnesota, and South Dakota. And on February 23, 1986, in Plano an 18-year-old died by suicide exactly three years to the day after the town's first cluster suicide.

Why is February the month of teen suicide clusters? Is it because it follows the allegedly depressing and stressful time of family holidays and unfulfilled vacation hopes for some teens? A closer look at the teen cluster suicides of the 1980s provides some suggestions.

Plano

The decade began when twelve teens killed themselves in the northern Denver, Colorado, suburb of Loveland and twenty youths died by suicide in Gardiner, Maine, within an eighteen-month period in 1980–81. In 1982 in Milwaukee County, Wisconsin, three youths died from suicide within days of each other. In August 1982, Cheyenne, Wyoming, was shocked when three of its teens killed themselves. Then three adolescents died by their own hand over one weekend in Groveport, Ohio, which liked to call itself "Central Ohio's Hometown." But no one was prepared for what would happen in Texas.

Twenty miles north of Dallas, Plano was a small farming village of about three thousand people as it emerged from the 1950s. But in a short two decades the soybean and cotton fields gave way to the spread of housing subdivisions and shopping plazas. In 1970 the population numbered 17,000. In 1980 it had reached 72,000, and by 1985 over 120,000. From all reports, the population has continued growing by 10,000 people a year.

Late in the 1970s the *Los Angeles Times* said Plano was "the quintessential Sunbelt city," and *Texas Monthly* commented: "There stands on the Texas plains a perfect city." *Newsweek* in 1983 observed: "Plano is one of the 'pop-up' communities that began to dot the Sunbelt in the seventies, as upwardly mobile young executives in search of the good life moved in from the foundering cities of the East."

But the city was far from perfect. The fast-paced, white-collar suburb of Plano soon showed the darker side of high achievement. The number of divorces, previously low, jumped to a thousand a year in the early 1980s. Most people who had come to Plano left because of the mobility inherent in their middle management jobs. Large segments of the populace had lived less than three years in the sprawling community when their teens began dying. After the deaths started, everyone started noticing the Sunbelt rootlessness, the competitive pressures, the incidence of substance abuse and alcoholism. But by then it was too late for the children. Plano found itself in the grip of a suicide cluster.

It began with Bill Ramsey and Bruce Carrio. Their story is the story of Plano. Bruce and his family moved from Rochester, Michigan, in June 1982—their fifth move. That first summer Bruce played with his computer and watched television sitcoms, usually *The Brady Bunch.* In September, after he started attending Plano Senior High School, he met Bill Ramsey. They became fast friends and hung out at places like the McDonald's near school and the popular local video arcade, Texas Time Out (TTO). They became known as "the Two Bs." They were fun to be around.

Then something happened to Bill, reportedly after he saw the movie *Pink Floyd—The Wall.* The movie is about a rock star's construction of a wall around himself. Bill began to build his own wall. Soon Bill took to wearing boots and a leather jacket. He also started writing dark poems he would share with Bruce, such as:

Death is painless, quick
As a whisper on the wind
Silently calling.

Bruce got a leather jacket also.

On February 19, 1983, Bill, Bruce, and another friend, Chris Thornsberry, met at a local pizza joint, Chuck E Cheese's. Like TTOs, it was filled with video games and the noise of rock music. The Two Bs and Chris decided to have a drag race. It was Chris's 1973 Corvette against Bruce's 1972 Skylark, out on one of the long and hot blacktops that line the country around Plano. Bill, with flag in hand, was set to give the signal letting them know when to let it rip.

But then something bizarre happened. Bruce's car never left the starting line, and Chris's Corvette swerved and struck Bill. Chris started screaming, "Bill, are you all right? Are you all right? Bill, are you all right?" Bill Ramsey, 17, was not all right. Rushed to Plano Emergency, he was dead by 5:30 A.M. the following morning.

One of the Two Bs was dead, and Bruce was very upset. He became withdrawn and more and more depressed about the freak accident. He would quote a Pink Floyd song to his friends and say he would see Bill again "some sunny day." The day after Bill's funeral, Bruce decided to make good on his words. After work, turning into the Carrio driveway, Bruce's mother was startled to see Bruce's car in their garage, an unusual place for it. Seeing his feet sticking out the back window of his car, she thought at first he had fallen asleep. But something was wrong. The cassette tape player was playing a Pink Floyd song, "Goodbye Cruel World," there was the odor of gasoline fumes, and the motor was still running. Bruce Carrio, 16, was pronounced dead of carbon monoxide poisoning on February 23, 1983. Bruce's rootlessness continued after his death. The Carrios told reporters they cremated Bruce because they did not know where to bury him. "Where is home?" they asked painfully.

A mere six days after Bruce's suicide, on March 1, Glenn Currey, 18, killed himself by carbon monoxide poisoning in his parents' garage. Like Bruce and Bill, he, too, had been a Plano High School student, but was not friendly with them. He had recently broken up with a girlfriend, and friends wondered if this was what had propelled the suicide, although, of course, it is never just one thing. It was clear, though, that he had patterned his suicide closely after Bruce's, even down to having music playing as he died of asphyxiation.

The town was in shock and community action groups were formed, but the suicides continued. On April 18, Henri Doriot, 15, shot himself with a .22-caliber rifle. Pinned to his bulletin board were news items about the Two Bs' deaths and a sketch labeled "The Ghost of Death." Meanwhile, more than a dozen other young people had attempted suicide since Bruce's death. The methods were as different as the youths themselves. One young male tried to use his own shirt to hang himself and a young female sliced up her chest with a pair of scissors.

Soon the word-of-mouth knowledge of their deaths had the local press, then the national media, turning its attention to the suicide clusters of Plano. During the week of August 15, 1983, a national newsmagazine did a major story on the growing Texas city and its wave of teen deaths. The spotlight was on Plano's adolescents. Tragically, within a week, three more Plano teens would be dead from suicides.

On August 17, Mary Bridget and John Gundlah, both 17, died of carbon monoxide poisoning while sitting in a car in the garage of a house under construction. They left a suicide note explaining they had been under pressure to break up but had decided they would rather die than end their relationship. Soon after the Bridget-Gundlah suicide pact, Scott Difiglia, 18, apparently despondent over breaking up with his girlfriend, shot himself on August 22 with a .22-caliber rifle. He died the next day at Plano's Presbyterian Hospital.

Almost exactly a year to the day after Bill Ramsey's death and Bruce Carrio's suicide, Plano recorded another suicide cluster death. On February 13, 1984, David Eugene Harris, 14, friendly and bright, a computer whiz, came home to parents who loved him, put their .357 Magnum to his head, and killed himself. The only thing his father could figure out that might have been bothering David was his new braces. Sadly, the reasons for suicides do not dwell in the land of logic and pain of grieving survivors. Here was the anniversary phenomenon at work, in which the tragic remembrance of a loss on its yearly anniversary calls forth action, sometimes similar action, by the vulnerable.

Plano's eighth youth suicide occurred on May 12, 1984. Then

twenty-two suicide-free months passed until February 23, 1986, when, on the exact anniversary of Bruce Carrio's suicide, an 18-year-old senior who had previously attempted suicide died of carbon monoxide poisoning. Once again the flag at Plano High School flew at half-mast and the teens at the shopping center and TTO scratched their heads. In whispers they wondered why death had visited them again.

The adults in the community responded with funding and organized efforts at prevention. A twenty-four-hour hotline and a community crisis center now exist in Plano. Guidance counselors have been added at the elementary-school level, and student groups such as SWAT (Students Working All Together) and BIONIC (Believe It Or Not I Care) have been set up. Police officers hold regular office hours in the schools, meeting casually with anyone who wants to talk.

Although the mystery of Plano's cluster remains, some have ventured insights. One Plano family therapist, Glenn Weimer, tends toward the contagion theory in explaining the series of suicides: "I had an adolescent group in the other day, and the kids all agreed that if the first suicide hadn't occurred, the others wouldn't have, either. I think they are probably right."

An article in *Rolling Stone* in 1999 stated: "For years, whenever city officials showed up at conventions, it was, 'Oh, Plano, the suicide capital.'" The article actually examined another, more subtle form of copycat phenomenon that visited Plano in the 1990s, an epidemic of deaths from drug overdoses among the young people of the town. Mike Gray's article, entitled "Texas Heroin Massacre," said it all in its subtitle: "The Jocks and Preps of Plano, Texas, Couldn't Get Enough of a New Drug. By the Time They Found Out What the Fine Brown Powder Really Was, Kids Had Already Started Dying." Gray documented how death came to Plano again in 1996–97. By November 1997, over a hundred teens and people in their twenties had been rushed to emergency rooms. Some had died; 16-year-old

Erin Baker, a Plano Senior High junior, became victim number thirteen from the heroin poisoning. Gray noted that in 1998, with the death of David Allen, 21, of Bedford, Texas, "the body count for the northern suburbs of Dallas and Fort Worth rose to at least thirty-four."

Plano remains a cluster "hot spot" that demands the attention of local officials who refuse to let their guard down.

Clear Lake

The city of Clear Lake, Texas, near Houston, was the setting for another suicide cluster. The community of nearly 40,000 is the site of the Johnson Space Center, and until the early 1980s it was truly a space-age boomtown. But those days have gone. Two years before the deaths of the seven space shuttle *Challenger* astronauts cast a pall over the city, six teen suicides took place in Clear Lake.

In 1984, on August 9, the chain of suicides began when Warren Paul Kuns, 19, shot himself in the head while he sat in his car. Kuns was the first of three friends, all high school dropouts, to kill themselves. Six weeks later, on September 17, Kuns's buddy Sean Woods, 19, shot himself in his pickup truck. At the time Woods was moving his possessions out of his parents' home. Woods reportedly believed in reincarnation and felt he would return. Soon after Woods's death, another 19-year-old friend, Wesley Tiedt, hung himself from the top of the stairs at his home. A fourth 19-year-old friend of Kuns, Woods, and Tiedt was under psychiatric care during mid-October 1984. He was present at Woods's suicide and told police he had formed a pact with the others to kill himself.

During the week after Tiedt's suicide on October 4, three other teens beyond the Kuns-Woods-Tiedt circle of friends would take their lives. On Saturday, October 6, 15-year-old Lisa

Schatz killed herself. On Tuesday, October 9, Gary Schivers, 16, hanged himself in his parents' garage. And finally on Thursday, October 11, ninth-grader Darren Thibodeaux, 14, shoved towels under the closed doors of his family's garage, turned on the engine of the family car, crouched next to the exhaust pipe, and died. His 17-year-old sister discovered his body lying behind the car. While young Darren was dying that Thursday afternoon, a team of psychologists was counseling students at nearby Clear Lake High School, and Gary Schivers was being buried.

Needless to say, the community was alarmed by the deaths and feared more. As rumors circulated that perhaps as many as twenty to thirty teens in the school district might be involved in a suicide pact, police and school officials were trying to dispel such talk.

On Monday night, October 15, psychologist Rion Hart met with five hundred parents at Clear Lake High School. He told them that he thought the wave of suicides might have run its course, but warned them not to let their guard down. Some angry parents shouted that they thought the school's hard grading system might be putting pressure on the teens. But not everyone believed this to be true. One senior, Paul Kinze, 18, rose and told the audience he felt it was not "drugs, grades, or girlfriends" that was to blame for the deaths but a "lack of communication between parents and kids."

In the years following the cluster, three psychologists were added to the five already on the Clear Lake school district's staff. High school counselors were trained to look for the warning signs of suicide risk, and junior high personnel also underwent training. The suicide cluster of Clear Lake apparently ended, or at least the media never reported any more suicides.

But Clear Lake would be in the news again because of deaths and near-suicides. On June 20, 2001, Andrea P. Yates, a 37-year-old mother of five, drowned to death her five children—Noah, 7, John, 5, Paul, 3, Luke, 2, and Mary, 6 months old—in the bathtub of her Clear Lake home. A stay-at-home, home-schooling mother with a long, disturbing history of suicide attempts, severe postpartum depression, and the more serious condition of postpartum psychosis, Yates was on suicide watch in her jail cell, awaiting her trail, which occurred in 2002.

During the Yates trial, forensic psychiatrist and *Law & Order* consultant Park Dietz testified that Yates was perfectly sane when she drowned her kids. Dietz based his argument on the fact that the program *Law & Order* was Yates's favorite program and that she planned her children's murders after watching an episode in which a mother drowns her kids, then claims postpartum depression (as Yates was doing) and is acquitted. Dietz theorized that Yates used the show as a blueprint to escape her rotten life and marriage.

But Suzanne O'Malley, an investigative journalist who writes for the series *Law & Order,* told Yates's lawyer that no such episode had ever been written. Yates was found guilty on March 12 and sentencing was to follow. The night before sentencing, Yates defense attorney George Parnham had Dietz admit to false testimony, raising grounds for a mistrial and forcing prosecutors to give up the death penalty. On March 16, 2002, Andrea Yates was spared the death penalty and sentenced to life in prison for drowning her five children. After sentencing, Parnham told O'Malley that she had saved Yates's life.

Other mothers would copy Yates's drowning of her children in the months that followed. On September 18, 2002, U.S. Army specialist Lillie Morgan drowned her son Joshua, 3, and Jazmin, 2 months old, in her Berlin, Germany, bathtub. There were others.

Peekskill and Beyond

Peekskill, New York, sits peacefully at the end of a narrow valley, on hills that slope abruptly down to the shoreline of the Hudson

River. These hills are white, and locals sometimes refer to them humorously as "the White Cliffs of Peekskill." But living in Peekskill is no joke. In the 1980s it was one of the poorest cities in wealthy Westchester County. Today the community still lives in the shadow of the Indian Point Nuclear Power Plant and, during the 1980s, had the misfortune of being picked to host the area's massive recycling facility.

Even the city's name sounds difficult and violent. Actually, Peekskill is derived from Peek's (more properly Peeck's) Kill, the creek that runs along its northern borders named for Jan Peeck.

Described as "surprisingly rural" as recently as the 1940s, forty years later Peekskill was being transformed into one of those marginal metro-suburban retreats for those employed in the Greater New York City area. The city still tried to retain some of its country charm, despite its urban evolution. In the center of Peekskill, for example, there is Chauncey M. Depew Park. An attorney and businessman, Depew was born there in 1834. By 1885 he was the president of Cornelius Vanderbilt's New York Central Railroad. In 1899, Depew was elected to the United States Senate and gained a reputation for his oratory. The park was seen as an appropriate tribute, as Depew enjoyed appearing in public and liked large gatherings. Depew Park in Peekskill figured in the beginnings of a suicide cluster that would shake the sleepy New York City suburbs to their foundations. Before the cluster was over, adults were reexamining their lives and relationships with their children.

The New York cluster started innocently with a boy playing in Depew Park. On February 4, 1984, Robert DeLaValliere, 13, went to the park but, instead of playing softball as he usually did, remained distant and isolated from others. Slowly he disappeared into the more wooded area. As the sun sank over the horizon, he threw a hemp rope over the branches of a robust tree and hung himself.

The death was a mystery. DeLaValliere had had no history of

mental problems. He had scores of friends and was liked by many at Peekskill Middle School, where he was a seventh-grader. But two weeks before the suicide, educators noticed he had been having trouble in school: missed classes, academic difficulties, and fights with other students. These things were not typical of a boy who had done well in school and enjoyed going to the movies with his friends. One movie he had recently seen, which some said made a big impression on him, was *An Officer and a Gentleman*. A character that DeLaValliere seemed to have liked a great deal was a young Navy cadet who hangs himself in a motel bathroom. Local police told reporters that they thought DeLaValliere may have been imitating the cadet. Lieutenant James Nelson of the Peekskill Police Department commented: "You worry how the violence on television and in movies is affecting young people today, whether the music of today is too suggestive, and what role that might be playing on vulnerable kids."

Did another teen then imitate DeLaValliere? Ten days after his suicide, 14-year-old Justin Spoonhour picked a tree in back of his home and hanged himself. Spoonhour lived in Putnam Valley, five miles north of where DeLaValliere died. His mother graphically described in a *People* magazine article how she found her boy. "I turned my light on and saw Justin hanging from a tree," she wrote. "His eyes and mouth were open, and his tongue was swollen and protruding." As we have noted, this was Valentine's Day in Peekskill.

Once again parents and townspeople were shocked. Justin Spoonhour was not your typical teenager. He was quiet and reserved. He liked classical music and acted in Shakespearean plays. He dreamed of competing in the Olympics in archery and of singing in the spring chorale, in which he was to do a solo. Justin's mother, Anne, decided to talk to the media to let other parents know that sometimes the warning signs are not clear-cut. "A kid who's talking about which summer camp he's going to attend and what he wants as a graduation present doesn't sound like your suicide type," she noted. "This was a child who was thinking ahead to the Olympics. There's no sense of mortality in that."

But there was something going on inside Justin. He was teased by some of his classmates about his interest in the arts, and he frequently was angered by their ridicule. Anne Spoonhour noted her son was reserved and often kept things hidden deeply. She said he preferred to avoid confrontations. She wondered about all of this as she looked for clues as to why Justin had died by suicide. She did not blame Justin's classmates. Not having many friends, being isolated, and being closer to adults, he had just not fit in. Observing the specific symbolic date that Justin killed himself, his mother speculated as to whether her son felt he had nobody to love.

Anne Spoonhour spoke and wrote a great deal about her boy. She missed him intensely and did not want other mothers to have to go through what she did. "It's very much quieter," she noted. "There's an empty space." All she could hope was that something could be learned from his death and that the suicides might stop.

But the cluster month of February was not yet over. In nearby North Tarrytown, 19-year-old James Pellechi, using a shotgun, killed himself at his home on February 16. A week after Justin's hanging, on the date of February 21, Christopher G. Ruggiero, 17, hung himself in his bedroom closet with his own bathrobe belt. Rumors of denial circulated about this death. Some said that he had really been experimenting in autoeroticism, a form of masturbation. Others were certain it was suicide. The son of the Pelham Village fire chief of ten years, he was the youngest of seven children. The five-foot-eleven-inch, 160-pound star athlete was called the best player on the high school hockey team by Coach Ralph Merigliano. Right before Christopher's death, however, something seemed amiss in his life. He had been kicked off the team for a year by the Westchester Interscholastic Hockey League as the result of an argument with an official during a game. Some friends directly linked that event to his suicide.

On February 24, Arnold Caputo, 19, a very popular and bright Fordham University student, hung himself from a beam in the attic of his parents' quarter-million-dollar home. He was an excellent musician, and his band had just cut a new demo. But he was going into a slump; rejected by better-known rock groups, he got depressed. The day before he died, he told a friend that he could not take it anymore, but this coded message was difficult to decipher. One of his final requests was that when he died, he wanted to be buried with his guitar.

Brian Hart, 19, was the youngest of six children and lived in Bedford Hills. But sometime before March 14, he drove several miles to Oakwood Cemetery in Mount Kisco, attached a tube to the car's exhaust, and channeled the fumes into the vehicle. Police said he could have been dead for more than a day when he was found.

People pondering the suicides recalled that in 1983, a North Salem 17-year-old boy had hung himself three weeks after his girlfriend killed herself. They had quarreled at a drive-in. Did it have anything to do with the 1984 suicides? No one knew.

Through the spring and summer of 1984, Westchester County's teen suicides continued, despite the best efforts of prevention programs and extra hours of counseling. And the suicides had a familiar ring to them. The hanging scene from *An Officer and a Gentleman* seemed to haunt the first of these suicides and continued to be imitated in many of those that followed. For example, late in July 1984, Sean Scarborough, 20, of Yorktown, hung himself from a tree in the backyard of his family's Sherman Court home.

By fall, school officials in Westchester County had targeted prevention programs for sixteen of the forty-three high schools.

Nearby Rockland County started similar programs in nine of their high schools. More than twelve hospitals and mental health clinics started support groups. Experts on the warning signs of suicide lectured students, parents, and teachers.

But the suicides continued. During the early evening of September 11, 1984, Maureen Fitzell, 15, a high school sophomore, walked a quarter of a mile behind her family's Mahopac house and shot herself with her father's .22 rifle. Reportedly, she was the eleventh youth between the ages of thirteen and twenty in Westchester, Rockland, and Putnam Counties to have completed their own suicide that year. On October 4, another sophomore, Nancy McCarthy, 15, also killed herself behind her family's home. McCarthy burned to death in Lattingtown, Nassau County, when she apparently doused herself with rubbing alcohol, nail polish remover, and gasoline. Her parents, psychologist John and Egleand McCarthy, a business executive, were at work at the time.

As the year came to a close, the suicides did not. Steven Perro's mother discovered her 13-year-old son hanging in the attic of their New Rochelle home on October 17. He left notes saying he was saddened by all the family problems. Eighteen-year-old Robert Valentine was found by his sister at about seven P.M. on December 20 in the living room of their Haverstraw home; he had killed himself with a gunshot from a high-powered rifle to the head. Two days later a 21-year-old Mahopac man, John Billingharn, hung himself from a basement stairway.

On February 10, 1985, in response to the public concern about teen suicide clusters like New York's, ABC-TV broadcast the made-for-television movie *Surviving*. It is the story of a boy and girl who die by suicide by carbon monoxide poisoning. Two days after it aired, 17-year-old David Balogh of Tarrytown died in his car of carbon monoxide poisoning. The Sleepy Hollow High School senior was found at a nearby landfill, and officials noted his was the first suicide in 1985 since the wave of deaths in 1984. David had watched the TV movie, and his friends reported he said he thought it was "really good" and then had gotten "totally obsessed about it." David's enraged father seriously considered suing ABC. But the stories about young Balogh eventually faded away.

During the first week in August 1986, local New York media mentioned that a young man had been found dead in a high school in Westchester County. Apparently the youth broke into the school, took off all his clothes, and hung himself.

The events that unfolded in the three counties just north of New York City in the 1980s led to some of the most comprehensive funding for suicide prevention training late in the decade. Today this section of New York and Bergen County, New Jersey, have two of the lowest suicide rates in the country.

Leominster

Leominster's past is filled with some proud manufacturing milestones. By 1845 some two dozen factories produced plastic combs in Leominster. Before 1935, 75 percent of the piano cases in the United States were made in the north-central Massachusetts town. But in the mid-1930s the Depression began to take a toll on the city's industries. The days of plants turning out such diverse products as furniture, toys, buttons, fabrics, wool yarn, and paper boxes were over. During the 1980s, with a population dropping yearly from 35,000, Leominster remained a close-knit blue-collar town that had seen better times. Foster Grant, the sunglasses people, decided to pull up stakes and go to Mexico. Other manufacturers made similar choices.

And then the teens started killing themselves. In May 1984 two teenage boys deliberately crashed their car into a loading dock. In the next few months one youth killed himself while playing Russian roulette, one of his friends ended his life using a gun, and another teenager was struck and killed by a train. The word around town was that a majority of these deaths were suicides, but at the time the police were treating most of them as accidents.

Suicidologists long ago speculated that officially reported suicides were only the tip of the iceberg and that many "accidents" were really suicides. In 1938, in the book *Man Against Himself,* Karl Menninger pointed out that individuals who exhibit dangerously self-destructive behaviors may unconsciously want to kill themselves without taking responsibility for their own suicides. Norman Tabachnick published similar ideas in a 1973 book whose title says it all: *Accident or Suicide?: Destruction by Automobile.* And in the same year the Leominster cluster began, one of this country's foremost experts on teen suicides, Richard H. Seiden, director of research programs, Suicide Prevention and Crisis Intervention of Alameda County, wrote that "suicides tend to be under recorded because of the social, legal, religious, and economic stigma that still attaches to self-destruction."

The CBS-TV movie *Silence of the Heart* gave a graphic representation of just such an incident in which a teen boy died by suicide but whose death was first labeled as the result of an accidental car crash. Two days after this movie was nationally broadcast, Leominster experienced an event that would no longer let it deny it was in the midst of a teen suicide cluster.

On the morning of November 1, 1984, two 15-year-old girls slipped out of school unnoticed, drank a bottle of champagne, wrote notes of apology for what they were about to do, and then killed themselves. Melissa Christine Poirier and Melody Maillet, sophomores at Leominster High School, were found in Melissa's bedroom. Each girl had been shot once; a twelve-gauge shotgun used for skeet shooting was found nearby. Melissa's mother, Mariette, had come home for lunch, opened Melissa's bedroom door to let a kitten out, and discovered the tragic scene. Scrawled in lipstick on a mirror was a message from Melissa saying she loved her parents and did not want them to be sad. The girls wrote that their parents should not blame themselves "because we found the gun because if it wasn't that we would have used something else."

Their note also said: "Life sucks and then you die. Goodbye cruel world I'm leaving you now and thier's nothin [sic] you can say to make me change my mind! I love to die. I'd be happier I know it! So please let me go. No hard feelings."

On Friday, the day after their deaths, classmates wept openly in the halls of Leominster High School. The school held a moment of silence among its 1,700 students, and anxious parents flooded the office with calls to check to see if their children were in school. One teacher had to throw out the grades for a test he gave the class that day because everyone was in shock.

Since September 1984, according to press accounts in *The Boston Globe* and other local newspapers, Melissa had been depressed. She had gotten into a fight with two girls over a boy and received a black eye and fractured nose. She was afraid to go outside and would spend long hours looking out the window. In October she went to counseling to try to get over her sense of dread. It *seemed* to help. The day before Melissa killed herself, her mother noticed she was happier; she did not want to go see her therapist the next day. She even brought home a kitten. Before leaving school on the day of the suicides, Melissa turned in a science project. Science teacher Mark Siemaszko said, "She seemed in a good mood, compared with the mood she had been in."

But suicidal people often become quite happy right before they kill themselves, as they have a firm plan in mind and thus experience a sense of relief and joy. That's apparently what happened with Melissa. Such a swift mood shift into happiness before a suicide is completed is thus technically called "suicide euphoria" by suicide-prevention consultants. It often falsely fools those closest to the victim into thinking a "flight into health" has occurred. Actually, when the young person finally "decides" to end it all, they are also ending their pain and seeing a way out. A wave of euphoria may then be apparent for one to three days before the suicide.

Leominster was thrown into the national spotlight. The Sunday following the girls' suicides, headlines in newspapers blared that the community was "stunned" by a "rash of teen suicides." The town was subdued and awestruck by the events. Hundreds of students attended and mourned the two girls at their funerals, and one teacher said the deaths had a marked effect on some of their classmates. "They grew up a lot, matured a lot, took things more seriously," said science teacher Siemaszko.

Five months after Poirier found the bodies of her daughter Melissa and Melissa's friend, Melody, she joined forces with Susan Warner-Roy, a neighbor whose husband had hung himself, to draft a state bill that would put suicide education in public schools. They also raised money for daylong seminars on suicide at the junior high school and guest lecturers on suicide for public forums. Every Tuesday, Mariette Poirier held a counseling group for teens in her living room in those dark days.

After the girls' suicides, no teen suicides were publicized or no one killed themselves for almost a year, despite several attempts. Then in October 1985 a 15-year-old boy shot himself. John P. Finn was found in the hallway of a friend's home with a single bullet wound in his head and a .38-caliber handgun lying near his body. Determined that this new death would not attract the attention the others had, school superintendent Louis Amadio immediately closed all junior and senior high schools to the media. "Sudden death is . . . a community awareness problem. Everybody has to be more aware of problems confronting teens these days," Amadio said.

Finn's best friend was William J. Lovetro, 17. A few minutes before 1986 officially began, Bill Lovetro died. He killed himself by ramming his car into the concrete foundation of a factory, mirroring the first known death in this cluster.

Disturbed by the suicides, Leominster Mayor Richard Girouard called a meeting at the city hall auditorium and asked the town's students to attend. Only about twenty-five came. Then two Boston television crews showed up. The crowd was angry at the media for their stories about Leominster and its suicides, and let them know it. And the students were frustrated with the tired old answers when the mayor brought up drugs as if they were one of the major reasons behind the deaths. The students pointed instead to competition with friends and to pressures in school and at home. The more they talked, though, the more everyone realized that no one knew why any of the adolescents had died by suicide.

Mental health counselors held weekly sessions at Leominster High School to deal with the feelings that were sweeping through the school. On Thursday, March 27, 1986, they opened their session a little differently with a surprise announcement: Speaking to the entire student body, they told everyone there that the night before, George Henderson, 14, a freshman honor student, computer whiz, and member of the school's cross-country track team, had killed himself. The students and their teachers then observed a moment of silence.

Diane M. Henderson had discovered her son's body in his bedroom when she returned home from work shortly before six P.M. The family's twelve-gauge shotgun was at his side. He had died from a self-inflicted wound to the head. One neighbor said, "They were just an everyday, normal family. The family did everything together. They went canoeing. They went mountain climbing. You name it. They did it together."

"With every new one it gets more baffling," Mayor Girouard said after George's death. "This boy was a total surprise. He was an honor student with no apparent problems. Just a nice kid." The mayor said officials had been keeping an eye on some students who were having difficulties, but the Henderson boy was not among them. "Neither was the last young man who killed himself," Girouard said. "We were watching his friend, but not him. . . . It's gotten to the point where many of the kids are saying, 'If they want to kill themselves, let them go ahead and do it. It has nothing to do with me,' and it's very difficult to get past that attitude."

Meanwhile, some in the community noted that the problems were not going away. They had heard about fifty attempted suicides in the last six months and were deeply concerned by the latest incident. School and town officials said they had tried to prevent future suicides but were unclear why their effort had failed. "We just don't know why," noted Leominster High principal George J. Antonio. "We've tried a lot of things, but obviously we haven't hit on the hot combination." He knew, though, that the publicity had been difficult for the students, and he flatly refused to allow reporters to interview them. As one student put it, "Why can't they just leave it alone? We are not freaks." Two days after the death of George Henderson, guidance counselors visited homerooms. Then school went into recess on Good Friday, and many took the day to ponder the recent suicides.

As spring moved into the rolling countryside around Leominster, town officials brainstormed new ideas to address the wave of suicides. Guest lecturers from the Centers for Disease Control were brought in. Mariette Poirier and Susan Warner-Roy's group, SPACE (Suicide Prevention Awareness Community Education), got fuller backing. The Leominster Youth Committee was formed. Numbering almost twenty members, including students, doctors, parents, public officials, clergy, and businessmen, the Youth Committee was brought together to tackle the difficult situation. "Somebody has got to do something," said Carolyn Barney, community relations director at Leominster Hospital and a member of the new committee. "I think this stands a chance of doing something positive. I don't think we're going to wipe out all the problems, but we're sure going to make a stab at handling as many of them as we can."

Leominster school superintendent Amadio made a phone call to Larry D. Guinn, director of student services in Plano, Texas, and asked for help. "It felt good to talk to and share information with someone else who has gone through it," Amadio said after his hour-long conversation. "What I like about the Plano approach is it doesn't focus on any kind of course called suicide prevention, but focuses on teenage stresses and self-esteem. And they emphasize how it's a community problem, not a school problem."

Early in June 1986, as the school year wound down, things seemed to be returning to normal. People were stepping back and trying to assess the events of the previous two years. The Massachusetts School Counselors Association acknowledged the great amount of work being done in Leominster High School. Guidance counselor Patricia R. Pothier was honored and cited by the association for her organization of counseling sessions for students needing to cope with Leominster's suicides.

But then on June 18 another shock occurred. A 20-year-old man who had moved to Leominster only a month before was found in his car, dead from a self-inflicted gunshot wound to his head. Michael Dionne had moved from the nearby town of Ashburnham. Police responded when a local resident reported he had heard a gunshot. They found Dionne in his car in the middle of the road. The car's engine was running, its lights on. Next to the young man's body was a rifle.

Police Chief Alan Gallagher said he was "making no connection" between Dionne's suicide and those of the teens. But others locally were wondering: Did people move there just to kill themselves? The remark spoke to the limbo in which people in Leominster found themselves. And another question was raised, as it had been at similar cluster sites: Would there be more youth suicides?

These two questions were soon answered with a bizarre suicide in September of 1986. A young man from Concord, New

Hampshire, chose Leominster as the site of his suicide, and he seemed to have imitated one of the first teen suicides in the cluster to fulfill his death wish. Like the two teenage boys who smashed their car into a loading dock, this young man from New Hampshire died by crashing his auto into a concrete wall at a shopping center. This "last" suicide of the 1980s cluster in Leominster left city officials wondering about their town's strange magnetism that appeared to pull the potentially suicidal to its borders.

Wind River

The general isolation, alcoholism, high unemployment, and de-spair found on the reservations of many native North Americans seemed to be underlying causes for one of the largest youthful suicide clusters during the 1980s, that of Wyoming's Wind River Reservation in 1985. The deaths began on August 12, when Reynold Wallowingbull, 20, used his socks to hang himself in the Riverton City jail. He was in jail after having been arrested for intoxication.

On August 16, Donovan Blackburn, 16, a popular student at St. Stephens School, hung himself from a tree with his sweatpants. Teachers remembered him as one of the brightest students, an out-standing athlete. Four days later a close friend, Darren Shake-speare, 14, was found hanging by baling wire from a tree. He had been at Blackburn's wake and threatened he would be next.

The fourth suicide was Paul Dewey, 23, who hung himself on September 13. The next day Edwin Norah, 22, was found hung, and four days after that Thomas Littleshield, 19, hung himself in the Riverton City jail. Roderick Underwood, 14, was the seventh suicide, and Levi Trumbull, 24, who hung himself on September 28, was the eighth. Two days later, a 25-year-old man hung him-self in a closet of his home. He used the drawstring from his sweatshirt. His sister discovered his body. Eight of the suicides were Arapaho and one was Shoshone.

On October 1, 1985, Salt Lake City television news reporter John Harrington and his cameraman Wayne Paige flew into the Wind River Reservation to report on the suicides. "Unbeknownst to them, the night before a ninth suicide victim had been found and feelings were fairly hostile," their news director John Edwards said. They had done some reservation interviews and then driven to the St. Stephens cemetery to shoot some outtakes on videotape. Although the graveyard looked deserted, as they set up their equipment, five carloads of Indians suddenly appeared. Before they knew it, the newsmen were looking down the barrels of several shotguns. Soon their cameras were smashed and their videotapes burned. After some tense moments the KTVX men were permitted to pack up the rest of their stuff and told to hightail it.

After the incident, tribal elders and leaders held a news conference to warn the media not to intrude on the grief felt by the reservation's families. Many clergy, school, and mental health officials announced they would answer no more questions from reporters. Counselors who had lived on the reservation all their lives had never seen such a crisis. They noted that since the beginning of the year, over fifty youths, including two young women, had attempted suicide. Yet another community was looking for answers to its suicide cluster.

"We don't have any reasons, and we're pretty frustrated," said Fremont County Coroner Larry Lee. "It's tragic. They haven't even lived and they kill themselves." Father Tony Short, a Jesuit priest at St. Stephens Mission, noted, "Indians have tremendous feelings. Anyone who thinks they're stoic is wrong. They have a lot of feelings that they keep inside and are not dealing with. People think liquor can loosen them up, but the problem is alcohol is not neutral." He also noted among the suicide victims "many come from extremely troubled homes."

Marjene Tower, a behavioral specialist with the Bureau of Indian Affairs, felt the suicides were "some sort of contagion that we don't understand. I've never seen this kind of epidemic before." Tower's most shocking discovery was the fact that all of the 14-to-17-year-old suicide victims were best friends, pallbearers at one another's funerals. Among the young men, they were all drinking buddies. She felt the impulse to commit suicide was "caught" like other diseases spread among closely related individuals.

Coroner Lee could not say if the deaths were linked. "Some of them were friends," he observed. "Some of them have attended the others' wakes. But they're all single suicides. As to the connection, I don't know if there is. It's just a domino effect." Obviously, Lee was talking about the copycat effect of the suicides.

Suicide prevention sessions were held weekly in the area schools during the fall of 1985, and students openly discussed the lack of recreational resources and the presence of alcohol on the reservation. On October 7 the community's Arapaho youth took part in a sacred tribal ritual that had in the past been used to ward off illness. The ceremony had been last performed in 1918, when the tribe was faced with an outbreak of Spanish influenza. Near the tribal sun-dance ground, four feathers, each with a red ribbon attached and each blessed with the Arapaho sacred pipe, marked the points of the compass to cleanse any unhappiness that might have prompted the suicides. Inside a tepee on the grounds, a tribal elder cleansed about a dozen members of the tribe at a time by tapping on the ground, painting each face with sacred red paint, and having them step over a burning herb. Hundreds of the reservation's students stood in lines outside the tepee, waiting to go before the elder.

After the ceremony allowed the youth to rediscover and rekindle their traditional ways and identity together, Wind River was calm. During the winter of 1985 to 1986, the ancient ceremony and a modern task force of agencies delivering family counseling seemed to have worked; no suicides took place.

Then on March 18, 1986, as spring began to warm the Wyoming air, an 18-year-old Arapaho youth hung himself. He became Wind River's tenth suicide since its cluster began. Dismayed, tribal leaders attempted not to dwell on the suicides and instead to address positive issues. As Danice Romersa-Kulia, director of the Shoshone-Arapaho Indian Children Welfare program put it, "We have to look forward. You can't always be looking over your shoulder at the past. "

Omaha

Like the cluster of 1983 in Texas and the 1984 cluster in New York, Omaha's 1986 chain of suicides began in February—but it received an enormous amount of national media attention. Over a five-day period, three students from Bryan High School killed themselves. The four-grade, 1,250-student high school is located on the outskirts of Omaha, in a white, working-class neighborhood. According to reports from their families and friends, the three did not know each other very well, but the quick succession of their deaths made everyone ask questions about the contagious nature of suicides among teens—the copycat effect in the wintry cornfields of the Midwest.

Michele M. Money, 16, died first, on February 3, 1986. School counselor Nancy Bednar said she was "a very pleasant girl. She wanted to be a counselor. She had a sensitive side." But the risk factors seemed to pile high on her as stressors such as her parents' divorce, her problems with her boyfriend, and a decision about whether to stay in school made her life unbearable. She overdosed on her mother's Elavil, an antidepressant. Friends recalled her always sunny nature.

Next was Mark E. Walpus, 15. Like Michele, his home situation was in turmoil because of a divorce, still relatively underdiscussed in the 1980s. He was a popular guy who spent his last winter working alone in his shop. Everyone thought he was on the way to college. Instead, he fired a bullet into his chest the day after Michele died. He left behind a suicide note.

Thomas E. Wacha IV, 18, was described as a fairly quiet loner who was deciding whether he really wanted to go to trade school. He had recently told a friend he was "disgusted with life." Captain Dick Mackley of the Sarpy County Sheriff's Department reported that on the morning of February 7, Tom had been involved in an automobile accident and had fought with his parents.° That night Tom died from a self-inflicted shotgun blast to his head.

Four other Bryan High students that we know about made serious attempts on their lives. On January 26, a 17-year-old male slashed his wrists and lived. Another 15-year-old boy took a drug overdose on February 5 and survived. The others made similar tries. As had happened before in other parts of the country, the community responded with sympathy and support. At Bryan, an emotional pep rally was held with the theme "Choose Life." Students wore yellow We Care at Bryan buttons and heart-shaped Choose Life stickers. Cheerleaders and bands performed and students linked arms and sang "We Are the World" during the hour-long event. Although some in Omaha labeled Bryan "Suicide High," in general the community tried to lend assistance. Burke and North High School students took huge banners to the pep rally to show their support for the high school. Principals from ten schools in West Omaha sent 108

°Fighting is often a hidden sign of suicidal or potential homicidal feelings, and may serve as a coded cry for help. Conflict, rapid mood swings, mishaps, and actual physical scuffles are frequent warning signs of concern of an at-risk and vulnerable person, as opposed to open clues about despondency or depression.

dozen donuts to Bryan. Joslyn School principal Sandra Pistone said, "We all want Bryan students to know that this is not just their problem. We're all in this together." Intensive counseling sessions were held for students and parents. Each homeroom teacher asked their students to pledge: "I will not make any big decisions, especially decisions concerning my health, safety, life and the feelings of my loved ones, without taking a day to think it over."

However, as often happens, anger soon surfaced as well. At a public forum, parents and other adults shouted down psychiatrist John Florian Riedler with comments about the lack of help in past times of need. Some Bryan students interrupted Riedler, accusing him of talking over their heads, and asked why teens had to die before help became available. Rumblings about "shutting the barn door after the horses have gotten out" were heard.

One of the first to jump in was Russell Walpus, 20, a Bryan graduate. "My brother was Mark Walpus, the one who died on Tuesday. The kids don't understand what you're trying to get to. It doesn't make any sense to them."

"We all do the best we can," Riedler told the overflow crowd packed into the school's six-hundred-seat auditorium. He added that he understood there was "a lot of anger" in the school. Riedler told the media: "Hysteria swept over this part of town last week. We're dealing with a confused bunch of people who are going through the regular stages of grieving." Needless to say, such actions and comments were not helpful. (During the 1990s, experts recommended that large assemblies not be held after suicides, because they inevitably ended up in shouting matches.)

Throughout Omaha in 1986, television reporters and other news media members combed the school hallways, interviewing students and peering into classrooms. Many students criticized the presence of television news crews. Press coverage began with a small Associated Press story on February 9, and by February 11, Omaha's suicide cluster had been featured in such papers as *The New York Times, The Boston Globe,* and *USA Today.* On Wednesday, February 12, ABC's *Nightline* devoted a segment to Omaha's wave of teen suicides. United Press International and Associated Press wire services ran stories through February 13. The media storm was in full gale.

"It's kind of upsetting to know that you get publicity for this kind of thing and not for something good like a good basketball team," said Kathy Stone, 15, the student council vice president.

The council's president, Dave Jeck, 18, observed: "I don't think that these suicides can be related specifically to our area. These suicides were caused by the same thing that causes every other suicide. They were depressed." He then added, "The first one may have set off the others. It may have put the idea in their heads that that is the way out."

School district psychologist Donna Chaney said, "Everybody involved—including the students—wants us all to get back to normal. Part of what we need to do is to restore calm."

By the middle of February, things were returning to normal, and various parts of the community that had been criticized were being seen in a new light. Local ABC affiliate KETV helped a suicidal youth get some assistance. The student, whose name was not released, left a desperate-sounding message on a teacher's answering machine. KETV made a plea for that specific student to call Omaha's Personal Crisis Hotline and spent the day broadcasting the telephone number. The student finally did dial the number and got help. Al Krumprey, director of the Personal Crisis Hotline, said their phones had been "ringing off the hook." Krumprey commented, "The suicides affect all of us here. They affect the psyche of the city."

As February ended in Omaha, a cautious tranquillity returned to the city. But people wondered: Why a suicide cluster, and why here? Barbara Wheeler, a member of the American Association of Suicidology, former director of Mental Health at Bergen Mercy Hospital and a crisis hotline trainer, summed up what a good many local folks were thinking. Although the three suicide victims had separate friends, different hobbies, and different Bryan High School activities, she noted their deaths might not be unrelated. The others might have seen the suicidal death as a solution. Wheeler concluded, "Suicide is the ultimate form of communication."

Spencer

Early in February 1986, Omaha was hit by three student suicides. Starting on February 9, the rest of the country was hit with a barrage of wire service and broadcast media stories on Omaha's suicide cluster. And on that date, Spencer, Massachusetts, was pulled into a vortex of teen suicide and suicide attempts. Before the month was over, one adolescent was dead by suicide, and eighteen others had made twenty-five attempts on their lives.

In the 1980s, Spencer was a town of eleven thousand. It is lost in the central part of Massachusetts, not far from the big city of Worcester, and just forty miles north is Leominster, well known for its own suicide cluster of the early 1980s. Spencer had been a manufacturing town involved in shoemaking since 1811, and was known as the birthplace of Elias Howe Jr., the inventor of the lock-stitch sewing machine. In 1986 it received attention for its cluster of suicide attempts.

According to Police Chief Robert A. Parker Jr., two of the early attempts were made on Sunday, February 9. At about four P.M., a 15-year-old high school freshman slashed her wrists. That night at around nine, a sophomore boy, 16, drank iodine. Both were rushed to area hospitals and recovered. Both were students at David Prouty High School in Spencer.

The next day 16-year-old Francis V. McNamara, a Prouty junior and football player, shot himself with a .22-caliber rifle in the second-floor bathroom of his Old Farm Road home. The next morning, Tuesday, he died at Worcester City Hospital. "I was shocked, because he was a super boy," said Diana Hart, 39, whose four sons played Little League baseball with McNamara.

"I just couldn't believe it. I didn't think anybody at the school would do it," commented sophomore Rick Arsenault, 15. He noted the football tight end hadn't appeared to be troubled, but then, "Frank wouldn't be the type to tell you what his problems were."

On the day McNamara died, Superintendent of Schools Philip F. Devaux held an assembly to meet with the students of the 750-pupil high school. Devaux announced that guidance offices and some classrooms would be open Tuesday through Friday of the following vacation week to give troubled students someone with whom to talk. He told the students that representatives from Tri-Link, a social service agency from Southbridge, would be available during the school vacation for parents as well as students. "We emphasized to them the need to communicate their feelings with their parents, school counselors, their peers, and teachers," Devaux said. "For the remainder of the school week all school district energies will center on assisting the students who have lost a classmate and a friend."

On the day after the assembly, counseling groups were set up at Prouty High School. Rumors had begun to circulate that as many as three other students had tried to kill themselves on Monday night, and school officials were worried. Also, questions were being raised about the actions of school officials: Advice had been given not to hold an assembly. Psychologist Pamela Cantor, then the president of the American Association of Suicidology, warned against encouraging a large turnout at the funeral. "In that way, a kid with no importance becomes important through death," she said. "Kids copy that." She cautioned that organizing the entire school to attend a funeral had not helped in previous cases. "Such a funeral is not about a celebrity event. It's about the death of a kid who made a tragic choice."

Nevertheless, on Thursday, February 13, more than two hundred parents and adults crowded into the cafeteria of David Prouty High School to discuss the recent events. Most expressed anger and upset over the media coverage of the story. As the parents' meeting was held, students conducted another meeting elsewhere in the school that was off limits to the press.

At the adults' meeting, school band director George Garber said Boston television stations had been aggressive in drawing comments from some high school students. Garber noted that the stations had never before reported positive stories from Spencer. The gathered crowd applauded his comments at length. Superintendent Devaux said that while some reporters had acted professionally, others had not. Devaux also expressed dismay at the fact that communication was so poor with the police, and some parents were concerned that no town officials had chosen to come to the meeting.

The social service workers found that the extent of the problem was deeper than imagined. The first attempt had actually occurred in December 1985, when a 14-year-old girl had tried to kill herself. Then, in January 1986, two 17-year-old girls attempted suicide. By the end of March, eighteen students had made twenty-five attempts, with five hospitalized in a month. The methods used included guns, iodine, nail polish remover, pills, hanging, and cutting.

Soon a strong network of friends was detected by mapping the relationships between the students who had made suicide attempts in Spencer's junior high school and high school. The friendship bond among them was extremely strong, but the interactions that held them together were generally negative. Making a suicide attempt was seen as one way to retain membership in the group. A number of high school students were linked to the junior high crowd who were friends of the 14-year-old who had attempted suicide in December. Tri-Link's positive intervention lasted six weeks at the school and turned a grave picture around. After they left programs they had set up continued and succeeded in giving individual attention to the still-troubled teens or those at risk.

Concern for teenagers in Spencer was high after the crisis waned. In March, Teen Action was formed. Anita L. Crevier said her idea for the group was born in the aftermath of young Frank McNamara's suicide. She told of how her daughter had comforted Frank's girlfriend after his death and expressed the notion that others could benefit from simply getting together. This prompted them to call ten friends to a meeting in their home. From this initial session came the idea to form Teen Action. Meeting twice a week at the Spencer Senior Center on Main Street, the group discussed the adolescents' problems, and each member suggested alternatives to suicide as a solution to the teens' concerns. Through basic problem-solving, Teen Action tried to get at the root of the town's suicides.

Teen Action was behind other projects as well. They had a question-and-answer column in the local paper and on a Worcester radio station. The group sponsored their dances and backed an effort to have teenagers added to the town boards as nonvoting members. Teens were actively sought out for their feelings and their concerns when public officials discussed issues that affected their lives.

Mankato

Situated in southwestern Minnesota, Mankato was a city of some 30,000 individuals in the 1980s. The town got its name from the Sioux word for the blue earth found in the vicinity.

Nestled in the Blue Earth River Valley, the lay of the land has had a lot to do with the future of Mankato. The two-hundred-foot-deep valley dictated that the streets run from northeast to southwest, paralleling the terraces of the sharp slope. The side streets then had to be constructed with a steep grade.

On February 6, 1852, three St. Paul men began building the town of Mankato after buying the land from Sioux chief Sleepy Eye. The uprising of four hundred Sioux in 1862 produced one of Mankato's major footnotes in history. Of the hundreds brought to trial, Abraham Lincoln pardoned all but thirty-eight. The simultaneous hanging of those thirty-eight Sioux was the largest legal execution that has ever taken place in the United States. You can still find a granite marker on the site of the execution, at the northwest corner of Front and Main Streets.

Another form of mass death visited the town 124 years later. In 1986, Mankato became the site of a cluster of suicides that one newspaper reported was "Minnesota's largest in memory." Interestingly, people in the area began to take note of it during the week Omaha received all the attention for its rash of suicides. In Mankato on February 11, young Diane Lamont had taken her own life, and folks grew concerned.

But Mankato's brush with teen suicide had really begun a month earlier. Bryan Javens, 18, shot himself to death in his bedroom on January 11. A champion wrestler and three-wheel racer, Javens was a senior at Mankato East High School. Not much was made about Javens's death, but it did receive a small write-up in a local paper. As usually happens in such towns, we can assume that, via word of mouth, Javens's suicide was well known among the youth of the community. Indeed, the short published report on his suicide was pinned to the headboard of Diane Lamont's bed, direct evidence of her attention to the media spread of the story. The 15-year-old Mankato East sophomore killed herself the same way Javens had: She used a gun in her bed. Police officials confirmed that they knew each other.

The Mankato suicides prompted local authorities to call two public forums. Three hundred people attended one forum, and eight hundred attended another. Mankato's citizens were upset. Experts on teen suicide discussed warning signs, officials tried to restore calm, but in general most residents were unsatisfied.

Then something weird happened on Valentine's Day. Someone got the community access cable television station to broadcast a message to Bryan Javens and Diane Lamont. The video valentine addressed to the pair read:

Hope you are having fun.
Glad you're together.
We miss you.
Love,
East High

Blue Earth County sheriff LaRoy Wiebold was outraged. He had the station pull the Valentine's Day message after he received a report that a copycat suicide pact had been formed by other teens. CCTV Channel 13 had to shut down for two hours to remove the video, and some townspeople complained the sheriff had violated the First Amendment. But others were happy with his actions and thought he might be onto something. The suicide pact report the sheriff received concerned the "11th of the Month Club." Rumors circulated that another Mankato East student would die by suicide on March 11. Sheriff Wiebold said he had "an intelligence report on the possibility of a copycat pact being formed by other young people."

Meanwhile, Mankato Mayor Herbert Mocol said that stories were going around "that there's going to be a suicide on the eleventh of each month. We've heard it again and again."

Kimberly Evers, 20, did not wait for the eleventh. On February 19 she died of carbon monoxide poisoning in her family's garage. She was one of four children and had graduated from Mankato West

High School in 1983. People said she had known Bryan Javens and Diane Lamont. Employed at fast-food restaurants in Mankato, Kimberly had graduated in December 1985 from a Minneapolis school for travel agents. Her boyfriend of three years, Tim Scheitel, was shocked by her death. They had planned to marry.

When the morning of March 12 came, there was a general sigh of relief that another suicide had not taken place. But when the Mankato *Free Press* decided to print an article reporting on the relief of the students and their families, the newspaper office was flooded with angry and concerned phone calls. One of them was from Audre Scheitel, mother of 17-year-old junior Tim.

From information at the public forums, Tim Scheitel's mother knew he was at high risk for suicide because of Kimberly's suicide. That was why she did not like the tone of the article. Tim's father noted that Tim's friends "did everything imaginable. They lined him up with girls, took him to parties. But what do you do when your young people deal with death? It's a pain so strong it can be all-consuming. You tell them you love them and you tell them there's a God and that's the best you can do."

Special attention was made to see that Tim was occupied and surrounded by friends on April 11.

But on April 26, 1986, Tim was alone at home except for his 11-year-old sister, Jessica. Their father, a rock musician, and their mother were at a Saturday night gig outside of Mankato. Early in the evening Tim went into the garage, left the door closed, and started the car. Thinking he might be trying to kill himself the same way his girlfriend had, Jessica told Tim she was sick. He turned off the car and stayed with his sister until he put her to bed at ten P.M. Then Tim Scheitel went back to the garage. His body was found on Sunday morning by his parents. He had died of carbon monoxide poisoning.

After Tim's suicide, a change seemed to come over Mankato.

Len Zimmerman, principal of Mankato East High School, said there would be no large assembly. "We've been told by psychologists that we shouldn't talk about it because the more publicity there is, the more chance you get the copycat effect," he said. The town's citizens were left with a feeling akin to that expressed by Sheriff Wiebold: "There are no answers. There are just questions."

After Tim Scheitel's suicide, there was a long calm in Mankato, but then late in 1986 another East High student died by suicide. Early on November 25, a 16-year-old junior was found hanged at her Mankato home. The young girl was the fifth youth suicide in Mankato, the fourth from the 940-student high school in one year. Police officials and high school personnel refused to comment on the latest suicide, saying they believed that publicity might prompt other suicides.

They were correct, of course.

The Bergenfield Four

By 1986, suicide clusters were popping out all over the United States and being chronicled in the media. Just a week after the Mankato suicide of Diane Lamont, two other upper midwestern teens would die by suicide on February 18. Sandra Stephenson, 17, of rural Jefferson, South Dakota, and John Meier, 18, of North Sioux City, Iowa, died in the closed garage at the Stephenson home. The cause of death was listed as carbon monoxide poisoning. Their deaths brought the number of suicides and murder-suicides in Union County, South Dakota, in one month to eight; most were farm-related. The next day Kimberly Evers, 20, killed herself in Mankato. Four days after that, an 18-year-old would die by suicide in Plano.

In March 1986, in the suburbs of Chicago, a series of teen suicides hit Shepherd High School in Palos Heights. Through the end of 1986, more suicides would revisit Wind River, Leominster, Mankato, and the Peekskill area.

The year 1987 would open with a cluster of three young males killing themselves within a three-week period in January in Newton, Massachusetts. In February, rumors circulated in an Inuit village near Bethel, Alaska, of a teen suicide pact as officials were still coming to grips with the fact that eight youths had killed themselves in recent months. Similarly, Broken Arrow, Oklahoma, realized that eight young people had died by suicide over the previous six months.

On February 18 and 24, 1987, the nation was startled by the news out of Kansas City, Kansas, that two O'Hara High School seniors, both students in a class called Death and Dying, had died in separate incidents of self-inflicted carbon monoxide poisoning. The method of death by car exhaust was being widely copied in these clusters, despite the fact that suicide by guns is the number one method of suicide for individual male and female young people.

Then on another eleventh of the month, that of March 1987, "Bergenfield" happened. This New Jersey town of closely packed houses lies just north of New York City in Bergen County. Just as the name Columbine in the 1990s would take on the dual meaning of a place and an event, so did Bergenfield denote both a location and the most publicized suicide cluster of the 1980s.

The growing storm began many months before in Bergen County. Rumors circulated that a suicide pact involving as many as eighteen people had taken place in a young person's backyard; they vowed that if one died, they all would. They called themselves The Burnouts. Then Joe Major, the leader of the group, fell—some said jumped—two hundred feet to his death off the Palisades Cliffs along the Hudson River in September 1986. Police labeled it an alcohol-related accident. They used the same word, *accident,* when three of Major's friends died, two of whom died in separate incidents in which they were struck by trains, and another who walked into a pond and drowned. All three had been drinking alcohol. The reality is that all of these may have been hidden suicides.

On the evening of March 10, 1987, Cheryl Burress, 17, decided to not go out on her date with Matt Reiser. Instead at 6:30 she called him to cancel. "We can't get together tonight," she told Reiser. "We're going to visit Joe." Reiser assumed that the "Joe" she meant was Joe Major, and that Cheryl was merely going to Major's grave, as she often did. Cheryl's younger sister Lisa, 16, had dated Joe Major for six months before his fall and was still skipping classes to visit his grave.

Cheryl and Lisa decided to drive around town with two young men, Thomas Rizzo, 18, and Thomas Olton, 19, that night in March. The two had also been friends of Joe Major's; one had seen him fall from the cliff. Both had recently cut up their wrists. All four teenagers had been having trouble in school: Three had dropped out of high school, and one had recently been suspended. That evening the two young men were using cocaine and alcohol; the two young women, just cocaine. At around three A.M. they stopped at the Amaco station on Washington Avenue, purchased three dollars of gas for Olton's brown Camaro, and asked the attendant for the auto vacuum hose. He said no.

The four then drove to a nearby apartment complex, Foster Village, off of Washington Avenue. They parked in a hangout many of the kids had been using, a thirteen-car garage, No. 74, that had been empty for at least a month. They then closed the garage door, locked it, left the car windows open, and kept the engine running. They wrote a note, which they all signed, asking to be buried together. The four were found dead many hours later by a tenant leaving for work. (They were not buried together.)

The media blared the news. Banner headlines several inches high told of the "Bergenfield Four." Bergenfield (population

25,600 in 1987) exists in the backyard of the media's epicenter, New York City. The story of the "pact" suicide was broadcast from coast to coast and soon around the world. It had a traumatic effect on the local youth. A group of them showed up the night after the suicides and spray-painted the pastel blue garage door black.

One week after the four youth died, a police officer was walking by the same garage, No. 74, and discovered a young man and young woman in a car attempting to gas themselves to death. They were rescued and survived. In the year that followed, more than eighteen suicides took place.

The overwhelming national publicity from these four suicide deaths triggered copycat suicides elsewhere across the country. The day after "Bergenfield," two young women were found to have killed themselves by carbon monoxide in Alsip, Illinois, a suburb (population 17,000) south of Chicago. Karen Logan, 17, and her friend Nancy Grannan, 19, were discovered dead in Grannan's car, which was idling in a closed garage attached to the Logan home. "Logan clutched a stuffed animal and a rose, Grannan held an album of her wedding photos," observed *Time* magazine a week after the tragedy. "On the dashboard of the car, the two had left nine sealed letters to friends and relatives, as well as two notes stuck under the windshield wipers. Said Alsip police chief Warner Huston: 'The publicity surrounding the Bergenfield incident probably gave them the impetus.' "

High school seniors, one each from Sumner, Washington, La Vista, Nebraska, and Moline, Illinois, died using the same method as the Bergenfield suicides. At least nine suburban teens from the Chicago area, two 20-year-olds from Staten Island, New York, and Clifton, New Jersey, a 17-year-old from Arlington, Virginia, and many others all died by suicide by carbon monoxide poisoning in the wake of the March 11 events in New Jersey.

No national organization tracked these deaths, but I surveyed every newspaper in the country in the course of my university suicide project at the time. I found that twenty-two media-noted suicides of young people by carbon monoxide in cars had taken place in two weeks, forty-seven in a month—which is over and above the normal numbers to be expected in the same time period using this method. This was an excessive number of suicides, above the normal rate, taking place nationally. Many other teens were killing themselves or attempting suicide by other methods as well, of course.

Within weeks a suicide hotline was established, intervention and prevention programs created, and good community cooperation undertaken in Bergenfield. Today the town has some of the best school and community suicide prevention programs in the nation.

On another level, however, the Bergenfield Four live on. Most teens are aware of the incident, and for several years one of the most popular cars for teens to own was a Camaro. The Washington Avenue Foster Village location of the suicides is a mecca for visitors. And although local residents have switched around numbers on the garages, people still search for No. 74.

The end of the 1980s saw more suicide clusters and copycats. In Dade County, Florida, thirty-seven suicides were recorded at the secondary school level in the 1988–89 school year. In "Suicide clusters: an examination of age-specific effects," published in 1990 in *American Journal of Public Health,* authors Madelyn S. Gould, Sylvan Wallenstein, Marjorie Kleinman, Patrick O'Carroll, and James Mercy found that clustering was "two to four times more common among adolescents and young adults than among other age groups."

Suicide clusters, the reality of which had been denied just a decade earlier, were now seen as all too real. Finally people realized that suicide clusters among teens actually leaped from one community to another and were fanned along by the media.

CHAPTER NINE

Murders and Murder-Suicides

The copycat effect is a highly volatile phenomenon, spreading much like a match fire set to gasoline dripping across a service station lot. Individual violent acts portrayed in the media tend to spawn similar incidents in the days and weeks that follow, though the subsequent events may be murder-suicides, mass murders, or mass suicides regardless of the precipitating event. Copycat murders and murder-suicides are real. The media spreads the contagious behavior: imitation.

The very first mass-media murders produced the copycat effect. On August 31, 1888, a vicious killer began murdering middle-aged prostitutes and mutilating their bodies around Mitre Square in the Whitechapel area of London's East End. The newspapers gave the killer a name, and soon all straitlaced Victorians knew of the terror called Jack the Ripper. Feeding on a heightened interest in the vivid descriptions of the killings, the press churned out more and more articles on the subject. The telegraph, a new invention, enabled newspapers in London, throughout the United Kingdom, America, and the entire English-speaking world to print stories on the Jack the Ripper murders within hours of their occurrence. The change in media reporting brought about by the telegraph resembles what happened less than a century later, when CNN and other all-news channels began providing wall-to-wall news coverage to modern television viewers.

Newspaper reporters and crime tracts repeated in minute and graphic detail the facts about the killings that emerged from the inquests, and embellished the stories with a few falsehoods of their own. In October 1888, for instance, the world's first docudrama novel on the Jack the Ripper case appeared when J. F. Brewer wrote *The Curse on Mitre Square*, a Victorian fact-based ghost story that is vividly close to reality. By the time the last of the Jack the Ripper victims was cut up on November 8, 1988, five women had been killed and linked to the Ripper. The killing spree was brief and even the "body count" was relatively low, but the telegraph-hastened, press-driven coverage of the Jack the Ripper story created its own mythos.

The newspaper stories spawned a wave of rape-murders and other crimes in the wake of the reportage of the Ripper's Whitechapel slaughters. Sociologist Steve Stack noted that researcher Jean-Gabriel de Tarde, soon after the Jack the Ripper murders, wrote that a "suggestion effect" had taken place.

Jack the Ripper's newspaper-friendly name and the vast media attention he received in 1888 left a remarkable cultural footprint on today's society. As the Hollywood Ripper website has documented, the most prominent serial killer in popular culture has produced thirty-eight Jack the Ripper movies and television episodes from 1917 to 2001. By comparison, the second-most-discussed serial killer, Wisconsin's mass murderer Ed Gein, has inspired just seven productions in forty-five years—although two, *Psycho* and *The Silence of the Lambs*, are classics.

The Jack the Ripper story has created copycat killers down

through the years and into the twentieth century. Between 1975 and 1981, Peter Sutcliffe became known as the Yorkshire Ripper. Sutcliffe, a truck driver, stabbed and mutilated twenty women, with thirteen fatalities. The murderer was a Jack the Ripper imitator, and the murders were done in a fashion to copy the Whitechapel killings. Subsequent reports suggest that murderers then copycatted Sutcliffe, the imitation cycle feeding on itself from one celebrity copycat to the next.

Murders as Suicides, Suicides as Murders

Homicides are sometimes referred to as suicides turned outward, suicides as homicides turned inward. Sigmund Freud, despite his fall from grace during the rise of feminism in the 1970s and the notion that some of his theories are sexist and outdated, had some interesting insights that inform any examination of the interplay between murder and suicide. His conceptualization of suicide was as the murder of one's self. Freud's granddaughter, non-Freudian feminist Sophie Freud, Ph.D., whom I studied under at Simmons College, said it well in her appropriately named "The baby and the bathwater: Some thoughts on Freud as postmodernist," in *The Journal of Contemporary Human Services* (1998). She observed that Freud's extensive work on the unconscious, however flawed, helped students of psychology to see that "surfaces mirror only one aspect of human motives, and that each visible aspect of human behavior carries within it, its very opposite."

Exploring the thin line between homicide and suicide, the American psychiatrist Karl Menninger—founder along with his father, of the well-known Menninger Clinic and author of *Man Against Himself* (1938)—extended Freud's thoughts on suicide as "murder of the self." Menninger wrote: "Is it hard for the reader to believe that suicides are sometimes committed to forestall the committing of murder? There is no doubt of it. Nor is there any doubt that murder is sometimes committed to avert suicide." In *Man Against Nature,* Menninger formulated what has become known as the "Menninger triad" for looking more deeply into suicidal thoughts and behavior. He found that suicidal individuals may share three aspects: (1) They wish to die (commit suicide); (2) they wish to kill (commit homicide); and (3) they wish to be killed (commit victim-precipitated homicide, or more commonly known today by the confusing terms *suicide by cop* and *blue suicide*). This is best illustrated in cases of murder-suicide.

Murder-suicides in the 1970s and 1980s were regarded as a form of domestic violence, as this was a period of heightened gender-based awareness. For example, women committing murder-suicide tend to kill their children and then themselves. Men tend to murder their spouses or partners and then complete their own suicides. As Patricia Easteal demonstrated in her 1993 study *Killing the Beloved,* one third of spousal homicides in the U.S. and Canada end in suicide. Today murder-suicides are no longer seen as being one-dimensional, as just about domestic violence. They are examined in terms of dominance, politics, and the result of triggering the suicidal-homicidal confusion in the impulsive, despondent, depressed, and angry individual. The triggering mechanism is the copycat effect.

Publicity about a celebrity murder and murder-suicide serves as the spark to send a vulnerable, questioning, suicidal person in one of many directions. How the individual copes with the stresses leading to suicide, of course, varies from individual to individual, but by adding a model of behavior to the mix, via the media, pushes some people in a specific behavioral direction. As we have seen, David Phillips has found an increase in both suicides and murder-suicides following other well-publicized suicides and murder-suicides, including an increase in unrecognized aircraft accidents. Similarly, sociologist Steve Stack's 1989 study, the first ever on the effect of publicized mass murders and murder-suicides, showed the interplay between the media, murder, suicide, and murder-suicides. Stack explored their impact on lethal aggression by focusing on the stories of mass murder-suicides and mass murders that aired on two or three of the network news channels (ABC, CBS, and NBC) from 1968 to 1980. Stack found that mass murder-suicides are significantly associated with increases in the suicide rate. He also noted that one special type of mass murder, publicized gangland mass murders, were associated with increases in suicide.

Waves of Murder-Suicides

The copycat effect is so predictable, and the media coverage of these events so thorough, they can almost be observed as they occur. For example, on Friday afternoon, May 16, 1986, former police officer David Young and his wife Dorris took over the Cokeville, Wyoming, Elementary School and held 150 students and teachers hostage. The siege ended when one of the Youngs' homemade gasoline bombs went off, killing Dorris and burning scores of fleeing, screaming children. David Young then turned his Colt .45 on himself.

This nationally broadcast suicide was followed by the killing that night of five people at a bar and nearby convenience store in Colorado Springs, Colorado. When cornered by police, the killer, plumber Gilbert Eugenio Archibeque, shot himself once in the head with his .237-caliber handgun at two A.M., Sunday morning, May 18, 1986.

The news media dwelled on the deaths, murders, near-murders, and suicides in the western states of Wyoming and Colorado from Friday, May 16, 1986, through Sunday, May 18. These front-page murder-suicide stories, if Phillips's theory about a follow-on increase in plane crashes is correct, should have led to some "disguised suicides" soon afterward. It seems they did. On Monday, May 19, newspapers such as *The Washington Post* and *The New York Times,* as well as the major wire services, noted that the weekend had been one of the bloodiest in recent history in terms of small private plane crashes. Seventeen people had died and seven were injured in noncommercial aircraft accidents in New Jersey, Georgia, Oregon, Indiana, and California. Meanwhile, in Temecula, California, two other people had died in a hot-air balloon crash that left a third occupant critically injured.

Murderers who kill themselves often copy murder-suicides. In October 1998, Ronald Jonker, 32, using his car's exhaust, killed himself and his three children, David, 7, Aaron, 5, and Ashlee, 17 months, on the northern outskirts of Perth, Western Australia. On July 3, 1999, a 25-year-old mother of five, Barbara-Anne Wyrzykowski, took Mark, 8, twins Sarah and Luke, 5, Jessie, 4, and Jayde, 1, for a drive in the family's seven-seater van to a remote area in a dense state forest a few miles southeast of Perth. She killed her children and herself by gassing. During the week of July 19, 1999, unemployed laborer Mark Heath took his four children—Sarah, 8, Holly, 6, Jak, 4, and Kaleb, 2—to an isolated bush area hundreds of miles south of Perth and connected a hose to the car's exhaust. On Saturday, July 24, 1999, all five bodies were found in the car, dead from acute carbon monoxide poisoning. "That twelve children could have been murdered by a parent, in three separate incidents, in the space of less than a year, within the same region of one state" was shocking for Australia, observed World Socialist website reporter Linda Tenenbaum on August 10, 1999.

Another remarkable cluster of familicides took place during a one-year period in the Pacific Northwest, and included two of the largest mass killings in Oregon's history. In December 2001, Christian Longo killed his wife and three young children and dumped their bodies into shallow waters off Oregon's central coast. For a week beginning December 19, authorities pulled their bodies from the sea. Christian's wife, Mary Jane Longo, 34, and son Madison, 2, were found inside a suitcase; Zachery, 4, and Sadie, 3, had weighted pillowcases tied to their bodies. Longo was arrested in Tulum, Mexico, three weeks after the first body drifted to the surface. He was charged with aggravated murder. On February 23, 2002, Robert Bryant murdered his wife and the family's four children and then fatally shot himself at his home in McMinnville, about thirty-five miles southwest of Portland, Oregon. Almost exactly one year after Longo killed his family, a similar killing took place in Tillamook State Forest, seventy miles south of the Longo murder site. Tillamook and Lincoln counties share a border, a coastline, and the Coast Range ridges. On the morning of the winter solstice, December 21, 2002, hunters in the Tillamook State Forest led police to the body of Renee Morris, 31. By nightfall, police found her three children, Bryant, 10, Alexis, 8, and Jonathan, 4, nearby. Two days later the Tillamook County district attorney charged 37-year-old Edward Morris with seven counts of aggravated murder in the death of his family. Police caught him on January 4, 2003. The stark parallels between the Longo and Morris cases jarred even veteran investigators—so much so that "detectives haven't ruled out that Morris could be a Longo copycat," said Beth Anne Steele, spokeswoman for the FBI in Portland, Oregon.

"It's extraordinary," said Charles Patrick Ewing, a law professor and forensic psychologist at the University at Buffalo Law School. "It really defies all probability that you would have that many in that short period of time. I call it sort of a contagion theory. When something like this happens and becomes public knowledge, it makes it more likely that it's in their consciousness."

While Andrea Yates, who drowned her five children in her Clear Lake, Texas, home, stood trial in February 2002, Julie Ostrowski, a Women's ENews reporter, observed: "And while the

Yates case was generating extensive coverage, the media hardly noted the case of Adair Garcia, a 30-year-old father of six living near Los Angeles, who was arrested on February 21 for murdering his five children, ages 2 to 10. 'Apparently despondent over marital troubles,' he 'allegedly lighted a charcoal grill . . . in the living room of the family's home,' the *Los Angeles Times* reported." The media has only enough attention for one murder-celebrity at a time.

On March 12, 2002, as the suicidal Andrea Yates was being convicted of drowning her five children, Royal Canadian Mounted Police "began their grim search for the remains of six Vancouver Island children who died in a suspicious house fire," wrote the *National Post's* Brad Evenson. "Their father was charged yesterday with six counts of first-degree murder. Two days later, the search for Toronto two-year-old Alexis Currie ended when her father led police searchers to her body. The same day, a Smiths Falls, Ontario, father was charged with killing his daughter."

It is obvious the Yates trial stirred up a hornet's nest of underreported and thus little noticed copycats. The media does not report extensively on this process.

Suicide Bombers

Suicide terrorism has been on the rise around the world since the 1980s. The Western media today is mostly concerned with Mideastern suicide bombers. The use of individuals willing to die to kill their "enemy" is, of course, nothing new. The kamikaze, whose name means "divine wind" in Japanese, after a typhoon that sank ships filled with invading Mongols in 1281, is clearly an example of preconceptualized murder-suicides for a cause.

Five thousand young Japanese airmen may have died in kamikaze missions during 1944–45. The Japanese command at

Clark Field, north of Manila, organized the initial kamikaze pilots. The first suicide attack was lead by Captain Yukio Seki on October 25, 1944, during the battle off the central Philippine island of Leyte, when he died by suicide when sinking the American aircraft carrier *Saint Lo*. Over fifty ships were sunk and many American lives lost by kamikaze attacks in the Pacific arena, including the sinking of ships like the USS *Bunker Hill* and the USS *Essex*. Half of the twenty-six planes in Seki's initial group, for example, were designated for suicide; the other half were not but would crash their planes into the destroyers and aircraft carriers as they were being shot down or faced almost certain death anyway. Japanese pilots were trained in special schools that employed brainwashing techniques to condition the potential kamikaze pilots for their eventual missions. While some pilots were ordered to be kamikazes, others would simply copycat their fellow pilots.

Suicidal-homicidal behavior requires a strong sense of purpose, which is in itself contagious and may lead to "volunteers" of this kind. The suicide bombers of Hamas serve as models of acceptable behavior among their peers, which is via the copycat effect. All of which leads to a normalizing of terrorism.

In 2002, *National Review* online editor Jonah Goldberg, a conservative, commented on liberal senator Patrick Moynihan's 1993 essay "Defining Deviancy Down" to make some points about the media's normalizing of terrorism. Goldberg's and Moynihan's insights apply here in understanding how the media makes "celebrities" of events, which then serve as cultural icons that are held up for emulation by followers. In this way copycats are produced. Calling the essay "one of the most influential articles of the last decade," Goldberg notes that "Moynihan argued that deviancy—crime, mental illness, out-of-wedlock births, etc.—had become so rampant, had so thoroughly soaked into the culture, that we simply had to redefine the abnormal as normal to cope."

"Moynihan's most famous example was the St. Valentine's Day Massacre," noted Goldberg. "That event was a major turning point in American history, credited with helping to convince Americans to abandon Prohibition . . . The actual details? Four gangsters murdered seven gangsters. In the early 1990s, Moynihan noted, Los Angeles suffered from the equivalent of one St. Valentine's Day Massacre every weekend. And, of course, we can say much the same about suicide bombings in Israel."

What we sometimes lose track of is that it wasn't always this way. We didn't always live in a world of suicide bombers. There is mounting evidence that suicide bombings, because of the media attention they receive, the fear factor they create, the terrorism and copycats they produce, achieve some of the goals of their suicidal-homicidal acts. The media are not to blame for this, but the media—and how they can be used—have certainly become a part of the process.

University of Chicago professor Robert A. Pape's 2003 *American Political Science Review* paper "The Strategic Logic of Suicide Terrorism" looks for insights into suicide bombers beyond the quick explanations of religious fanaticism and impoverished backgrounds. Pape examined all 188 suicide terrorist attacks worldwide from 1980 to 2001. He showed that "suicide terrorism follows a strategic logic, one specifically designed to coerce modern liberal democracies to make significant territorial concessions. Moreover, over the past two decades, suicide terrorism has been rising largely because terrorists have learned that it pays. Suicide terrorists sought to compel American and French military forces to abandon Lebanon in 1983, Israeli forces to leave Lebanon in 1985, Israeli forces to quit the Gaza Strip and the West Bank in 1994 and 1995, the Sri Lankan government to create an independent Tamil state from 1990 on, and the Turkish government to grant autonomy to the Kurds in the late 1990s. In all but the case of Turkey, the terrorist political cause made more gains after the resort to suicide operations than it had before." Pape's findings are that the suicide attacks are always part of organized campaigns, that the targeted areas are always democracies, and that the ultimate goal of the attacks is to force democratic governments to withdraw from occupied territories. Suicide bombers employ the media, its death news, as horror-driven entertainment to broaden the message.

Pape distinguishes between "demonstrative terrorism" and "suicide terrorism." He acknowledges that the number one goal of "demonstrative terrorism" is to gain "publicity, for any or all of three reasons: to recruit more activists, to gain attention to grievances from softliners on the other side, and to gain attention from third parties who might exert pressure on the other side." He reminds everyone this form of terrorism wants "a lot of people watching, not a lot of people dead." On the other end of Pape's terrorist continuum lies "suicide terrorism." While Pape acknowledges that this kind of terrorism can also be used for demonstrative purposes, he senses they are mostly dying and killing as many people as possible, as "coercion is the paramount objective of suicide terrorism."

The trigger event that reignited the small series of suicide bombers after the Oslo Accords of September 13, 1993 is the murder and "suicide by crowd" known as the "Hebron Massacre," carried out by Baruch Koppel Goldstein on February 25, 1994. An immigrant physician from New York City, Goldstein became a Jewish settler at Kiryat Arba, a suburb of Hebron, five minutes from the Cave of Patriarchs and the heart of the city. Established in 1971, Kiryat Arba was the first renewed Jewish community in Judea and Samaria. Goldstein picked the date carefully for his attack; it was Purim, the fourteenth day of Adar, a day in Jewish history linked to Jews overcoming their enemies, on the eve of the Jewish sabbath and, for Muslims, the middle of Ramadan. Baruch, wearing his officer's uniform, appeared at the al-Ibrahimi mosque with his Galilon rifle during Sabbath prayers. The shrine, the traditional burial place of the biblical

Abraham, is also revered as the Cave of the Patriarchs, the Hebron site holy both to Muslims and Jews. Thinking he was preventing the deaths of hundreds of Jews living in Hebron, Goldstein fired away, killing twenty-nine Muslims. Bystanders apparently killed Goldstein, although his operation clearly was a "suicide mission," as he left notes saying he was not coming back. Immediately rioting broke out, which led to the deaths of another twenty-six Palestinians and two Israelis.

The media—American, Israeli, and English-speaking—immediately presented Goldstein as a "lone nut." It was only years later that a few online articles would quote his father as saying that days before his son's attack, loudspeakers on mosques in Hebron had been blaring forth a clear message to Muslims: "Itbach el-yahood!" ("Slaughter the Jews!") Goldstein had grown upset and fearful of a rumored attack by terrorists against the settlement Jews.

Hamas announced in March that suicide bombings would resume. On April 6, Hamas set off a car bomb in Afula that killed eight and wounded forty-four. Hamas said their attack was revenge for Goldstein's killing of twenty-nine Palestinians. On April 13, Hamas next used a belt bomb that killed five and injured thirty in Hadera, north of Tel Aviv. The PLO suspended peace talks with Israel, and then quickly, on May 4, 1994, Israel agreed to a withdrawal of military forces from the Gaza Strip and Jericho. All of these events support Pape's theories that suicide terrorists are intermittently reinforced for their acts. However, Hamas's suicidal reaction was directly linked much more with the overt, media-driven reaction to the Hebron Massacre. It was a publicity event, and Hamas responded with high-profile suicidal missions.

We do not have to go through the 188 recent suicide-bombing events to understand what is happening. These events cluster and are linked by the copycat effect. There is now widespread recognition of that fact. In 1980, Manus I. Midlarsky,

Martha Crenshaw, and Fujio Yoshida talked of this process in their *International Studies Quarterly* journal article "Why Violence Spreads: The Contagion of International Terrorism." And in 1985, Kent Layne Oots and Thomas C. Wiegele proposed a model of terrorist contagion in their "Terrorist and Victim: Psychiatric and Physiological Approaches from a Social Science Perspective," in *Terrorism: An International Journal.* They found that potential terrorists become aroused and accept the use of violence after observing media presentations of terrorism. They noted that the potential terrorist "need only see that terrorism has worked for others in order to become aggressively aroused."

Philip Marsden, a contagion psychologist and visiting research fellow at the University of Sussex at the time, saw the danger after 9/11 and said: "The political and media reaction to the recent terrorist attacks in the U.S. could trigger a spate of copycat terrorism." Marsden boldly stated that "copycat terrorism makes compelling sense when we understand the simple but deadly psychology of contagion. A phenomenon of 'disinhibition' can occur when suicidal or murderous thoughts—inhibited by conscience, uncertainty or fear—are exposed to what is perceived as the positive consequences of suicide or murder. When this happens, the mental conflict between urges and inhibitions may be resolved, resulting in a suicidal and possibly murderous mind being made up. Thought is free to become deadly action. With a perverse irony, the global attention and blanket media coverage accorded the U.S. terrorist attacks may actually help make up some desperate minds and legitimize future murder-suicides."

A perverse irony, indeed.

CHAPTER TEN

Going Postal

A micro-war of murder-suicides, fueled by the copycat effect, has been raging for years in the American workplace. Ever since 1986, this micro-war has been known by an all-too-familiar two-word phrase where the phenomenon got its start: *going postal.*

The episode that gave a name to such events involved Patrick Henry Sherrill. Neighbors described him as a strange man. He would ride around town, unaccompanied, on a "bicycle built for two." A loner without friends, Sherrill lived with only his pit bull after his mother died in 1978. He wore battle fatigues most of the time and told people he had served in Vietnam, although he hadn't. He had been in the Marines, however, and was a good marksman, reaching the level of "expert" with the M14 and the pistol. He continued in the Air National Guard, then the 507th Tactical Fighter Group, then returned to the National Guard. He even completed a nine-week-long firearms course to become a weapons instructor, fulfilling that role eventually. He liked weapons and seemed comfortable in quasimilitary settings. For three years Sherrill sought employment with the United States Postal Service (USPS). Finally, in 1985, he landed a job as a substitute letter carrier. Never one to mix well, Sherrill was a bomb waiting to go off.

Edmond, Oklahoma

On August 19, 1986, two postal supervisors got into an argument with Sherrill, apparently over some disputed leave time. After eighteen months at the post office, he felt he might be suspended or even be fired. The next day Sherrill launched the phrase *going postal* into the American lexicon.

Sherrill, 44, arrived at the Edmond, Oklahoma, post office a few minutes before seven A.M. on August 20, 1986. He walked in wearing his normal summer uniform—shorts, high kneesocks, and a shirt, which that day was already soaked through with sweat. He was carrying a .45-caliber semiautomatic pistol in his right hand and had in his postal bag another .45 and about one hundred rounds of ammunition. In the course of fifteen minutes he killed fourteen postal workers, mostly male supervisors and women coworkers, wounded six others, then killed himself. The supervisor who had disciplined Sherrill overslept and didn't make it to work on time; his life was spared.

The media quickly tagged Sherrill's snapping under pressure and killing his coworkers in a rampage at work as *going postal.* The phrase is comparable to others denoting unpredictable and outrageous behavior, such as *going berserk* (1908), *going crazy* (1930), and *going ballistic* (1971).

Sherrill's fifteen minutes of infamy spawned a series of copycat attacks that still haunt us today. The ripple effect of the Sherrill event reached Australia. Like the U.S., Australia had its own first prominent postal-related rampage during the same time period. On December 8, 1987, Melbourne law student Frank Vitkovic, wearing a fatigue jacket and carrying a high-powered rifle, ran through an Australian Post Office building, killing eight and injuring seventeen. He was tackled on the tenth floor of the building and his rifle was wrestled away, but Vitkovic escaped, only to leap to his death from the eleventh floor. (Vitkovic is said to also have been an Australian copycat of Julian Knight, who had killed seven and wounded nineteen, in sniper fashion three months earlier, on August 9, 1987. Knight was a copycat himself, as he was an admirer of Texas Tower sniper Charles Whitman.)

The U.S. media did not treat the issue of workplace violence as a "national issue," until after Sherrill's "going postal" became a cause célèbre. After all, this shooting was more than a "local" event: The USPS is a federal government agency. If it's a work shooting, it's irrational, the media reasoned; but if it's postal, that's not local, it's national. So after Sherrill, every time a postal shooting happened, publicity about it snowballed and before long the notion arose that stressed-out postal workers were vulnerable to the copycat effect.

Before Edmond

Others had "gone postal" before Sherrill, of course, but the media had treated their acts as the random and isolated actions of deranged individuals. The very first "modern" postal shooting on record actually occurred on August 19, 1983—oddly enough, preceding Sherrill's killing spree by almost three years to the day. This earlier incident involved a Johnston, South Carolina, post office employee named Perry Smith. His son, also a postal employee, had died by suicide nine months before, and since then people at work seemed to have no understanding of Smith's pain. Instead, Smith felt the postmaster had it in for him. When word spread that August 19, 1983, would be postmaster Charles McGee's last day on the job, Smith felt his chances of confronting McGee slipping away. So Smith came to work, gun blazing, on August 19, and chased McGee across the street and into a little neighborhood store, where Smith fired two twelve-gauge rounds into McGee, killing him. Two other postal workers and a police officer were wounded in the spree before Smith gave up to the injured officer. Smith was convicted of murder in a South Carolina court and sentenced to life in prison.

Four months later, postal worker James H. Brooks would commit a very similar crime on December 2, 1983. That day Brooks confronted Anniston, Alabama, postmaster Oscar Johnson about his criticisms of him, then left the post office, got a .38 out of his car, and returned to shoot the postmaster in the forehead. Shouts of "Get out! Jim's got a gun!" went up throughout the postal facility. Johnson would later die at a hospital. Another postal employee, Butch Taylor, was hit in the arm and stomach; he survived. The shooter surrendered peacefully when the police arrived. Brooks was convicted of first-degree murder in federal court and sentenced to life in prison. Under federal law, individuals serving life sentences cannot be paroled.

A little more than a year later another postal incident occurred. Twelve-year veteran mail sorter Steven Brownlee, who sometimes heard voices and didn't have many friends, was attracted to another postal worker named Bettye T. Eberhart. Brownlee became extremely upset when, in early March 1985, Eberhart's estranged husband killed her in her Decatur, Georgia, home. Brownlee was heard to mumble, "Somebody must pay for Bettye's dying." On March 6, 1985, soon after two P.M., Brownlee took a .22 handgun and killed his supervisor Warren Bailey and coworker Phil Sciarrone, then struggled with other postal workers, wounding Doug Adams before he was subdued. Police arrested him soon afterward. The post office opened the next morning.

This incident occurred at the main post office at Hapeville, near the airport, in Atlanta, Georgia. One of the career employees at the post office that day was Ron Denney. Soon after the

Brownlee spree, Denney was promoted and decided to move away from the urban setting so he and his wife, another postal employee, could feel safer. Judy Denney had just been working at her new postal location for four days when Patrick Sherrill of "going postal" infamy killed her in Edmond, Oklahoma, just sixteen months after Steven Brownlee's murderous rampage. (Brownlee, incidentally, was found not guilty by reason of insanity; he remains in a mental facility in Georgia today.)

Ten weeks after the Brownlee shootings, mail carrier David Perez (a pseudonym) got into an argument with supervisor George Grady at the main post office in Manhattan on May 31, 1985. When postal clerk Carlos Siratt tried to break up the fight, Perez, 45, pulled a .30–30 rifle from his mailbag and shot Siratt in the chest. The clerk survived and David later surrendered to police after holding Grady hostage for two hours. Perez went to trial, and on January 30, 1986, a judge dismissed all charges except assault, sentenced him to five years of prison, then suspended the sentence, gave Perez five years' probation, and set him free.

These four shooters—Smith, Brooks, Brownlee, and Perez—all caused critical incidents at post offices before Sherrill's rampage in Oklahoma. While the national media had not focused much attention on these early stories, within the postal service, certainly, word of the problem was spreading.

After Edmond

Once Patrick Henry Sherrill killed fourteen in his postal killing spree in Edmond, Oklahoma, the incidents began to pile up quickly.

Ever since Dominic LuPoli got his job at the Incoming Mail Center for the Boston-area post offices in 1986, he had been obsessed with Lisa Bruni, who also worked there. But she wasn't interested, never dated him, and grew concerned about LuPoli's sexually explicit comments, notes, and other inappropriate actions. She complained to supervisors and asked for shift and/or location transfers to avoid a growing number of nasty interactions with LuPoli. On the evening of June 28, 1988, she wrote a "To Whom It May Concern" letter and sent copies to her union, the postal inspector's office, and her supervisor. In it she stated that she felt threatened by LuPoli and was concerned for her safety, noting: "I greatly fear an incident similar to the one in Oklahoma is possible here . . . I am not the only employee to make this sad observation." On June 29, 1988, Dominic LuPoli, 40, fatally shot Lisa Bruni at the Incoming Mail Center where they worked, then drove to Revere Beach Boulevard and shot himself dead as police approached his car.

On December14, 1988, Warren Murphy, an employee at a New Orleans post office, wounded two coworkers and his supervisor with a shotgun, then took a fourth female employee hostage. Supervisor Leonard King, who had been shot in the face, would lose his right eye from the shotgun blast. After a thirteen-hour police standoff, Murphy finally surrendered. He was found guilty of kidnapping and assault with intent to commit murder. Judge Veronica Wicker sentenced Murphy to sixteen years in prison.

Within a five-month period between November 1988 and March 1989, four postal workers in southern California died by suicide. Few did it as dramatically as Don Mace. "By the time you receive this, I should be dead," wrote ten-year veteran postal worker Mace in March 1989, in a letter to local newspapers. He dropped the suicide letters in a mailbox on March 25, 1989, then dressed in his postal uniform and went to his workplace, the Poway Post Office. From all reports, Don Mace, 44, walked quietly into the San Diego–area postal facility, took out his .38, and shot himself in the temple.

On January 19, 1989, Alfred J. Hunter III, a Boston postal

worker, went into a Salisbury, Massachusetts, gun shop and bought an AK-47 assault rifle. Speaking of the Stockton, California, school shootings, which had occurred that day and in which five Asian kids were killed, Hunter, a Vietnam vet, told an acquaintance: "I really like what happened there. I need a gun. I really want one." On May 9, 1989, Purdy took his new AK-47 and a full box of ammunition, killed his Filipino wife, and stole a two-passenger Cessna 152. For over three hours Hunter dive-bombed the USPS's South Annex, where he worked. He strafed the building with fire from his AK-47 but never hit anyone. He also fired on the skywalk of the Prudential Tower, in the heart of Boston. Police feared he was going to crash into that gigantic skyscraper, but then Hunter took the plane to Logan Airport, and flew directly at the air traffic control tower a few times. Finally, just as suddenly as it had begun, Hunter landed the plane and surrendered to police. For three years Hunter remained in Bridgewater State Hospital, until he was found competent to stand trial. He has been in and out of courts for years, awaiting his fate.

While in the Marines, John Merlin Taylor learned that his young sister, homecoming queen JoAnn, had killed their abusive father when he attacked their mother on June 12, 1958. After his service, Taylor stayed away from his large Missouri clan and settled in Escondido, California. He got a job at the post office, as so many ex-military men do. During July 1989, John Taylor thought he was under investigation for stealing mail. He told fellow workers that he hoped there would be no violence like that which had occurred in Edmond, Oklahoma, three years before. Then on the morning of August 10, 1989, Taylor killed his wife with a Sturm Ruger .22 semiautomatic pistol while she was asleep in their bed. He then drove to the Orange Glen post office, killed two colleagues, Ron Williams and Dick Berni, and wounded two others before killing himself in the rear of the building.

The 1990s saw no letup in the postal killing sprees. And often the killers cited the Patrick Sherrill rampage of 1986 as the model for their behavior. After nine years of working for the U.S. Postal Service, Joseph M. Harris began having trouble with Carol Ott, his night-shift supervisor in Ridgewood, New Jersey. Then, after a series of threats, Ott fired Harris in April 1990. On the night of October 9, 1991, Harris wrote an open letter saying how he had been unfairly treated by the post office and mentioned the Patrick Sherrill rampage of a few years earlier. The next morning, on October 10, 1991, Harris put on a black Japanese outfit, grabbed his three-foot-long samurai sword and various guns, and went to Ott's Wayne, New Jersey, home, where he killed her with the sword and her partner, Cornelius Kasten Jr., with a .22 pistol. Then Harris went to the Ridgewood post office and killed two mail handlers as they arrived for work. He was found guilty of murder and received the death penalty for killing Kasten (but only life for the postal workers). Harris would die on September 26, 1996, after suffering severe cranial bleeding in his prison cell.

Just five weeks after the Harris rampage, Thomas McIlvane, an ex-Marine champion kickboxer with a black belt in karate, was fired for swearing at his supervisor as well as threatening other clerks and fighting with customers at the Royal Oak, Michigan, post office. Upset about losing his job, McIlvane repeatedly warned that he would make Pat Sherrill's massacre at Edmond look like "Disneyland" or "a tea party." One of McIlvane's ex-supervisors was so disturbed by the threats that he asked the USPS security division in Detroit for protection, but the request was denied. Some of McIlvane's coworkers took the problem so seriously that they drew up escape plans. The day after McIlvane's request for reemployment was denied, he took his revenge. On November 14, 1991, McIlvane walked into the post office with something hidden under his raincoat. Within moments he proceeded to kill four supervisors—including the one who had asked for protection—and wounded five employees with a sawed-off .22-caliber Ruger semiautomatic rifle. McIlvane then killed himself. The postal inspector's office—which, according to researcher Don Lasseter in *Going Postal: Madness and Mass Murder in America's Post Offices*, "had repeatedly ignored or turned away requests for help to deal with McIlvane's threats by claiming inadequate available security staff to provide protection of the frightened managers, suddenly found all the staff they needed to post guards around the Royal Oak facility, *after the massacre*" (Lasseter's emphasis).

The U.S. Congress was upset enough about the McIlvane incident to appoint a full-scale commission to study what had gone wrong. On June 15, 1992, the U.S. House of Representatives' Committee on Postal Office and Civil Services released a study, *A Post Office Tragedy: The Shooting at Royal Oak*. The report said there had been twenty-one firsthand accounts of threats from McIlvane that he might do something, but it also talked of the harsh management style at the post office in Michigan and the paramilitary character of the USPS generally. (In the post-Vietnam era, many ex–military officers became postal administrators in a system that gave preference hiring to Vietnam vets. It would prove to be a volatile mix.) This congressional report acknowledged that the Royal Oaks incident was one of nine "violent happenings involving present or former postal employees since 1983" and that it followed by only a month the "shooting incident in Ridgewood, New Jersey." The report's number one recommendation was for better preemployment screening.

Meanwhile, in California, individual postal worker suicides continued. Some said that nine-year USPS veteran Roy Barnes, 60, was worried about his work being cut back. On June 3, 1992, shortly after lunch, he stood up in the middle of his work area at the Sacramento post office in Citrus Heights, pulled a .22-caliber pistol from his pocket, and fired it at his chest. He was declared dead on arrival at the hospital.

More postal events occurred in rapid succession even as the media and the USPS increased their scrutiny. The transmission of the idea from one event to the other was crystal clear. At 8:45 A.M. on May 6, 1993, Larry Jasion, 45, who worked in the postal motor pool in Dearborn, Michigan—just fifteen miles from Royal Oaks—strolled into the garage area with a shotgun in one hand and a pistol in the other. He then killed coworker Gary Montes and wounded two others before putting a bullet in his own head.

How much more confidently could the copycat effect be demonstrated? Four hours after the Jasion postal shootings were on the news, on May 6, 1993, postal worker Mark Richard Hilbun, 38, began his own rampage. He first murdered his mother; then the man who once showed up at work wearing his green underwear over his clothes went on to the Dana Point community post office near Los Angeles and shot two workers, killing one, Charles Barbagallo, a coworker who had befriended him. Hilbun was convicted and sentenced to nine life sentences, plus an extra eight months for animal cruelty for slitting the throat of his mother's dog. Judge Everett Dickey wanted to make certain that Hilbun never got out of prison.

In 1993, at the time of the Jasion and Hilbun postal rampages, Christopher Green legally purchased a 9mm Taurus handgun. Green had worked cleaning the Montclair, New Jersey, post offices from July 16, 1992, through April 25, 1993. Then on March 21, 1995, Green, 29, took his gun to the substation near the four P.M. closing time and killed the two postal workers and two customers. He thought he had killed a third customer, but David Grossman survived. Investigators were skeptical of Green's motive: He owed back rent on his expensive apartment. After pleading guilty to the charges, the judge gave Green five life sentences in federal prison with no chance of parole.

The spring of 1995 saw the horror of the Oklahoma City bombing and the beginning of "the trial of the century" on the

O. J. Simpson double-murder proceedings. Sixteen miles east of the Simpson courthouse, another drama unfolded. On July 10, 1995, postal worker Bruce William Clark, 58, walked up to his supervisor, James Whooper III, in the processing center at City of Industry, California; Clark pulled a .38-caliber handgun from a paper bag and shot Whooper in the chest and face, killing him almost instantly. Clark's coworkers grabbed him, wrestled the gun away, and turned him over to Los Angeles County sheriff's deputies. The 58-year-old was sentenced to twenty-two years in prison without parole after plea-bargaining to a second-degree murder charge.

Two weeks after the Clark shooting—and a dozen years after the Pat Sherrill "going postal" incident in Edmond, Oklahoma—the U.S. Postal Service instituted a new policy: Any employee entering a post office with a gun would be fired. Five weeks after the new postal workplace guideline was announced, another postal shooting occurred in Illinois. On August 29, 1995, Dorsey S. Thomas, 53, living in a delusional and paranoid world, walked into his place of work at the Palatine, Illinois, post office, and shot and wounded two men with whom he regularly joked and ate lunch. He thought they had raped him twenty-one months previously. Both men recovered but remained disabled. Thomas, 53, was sentenced to serve sixteen years in federal prison.

On August 13,1996, the news from New Egypt, New Jersey, told of letter sorter Rodger Johnson, 44, who was arrested after a search of his booby-trapped home revealed explosives, gas grenades, eighty-five guns, and thousands of rounds of ammunition. Two days later, at the main Paterson, New Jersey, post office, 38-year-old postal employee Danny Isku confronted his supervisor, Jerry Peterson, and USPS labor representative Richard Anastasi, then pulled a 22.-caliber Ruger semiautomatic gun out of a brown bag. Peterson and Anastasi jumped Isku, who had had enough teasing over his short stature and speech impediment. Peterson was wounded in the hand and Anastasi broke his hand, but Isku was subdued and arrested.

Before the year's end, on December 19, 1996, Charles E. Jennings, 41, an eighteen-year U.S. Postal Service veteran, shot senior labor relations supervisor Jay Brown to death in a post office parking lot in Las Vegas. On September 2, 1997, Vietnam vet and twenty-one-year postal worker Jesus Antonio Tamayo, 64, shot his ex-wife and her friend at point-blank range in a crowded Miami Beach post office, then went outside, looked up at the sky, and shot and killed himself. In Milwaukee exactly one year to the day after the Jennings incident, on December 19, 1997, Anthony Deculit, 37, killed a postal coworker Dan Smith and wounded two others before killing himself as a colleague pleaded, "Don't do this." A mere five days later, on December 24, 1997, fired postal worker David Lee Jackson, 42, held seven hostages at a postal mail-sorting facility in Denver for nine hours before everyone was freed unharmed. On April 17, 1998, at a post office in northwest Dallas, 27-year-old recently hired letter carrier Maceo Yarbough III fatally shot LaVina Kelley-Shaw, 34, a mother of three and postal clerk for fifteen years. On October 6, 1998, in Riverside, California, nine-year veteran postal worker Joseph Neale, 48, took the mayor and two city council members hostage, then waged a gun battle with police officers. Five people, including a policeman and the gunman, were wounded. Mayor Ron Loveridge said: "It was surrealistic, something you'd see in a movie or on television . . . and you also recognize that you may or may not leave that room."

On April 10, 2001, three employees at the USPS bulk transfer center in Kearney, New Jersey, sustained injuries when Ethiopian immigrant Michael Teklai, a U.S. resident since 1994, slashed them with a knife. He was carrying a gun but didn't use it. When he came in, he activated a metal detector and someone yelled: "He's got a gun." Three Kearny police officers found Teklai in a locker room, stripped down to his underwear and covered in his own blood, said Terrence Hull, a county prosecutor. Teklai had cut his left wrist with one of his two folding knives and was pointing his gun at the officers, Hull said. "He approached the officers, and he was instructed to drop his weapons. When he didn't, all three officers discharged their weapons," Hull told the Associated Press. Teklai died at the postal facility.

A Myth?

As the 1990s drew to a close, postal shootings were being discussed on websites, and Don Lasseter's book *Going Postal: Madness and Mass Murder in America's Post Offices* (referred to above), saw publication. This brilliant book shows the good, the bad, and the ugly of the unfortunate victims, the killers, and the United States Postal Service. The book was not received well by the USPS, as Lasseter focused on the harsh management polices that make some post offices not much more than ticking time bombs. The book documents the copycat effect for the whole phenomenon of "going postal," detailing the media's and the USPS's responses to deflect the attention elsewhere.

As it turns out, the USPS had pulled together another commission to study the problem of postal shootings. Their report was less than earthshaking, but it definitely indicated that a public relations campaign was in full swing. In essence, *The Postal Service Commission Report on a Safe and Secure Workplace* disclosed that "going postal" was a myth. "Postal workers are no more likely to physically assault, sexually harass or verbally abuse their coworkers than employees in the national workforce," said the work group.

This "independent" United States Postal Service Commission on a Safe and Secure Workplace was headed by Joseph A. Califano Jr., chairman of the commission and president of The National Center on Addiction and Drug Abuse at Columbia

University. Califano presented the 249-page report to the post-master general in August 2000 after two years of study.

The report said that twenty-nine homicide cases had occurred at post offices between 1986 and 1998 and that former or current postal employees—all of whom, they said, were violent criminals or suffered from mental illness and should not have been employed by the USPS—had committed fifteen of the shootings. On the other hand, they noted that postal workers were only a third as likely as those in the national workforce to be victims of homicide at work (0.26 versus 0.77 per 100,000 workers annually from 1992 through 1998). "Comparing industries, retail workers are eight times likelier than postal employees to be homicide victims at work; comparing occupations, taxi drivers are 150 times likelier than letter carriers to be homicide victims at work," the report said.

Critics countered that while taxi drivers and employees of liquor stores, gas stations, and grocery stores may die more often than postal workers, in all of those situations, clearly, it was not their coworkers killing them. They also pointed out that homicide was the second leading cause of death for postal workers, clearly an unacceptable situation for postal employees. The database for the study was also rather selective: They failed to include, for example, the Christopher Green killings, because they judged that it had happened during a robbery.

The goal of the study was clear: "We hope to shatter the myth, so postal workers can sleep a little better at night," said Alyse Booth, spokeswoman for the commission. The problem was essentially illusory, in other words. Besides, since 1998, the panel said, the USPS had taken steps to better screen employees and increase security at post offices.

Sadly, the commission failed to look into behavior contagion, imitation, and the copycat effect. The USPS simply stuck its head in the sand.

The U.S. Postal Service has continued its crusade against the use of the phrase *going postal* into the twenty-first century. After the Fox network aired a promotion for an upcoming episode of *Mad TV* that showed two postal employees brandishing guns and talking about shooting as customers cower, the USPS went on the offensive. Their response on December 10, 2003, that the skit was "unfair" and "an insult to every man and woman in the Postal Service" appeared on most television news programs in the United States and in newspapers from the *Atlanta Journal-Constitution* to the British paper *The Guardian.* Postal officials asked their 750,000 workers to contact the head of Fox Entertainment Group to complain. A Fox spokesman replied that *Mad TV* was "an equal opportunity offender." In a little over a decade the term *going postal* had gone from grim reality to a joke for public consumption.

Perhaps prodded a little by USPS admonishments, the media began to shift its focus away from the specific—postal shootings—to the more general issue of "workplace violence."

A Post–"Going-Postal" World

Due to the USPS's counter–public relations efforts, the media's attention seemed to drift from "going postal" incidents to mass-murder rampages in other settings. (Mass murders are different from serial killings: Serial killers, like Jack the Ripper, kill over time; mass murderers and rampage killers kill several people within a very limited time frame.) With modern Americans introduced to mass murders with the popularization of "going postal" events and terminology, the leap to "workplace violence" incidents in general was a direct one.

Examples from the late 1980s and 1990s range far beyond the confines of post offices. Workplace violence occurred at brokerage firms, warehouses, assembly lines, and construction companies. Even the Connecticut Lottery Corporation was not safe from workplace rampages. Most shooters were suicidal, and in half the incidents they ended up dying by their own hand or by "suicide by cop." It was rather apparent, too, that these acts were triggered by prior incidents. Once one workplace incident occured, another often happened within two weeks.

The Multiviolence Copycatting

Before Joseph Wesbecker, 47, shot to death seven employees and himself in a workplace rampage at the Standard Gravure Corporation in Louisville, Kentucky, on September 14, 1989, he left behind at his home a *Newsweek* article about Patrick Purdy, who had killed five children and himself at a Stockton, California, school on January 17, 1989. Wesbecker even purchased the same model gun Purdy had used in his rampage, an AK-47 assault rifle.

Before George Hennard crashed his truck into Luby's Cafeteria in Killeen, Texas, on October 16, 1991, and sprayed it with gunfire, he had watched a documentary video at home about a similar mass murderer, James Huberty, who killed twenty-one people at a California McDonald's on July 18, 1984.

It became clear by the late 1990s that reports of workplace violence were not always followed by other copycats of workplace incidents a day or a week later but sometimes by other forms of mass and rampage violence as well. For example in the first week of November 1999, two workplace shootings on a Tuesday and a Wednesday shook the United States, which was already reeling from a long string of office and school killings for the year. In Seattle and Honolulu, the families of nine victims grieved as observers debated how to keep violence out of public settings traditionally considered safe. In Honolulu, seven people were shot to death when Xerox technician Brian Uyesugi walked into a second-floor meeting room of the Xerox's offices and opened fire. He shot all the victims at close range with a 9mm handgun. In Seattle the next day, a gunman shot and killed two men and wounded two others in a shipyard office. Wearing a dark trench coat over camouflage clothing, the gunman had walked into the Northlake Shipyard building and proceeded down a long hallway and into a back office before wordlessly opening fire and shooting all four men in the room with a 9mm semiautomatic handgun. Two 9mm guns, two Pacific Rim cities, two days of killings. Ten days later another school shooting occurred in New Mexico.

One type of copycat event was reinforcing another—and people were beginning to take notice.

In early July 2003, author Kate Randall, writing on the World Socialist website observed that "the past week has witnessed an uncommonly large number of violent incidents—including two workplace shootings, murder-suicides and multiple homicides. Three teenagers were also arrested for allegedly plotting a killing rampage. Between July 1 and July 8, twenty individuals were killed in these incidents and another fourteen wounded . . . Also on July 8, police found the bodies of four people, apparent victims of a murder-suicide, in a small, well-kept ranch-style home in Magnolia, N.J. . . . Another multiple shooting was discovered on July 8, this time in Bakersfield, California. The bodies of a grandmother, mother and three young children were all found shot dead in their home."

When such clustering occurs, with its mixed types of violence, the copycatting is spreading from one type of incident to another. "Absolutely, there's a copycat aspect to workplace violence," James Alan Fox, a criminologist at Northeastern University in Boston, told *The Christian Science Monitor* in 2001. "There's a copycat aspect to virtually all high-profile, high-visibility crimes."

The violence is everywhere and the media is gobbling it up, unconsciously spreading it in the process.

CHAPTER ELEVEN

School Shootings

Today's frenzied style of news coverage, with its wall-to-wall "live news," "breaking news," and "continuing coverage," has become a modern form of entertainment. The newsroom's addiction for its own "reality programming" is a relatively recent phenomenon. It all began with CNN, the first news-only network on television, which has been around since 1980. Under Ted Turner's leadership, CNN was a groundbreaking idea, but it soon became "traditional" in terms of its low-impact, factual reportage of the news. By the mid-1990s, other news services began to promote an even more graphic "breaking news" style that led to today's MSNBC, Fox News, and other "news" networks. Fox News Network is a babe in these woods, evolving from the news department at Fox TV at the end of the 1996 elections. Everyone is now forced to compete for the latest breaking horror story. The modern world has given the media just what it wants most.

"I Just Don't Like Mondays"

Media interest in adolescent suicide clusters reached a peak in 1987 with the Bergenfield incident. Then through the early 1990s, stories about teen suicides faded from the national television, magazines, and newspapers. But it was just a matter of time before the media would find a new, ever-more-sensational, *youth*-oriented death phenomenon. And that would be school shootings.

The "modern era" school rampages goes back to 1979 and Brenda Spencer, a 16-year-old girl allegedly addicted to violent films and killing birds with her BB gun. Her father had given her a .22 semiautomatic for Christmas. Spencer would later remark: "I asked him for a radio and he bought me a gun. I felt like he wanted me to kill myself."

On January 29, 1979, Spencer pointed her gun out her bedroom window at San Diego's Cleveland Elementary School across the street. She waited for the principal to open the school. At that point Spencer began firing on the students who were coming to school. For twenty minutes she had the students, teachers, and the crossing guard pinned down. During that period Spencer killed the school principal and the school's caretaker as well as wounding nine students, aged 6 to12. During the next two hours Brenda Spencer talked to the police and press before finally surrendering. Explaining to reporters what she had done, she said: "I just started shooting, that's it. I just did it for the fun of it. I just don't like Mondays. . . . I just did it because it's a way to cheer the day up. Nobody likes Mondays." She finally surrendered and was convicted on two counts of murder. Brenda Spencer is serving two twenty-five-years-to-life sentences.

The Boomtown Rats, an Irish rock group touring America at the time of the Spencer shooting, decided to write a song about the event. Labeled punks by the media, the Boomtown Rats were relatively famous at the time, being Dublin's answer to the Sex Pistols and the Clash. "I Don't Like Mondays" became their most successful and most enduring hit despite the fact that many American radio stations refused to play it. The song's writer, singer Bob Geldof, then left the group for a solo career and eventually played the lead role in Pink Floyd's *The Wall*. Geldof would go on to become a well-known rock promoter, organized the Band Aid and Live Aid benefit concerts, and cowrote the songs "Do They Know It's Christmas?" and "We are the World." Those in the music business even now call him Saint Bob (he actually holds an honorary knighthood) for his good deeds. Geldof, who has had a star-crossed and difficult life (e.g., divorces, his ex-wife's lover's suicide, her later death), has Brenda Spencer's killing spree and his success with "I Don't Like Mondays" to thank for his rise to fame. At the end of 2003 the media speculated that Geldof might seek to become the president of Ireland.

A decade would pass—almost to the day—before shootings at schools would start to be "news." On January 17, 1989, Patrick Purdy, also known as Patrick West and other names, returned to the school he had attended fifteen years before. But he wasn't interested in a pleasant homecoming. Instead, Purdy, wearing a T-shirt with the word *Satan* on it, opened fire at the playground of the Cleveland Elementary School in Stockton, California, killing five children and wounding thirty-five youngsters and a teacher with his AK-47. All were the children of Southeast Asian refugees. Purdy then turned the gun on himself and died by suicide.

Both the Purdy and Spencer incidents were atypical of the later school shooter pattern. Neither was a current member of the student body they attacked, and Spencer was female; all school shooters who caused fatalities in the late 1990s were males who were suicidal. But the era of school shooters was dawning, and it would clearly be a copycat blueprint attentively "followed," if not fueled, by the media.

Rage

Although it attracted no such recognition by the media at the time, America's "first" modern school shooting took place on Groundhog Day, February 2, 1996, in Moses Lake, Washington State. The Moses Lake killings set the pattern for what would follow in America: a student (not an outsider) killing other students and teachers. This is the horror—the danger from within of students killing students—that appears to have captivated the media. On that day, Barry Loukaitis, 14, dressed all in black, with boots and a long coat that hid his father's hunting rifle and two handguns, walked into his Frontier Junior High fifth-period algebra class at Moses Lake and started shooting. He had cut the pockets out of his long Western duster and was able to use the .30-.30 lever-action hunting rifle without taking his hands out of the long, black trench coat. Loukaitis killed two classmates, Arnold Fritz and Manuel Vela, and then severely wounded another, Natalie Hintz. Hintz, sitting beside the boys, was shot in the stomach, with the bullet traveling through her elbow and almost tearing her right arm off. Next, Loukaitis aimed at the back of his algebra teacher, Leona Caires, and killed her as she was writing an equation on the chalkboard. With the carnage around him and fifteen students in the room crying hysterically, Loukaitis calmly turned toward them, smiled, and said: "This sure beats algebra, doesn't it?" The line was a quote from the 1977 Stephen King (writing as Richard Bachman) novel *Rage*. Physical education teacher Jon M. Lane then rushed into the room, knocked the rifle away from Loukaitis, and wrestled him to the floor to end the shooting.

Loukaitis's mother told the jury at his widely reported trial that she had treated her son as a confidant, telling him everything. One of these things included her plans to kill herself in front of her ex-husband and his new girlfriend, whom she was going to kidnap and tie up on Valentine's Day, 1996. Using advice from *Rage*, young Loukaitis talked her out of it and encouraged her to write down her anger—"like a play"—thus following Stephen King's lead. Despite this bit of mature intervention, Loukaitis decided to turn his own suicidal feelings into a homicidal fury based on various cultural clues he had picked up himself.

Loukaitis had planned the shootings carefully, getting ideas, he said, from the Stephen King book. In it, a troubled high school boy takes a gun to fictional Placerville High School, kills his algebra teacher, Mrs. Underwood, another school adult, Mr. Vance, and takes the algebra class hostage. Police would find a collection of Stephen King's books in Loukaitis's bedroom, including his well-worn copy of *Rage*.

The *Rage* scenario had been played out before in real life. At Valley High School in Las Vegas, Nevada, on March 19, 1982, after algebra teacher Clarence Piggot refused to cancel a public speaking assignment, 17-year-old Patrick Lizotte gunned him down. Patrick also wounded two other 17-year-old students during his rampage. He left the school and was killed nearby during a shoot-out with the police. On January 18, 1993, Scott Pennington, 17, took his senior English class captive at East Carter High School in Grayson, Kentucky. He killed his teacher and a custodian. Pennington would tell investigators later that he read *Rage* only after the shooting. In 1997, *Rage* would be linked to another shooting. A copy of *Rage* was found in the locker of Michael Carneal, a high school shooter in West Paducah, Kentucky.

Stephen King discussed the role of *Rage* after the Loukaitis shootings and eventually apologized for writing the book, saying he penned it during a troubling period in his life. He said he wished it never had been published. Finally, in 1999, he told his publisher to discontinue publication and pull it off the stands. He told the *Today Show*'s Katie Couric: "I took a look at *Rage* and said to myself, If this book is acting as any sort of accelerant—if it's having any effect on any of these kids at all—I don't want anything to do with it, regardless of what may be the moral and legal rights and wrongs. Even talking about it makes me nervous."

Other pop-culture items influenced the Loukaitis rampage. He had rented the video of Oliver Stone's film *Natural Born Killers* (1994) seven times and got the idea for the long black coat and black outfit from that movie. From *A Fistful of Dollars*, starring Clint Eastwood, he crafted his hardened personal desperado manner. During the monthlong trial that began on August 24, 1997, the focus was on what became known as the "Pearl Jam Defense." Loukaitis had memorized the words and overly identified with the character in the rock video *Jeremy*. The 1992 video, played often on MTV, showed a shirtless boy who comes to school and leaves his classmates covered in blood. The video and song were based on an actual 1990 incident in which Jeremy Wade Delle, 15, of Richardson, Texas, walked into an English classroom at Richardson High School, put a gun to his head, and pulled the trigger, dying by suicide in front of thirty students. "Jeremy spoke in class today" became the famous line from the award-winning Pearl Jam video (the 1993 MTV Video of the Year) that young people across the country would say to each other. The media noted that the Delle suicide of January 8, 1990, appeared to come during the tail end of a media feeding frenzy on teen suicides. Where teen suicides ended, school shootings picked up.

In *Teenage Rampage*, British crime author Antonio Mendoza reflected on the fact that violence in American schools was really nothing new, but it changed with the Barry Loukaitis incident: "Loukaitis's rampage at Frontier Junior High in Moses Lake, Washington, was the first in a series of school assaults in rural communities during the late nineties that were chillingly similar and fearfully effective. All perpetrators were excessively well-armed, white, middle-class youngsters, and their meticulously crafted plans of attack yielded increasingly higher body counts. Their rosy cheeks, freckled faces and seemingly 'boy next door' looks made the perpetrators objects of worldwide media attention, changing forever the concept of school shootings."

In the Wake of Barry

The Loukaitis shootings reverberated in Moses Lake for some time and became the national model for future school rampages. Six months after the incident, a local 14-year-old broke into a home, yelled the name Loukaitis, shot off rounds from a hunting rifle, held a man hostage, and then gave up to the police. And almost a year after the Loukaitis killings, victim Arnold Fritz's cousin, Aaron Harmon, 14, a ninth-grader at Chief Moses Junior High School, shot and killed his 9-year-old stepsister, his mother, and himself at their Moses Lake home on December 7, 1996. Distressed over the death of his cousin—whom he considered a brother—at the hands of Loukaitis, Harmon decided to employ the same method for his rampage, a hunting rifle.

About a week after the Loukaitis shootings, on February 8, 1996, Douglas Bradley, 16, a student at Mid-Peninsula Education Center, a high school in Palo Alto, California, drove his car onto an outdoor basketball court, threw money out the window so a group of students would gather, and then fired on them with a .38 revolver, injuring three. He then turned the gun on himself, killing himself. On March 11, 1996, just before taking a quiz in an algebra class—a subtle link to Loukaitis—at the North Stanly High School, New London, North Carolina, Jamie Hurley, 15, took his own life with a 9mm pistol that he had hidden in his coat.

Two days later a copycat occurred overseas. On March 13, 1996, in Dunblane, Scotland, "loner" Thomas Hamilton, 43, entered a school kindergarten class and killed sixteen children, the class's teacher, and then himself. Hamilton, a dismissed local Boy Scout leader who had a history of unstable behavior, took four minutes to commit this rampage, one of the worst in the United Kingdom's history. Hamilton's age was atypical of the later copycat pattern of school shootings. Then on September 25, 1996, David Dubose Jr., 16, at the Dekalb Alternative School in Scottsdale, Georgia, used a .38 revolver to kill English teacher Horace Morgan.

After the Loukaitis incident, the next "nationally publicized" shooting took place on February 19, 1997, at Bethel Regional High School in Bethel, Alaska, which had been a hot spot of suicide clusters a decade earlier. When student Evan Ramsey, 16, was feeling suicidal in 1997, he went to two 14-year-old friends and asked them what he should do. The boys said that if he was going to kill himself, he should take some people with him. On February 19, Ramsey did just that, killing a star athlete, Joshua Palacios, and wounding two others with a twelve-gauge shotgun. Then Ramsey went to the administration office and shot and killed the principal, Ronald Edwards. State police arrived and ended the rampage; they also arrested as accomplices the two friends who had discussed Ramsey's plan with him.

Rural Rampages

By the fall of 1997 school shootings would become horribly routine, almost as if some kind of copycat contagion was occurring. Of course, it was.

On October 1, 1997, in Pearl, Mississippi, Luke Woodham, 16, a self-styled satanist and Adolf Hitler worshipper, stabbed his mother to death in the morning and then drove to his Pearl High School. There he used a rifle to kill two students, former girlfriend Christina Menefee, 16, and Lydia Dew, 17, and wound seven others. He stopped only because he ran out of ammunition. When he returned to his car for his other gun, the assistant principal disarmed him. Two members of his "Hitler group" were charged as accessories to murder; others were arrested on the basis of a conspiracy, but these charges were later dismissed.

Exactly two months later, on December 1, 1997, at Heath High School in West Paducah, Kentucky, Michael Carneal, 14, killed three students—Jessica James, 17, Kayce Steger, 15, and Nicole Hadley, 14—and wounded five as they participated in a prayer circle. Another student tackled the black-attired Carneal, and the police found that he had a pistol, two rifles, and two shotguns, along with 700 rounds of ammunition, all of it stolen. A copy of Stephen King's *Rage* was found in his locker at school.

On December 15, 1997, a similar scenario unfolded in Stamps, Arkansas. While hiding in the woods, Joseph "Colt" Todd, 14, shot two students as they stood in the parking lot. This appears to have been the direct model for the next shooting, also from Arkansas. On March 24, 1998, at Jonesboro, Arkansas, at the Westside Middle School, Mitchell Johnson, 13, and Andrew Golden, 11, both wearing camouflage, used rifles to shoot at their classmates and teachers from the woods. Four students— Natalie Brooks, 12, Paige Ann Herring, 12, Stephanie Johnson, 12, and Britthney Varner, 12—and one teacher, Shannon Wright, 32, were killed, while ten others were wounded outside as the school emptied during a false fire alarm set off by Golden. The boys had a van stocked full of ammunition and guns that they had taken from their relatives. The next day (March 25) in Coldwater, Michigan, and almost a week after that (on March 30) in Chapel Hill, North Carolina, an 18-year-old male and a 13-year-old female, respectively, shot themselves to death with guns at their separate schools.

About a month later, on April 24, 1998, Andrew Wurst, 14, killed teacher John Gillette and wounded two students and another teacher at the eighth-grade graduation dance at James W.

Parker Middle School in Edinboro, Pennsylvania. The banquet hall owner went after him, disarmed him, and held him for police, but the boy acted as if the whole thing were a big joke. On May 19, 1998, at Fayetteville, Tennessee, one student was killed in the parking lot at Lincoln County High School three days before he was to graduate. The victim was dating the ex-girlfriend of his killer, 18-year-old honor student Jacob Davis.

The imitation occurring in these copycat events was taking place on both a large and a small scale. On the macro level, the shootings were largely taking place in rural settings: in Washington state, Alaska, Mississippi, Kentucky, and Arkansas. On the micro level, all involved suicidal-homicidal young males with guns.

Three days after the Fayetteville incident, at Springfield, Oregon, on May 21, 1998, 15-year-old Kip Kinkel used a semiautomatic rifle to kill two students, Mikael Nikolauson, 17, Ben Walker, 16, and wound 22 others in the cafeteria of Thurston High School. He was disarmed and taken to the police station, where he withdrew a hidden knife. He claimed he wanted to die. Police officers who went to his home discovered that he had killed both of his parents and had booby-trapped the house with five homemade bombs, one of which he'd placed underneath his mother's corpse. His classmates had once dubbed him the student "most likely to start World War III."

On the same day, May 21, 1998, two hundred miles due north, at the end of the school day Miles Fox, 15, a student of Onalaska High School, Onalaska, Washington, took a young woman hostage from his bus to his home and died by suicide from a shot to his head. As the story aired on the radio and television, Ricardo Martin, 15, shot himself with a .38-caliber pistol and died on the campus of Rialto High School, in Rialto, California.

As the school year was ending, on June 15, 1998, a 14-year-old boy wounded one teacher and a guidance counselor in a school hallway in Richmond, Virginia. Both survived.

The fall of 1998 would be relatively calm, although copycat suicides would pop up in Texas again. A 15-year-old shot himself on January 1, 1999, in the locker room of Richland Hills High School, in Fort Worth. On January 21, 1999, in the locker room at Richland High School in North Richland Hills, Texas, 15-year-old Randall James fatally shot himself. And on April 16, 1999, Shawn Cooper, 16, of Notus, Idaho, rode the bus to school with a shotgun wrapped in a blanket. He pointed the gun at classmates and a secretary and then shot twice into a door and at the floor. He had a death list but told one girl he wouldn't hurt anyone. He surrendered.

Columbine

Then the nightmare of April 1999 occurred.

On April 20, 1999, Eric Harris, 18, and Dylan Klebold, 17, killed one teacher and twelve students and wounded twenty-three others at Columbine High School in Littleton, Colorado. Focusing their attack on the cafeteria, Harris and Klebold spoke German and wore trench coats as they reenacted scenes from *Matrix* and *The Basketball Diaries* in the nation's deadliest school shooting. They had plotted for a year to kill at least five hundred and blow up their school. At the end of their hour-long rampage, they turned their guns on themselves. Harris and Klebold appeared to have deliberately chosen the anniversary date of Hitler's birthday for their attack. At one point Harris and Klebold had also considered the highly important date of April 19—the anniversary of Waco and the Oklahoma City bombing—but transportation problems forced a delay in their plans. They finally carried out their attack on the twentieth, speaking German and "honoring" Hitler. (They had also discussed that after the attack, they would hijack a jetliner, fly it from Colorado, and crash it into Manhattan. This was two years before the terror of 2001.)

In the wake of the shootings in Littleton, the nation's schools were under attack by copycats. Some four hundred related incidents were reported in the month following the killings. "Across the nation after the 1999 Columbine tragedy," noted Court TV's Katherine Ramsland, "other kids called in bomb threats, wore trench coats to school, or used the Internet to praise what Klebold and Harris had done. Only ten days later, on April 30, people feared the eruption of some major event because that day marked Hitler's suicide in 1945. Schools in Arizona, New Jersey, Michigan, North Carolina, and DC closed to investigate potential threats. It wasn't Paducah, or Jonesboro, or Springfield that they wanted to imitate; the mantra was 'Columbine.' "

One week after Columbine, on April 28, 1999, one student, Jason Lang, 17, was killed, and one wounded at W. R. Myers High School in Taber, Alberta, Canada. This was the first fatal high school shooting in Canada in twenty years. The shooter was a 14-year-old boy. Exactly a month after Columbine, on May 20, 1999, in Conyers, Georgia, six students were injured at Heritage High School when classmate Thomas Solomon, 15, opened fire. No one died. Witnesses reported that Solomon placed the revolver in his mouth as if to shoot himself but did not pull the trigger.

On November 19, 1999, Victor Cordova Jr., 12, shot and killed Araceli Tena, 13, in the lobby of Deming Middle School in Deming, New Mexico. In Fort Gibson, Oklahoma, on December 6, 1999, four students were wounded as Seth Trickey, 13, opened fire with a 9mm semiautomatic handgun at Fort Gibson Middle School.

A year later experts began to reflect on Columbine and its aftermath. "It used to be the most common type of this violence was in the family," mass murder expert James Alan Fox told *The New York Times*. "Now it's no longer true. It's in the workplace and in the schools."

Kay Redfield Jamison, a professor of psychiatry at Johns

Hopkins School of Medicine and author of *Night Falls Fast: Understanding Suicide,* commented: "The link between suicide and homicide is a very real one, and it hasn't been studied nearly enough. It has always struck me about Columbine, people forget they died by suicide. And that's understandable—it was the least important thing from the public point of view."

Pondering Columbine and the murder-suicide rampages, Philip Cook, a professor of public policy at Duke University who has studied social contagions, told *The New York Times*: "The transmission mechanism seems to be nothing more or less than that it's an idea that's in the air. So you have these kinds of catastrophic consequences from what seems a minor change in the environment."

"Why do you get a lot of people doing the same thing?" asked Joseph Westermeyer, a psychiatrist at the University of Minnesota who has studied epidemics of explosive murder in other cultures. "I think there is this copycat element."

Columbine Goes International

After Littleton, the copycat effect involving school shootings went global. On December 7, 1999, in Veghel, Netherlands, a 17-year-old student wounded a teacher and three students. During March 2000, in Branneburg, Germany, a teacher was killed by a 15-year-old student, who then shot himself. The shooter has been in a coma ever since. On January 18, 2001, two boys, ages 17 and 19, killed a student in Jan, Sweden, in an unusual school shooting that shocked that usually nonviolent country.

In 2002, Europe was rocked with massive school shootings. In Germany on February 19, 2002, a young man at the factory from which he had been fired killed two in Eching. He then traveled to Freising and killed the headmaster of the technical school from which he had been expelled. He also wounded another teacher before killing himself. On April 26, 2002, at Erfurt, Germany, Robert Steinhaeuser, 19, stalked the halls of the Johann Gutenberg secondary school, looking for certain teachers. Before he was finished, he had killed thirteen teachers, two students, and one policeman and wounded ten other people. Then he killed himself. (Six weeks later a student who was in the school and witnessed Steinhaeuser's rampage died by suicide, according to German press reports of June 14, 2002.)

The German media would report that the Erfurt killings were not as impulsive as originally thought. Steinhaeuser deliberately chose the date of Rudolf Hess's birthday for the Erfurt school shootings. Hess, Adolf Hitler's deputy, was born on April 26, 1894, in Alexandria, Egypt. Hate groups throughout Germany, especially neo-Nazis, celebrate April 26 because it is Hess's birthday. Hess has become a hero of neo-Nazis. Today more neo-Nazis come to Hess's grave on August 17 than come to Hitler's grave on his birthday, April 20. The date of Hess's suicide, August 17, has also witnessed increased neo-Nazi activity (in the form of parades and demonstrations) in Germany, Denmark, Sweden, and other European countries in recent years. On August 17, 2001, for example, about eight hundred neo-Nazis marched to the Bavarian gravesite of Rudolf Hess, Wunsiedel, to mark the fourteenth anniversary of his death. Several of these banned marches have turned into confrontations with the police.

Three days after the Erfurt shooting, Dragoslav Petkovic, 17, killed one teacher and wounded another before killing himself in Vlasenica, Bosnia-Herzegovina. Then on July 1, 2003, a 16-year-old pupil killed himself in a German school classroom after shooting a teacher in the thigh. No other children or staff were injured in the incident in the secondary school in the northern Bavarian town of Coburg.

The international trend continues. On January 13, 2004, an economics teacher and deputy headmaster was shot in the head and killed at the Terra College canteen in The Hague, Nether-lands. The unidentified 17-year-old shooter was said to be a dis-gruntled student who had been suspended from school, accord-ing to a Radio 1 newscast. The country was in shock: This was only the second school shooting since 1999 in the Netherlands.

American School Shootings into the Twenty-first Century

School shootings continued in America after Columbine. The deaths by school shootings showed a gradual increase from 1996 to 1999, and then a sudden jump. In the post-Columbine era, school and city officials realized for the first time that dealing with at-risk youth—whether suicidal, angry, or impulsive—might prevent more school shootings. After Columbine, the United States Secret Service studied school shootings and, in March 2001, declared that zero-tolerance punishments, such as expelling students who wore trench coats, was the wrong ap-proach. That simply sent the youths out of the schools, only to return later with guns and cause a rampage. The Secret Service study mentioned that a majority of the student shooters were suicidal and knew about previous shootings.

Youth advocates began to discuss the excessive and often ir-responsible coverage of school shootings. Center on Juvenile and Criminal Justice president Vincent Schiraldi told Youth Beat reporters LynNell Hancock and Donna Ladd in 2002 that the media are creating youth-violence connections where they do not exist and giving the public a distorted picture of young peo-ple in America. "The media really have no clue as to how to deal with this at this point. And I'm not sure many in the media are concerned," he said of the "wall-to-wall coverage" of school shootings. "What's the plan here, guys?"

Suicide-prevention training increased, but the copycat factor received little attention. Before September 11, 2001, media attention seemed focused on what school shooting might be next. When the terrorist attack occurred, a virtual media blackout kept other violence out of the news. But, in fact, there were no shooting rampages in American schools during the entire scholastic year 2001–2002. Little did the media notice or comment on the fact that school shootings had decreased so precipitously when they weren't reporting on them.

CHAPTER TWELVE

The Message in the Music and the Musicians

School shootings, like other mass murders and suicide clusters, reflect the culture of the times. The role of the media takes many forms in such events, but perhaps nothing rules and mirrors the culture of adolescents the way music does. Yesterday's swing and jazz, as remembered in bebop, the Lindy, the shimmy, and the Charleston, have evolved into the music that fills our world today: rock and roll. New Wave. Punk. Heavy metal. Grunge rock. Hip-hop. Gangsta rock. Death rock. The beat, lyrics, groups, and individual artists are held in high regard. Rock-star look-alikes are everywhere. And the fashion follows the music in more than clothing. Attitudes and belief systems are born from the messages communicated or reinforced through teen music. What is the place of music and the musicians in the schema and messages of copycat acts? What does history convey in this harmonic sphere?

Gloomy Sunday

During the early decades of the twentieth century, music as a form of mass media affected people's lives and deaths. The story of "Gloomy Sunday" is a case in point.

In Hungary in 1933, composer Rezsô Seress and lyricist Laszlo Javor wrote a mournful tune they called "Szomorú Vasárnap," which is translated into English as "Gloomy Sunday." The song tells of a mourner who is thinking of ending it all because his lover has just died. The tune enjoyed moderate success but received little attention until 1936. Early that year Budapest police found a suicide note containing lyrics from the song near the body of shoemaker Joseph Keller. An investigation by the authorities discovered that the ballad had inspired a total of eighteen suicides. Specifically, two persons had died by suicide after hearing it played by a Gypsy band, a few killed themselves with the sheet music in their hands, and others died by suicide while listening to recordings of the Hungarian version of "Gloomy Sunday." Budapest authorities banned the song. After *The New York Times* ran the headline "Hundreds of Hungarians kill themselves under the influence of a song," it became known as the "Hungarian Suicide Song." Songwriter Seress tried to tame the song's impact by adding a third stanza, one that was dreamy and more positive, but it didn't work. The song continued to trigger suicides.

American producers, sensing a hot property, quickly became interested in the piece. They commissioned Sam M. Lewis (of "Five Foot Two, Eyes of Blue," "I'm Sitting on Top of the World," and "Absence Makes the Heart Grow Fonder" fame) to translate all three stanzas of the lyrics. Lewis is therefore credited as the lyricist in the English version of the song. By March of 1936, three records, by Henry King, Hal Kemp, and Paul Whiteman, were being promoted as "Gloomy Sunday, the Famous Hungarian Suicide Song." It would be the last hit and the last song that Sam M. Lewis would "write," although he would not die until years later, on November 22, 1959.

In the 1940s, "Gloomy Sunday" was recorded by the famous singers of the time: Billie Holiday, Paul Robeson, Artie Shaw, and Mel Torme. But the song didn't have the impact in America that it did in Hungary, according to standard reference works. Experts such as suicidologist Edwin S. Shneidman noted that it caused no suicides in the United States, even though its airplay was supposedly unrestricted. But according to authors Hal Morgan and Kerry Tucker in *Rumor!* and snopes.com's *Urban Legend Reference Page,* some experts (unnamed) attribute cases of suicide (up to "200 worldwide") in both the United States and Britain to the English-language version of "Gloomy Sunday," with a special note that many were "young jazz fans" who became depressed after hearing Billie Holiday's 1941 version of the song.

One famous suicide will always be very directly connected to "Gloomy Sunday." While the song did bring wealth to its Hungarian composer, happiness eluded him. At the age of 69, Rezsô Seress leapt from the eighth floor of his Budapest apartment building on a cold Sunday during the winter of 1968. His death will forever be linked to the song he wrote.

The song has received new notice in recent years. Sarah McLachlan recorded "Gloomy Sunday" in her album, *Rarities, B-Sides & Other Stuff* in 1996. In 1999, *Music and Vision Magazine* called "Gloomy Sunday" "the saddest song ever written." Then in 2001, in German, and in 2003, in English, director Rolf Schübel's film *Gloomy Sunday* began screening in art houses. But his "Gloomy Sunday" became the butt of unfortunate jokes. Film critic Roger Ebert wrote on June 20, 2003, that "if it is true that the title song drove hundreds to commit suicide, some of them may have merely been very tired of hearing it."

Ozzy Osbourne and "Suicide Solutions"

Suicide themes continued to be portrayed in popular music. Simon and Garfunkel's 1965 songs "Richard Cory" and "A Most Peculiar Man" are similar in terms of their despair and loneliness as a source of suicide. Elton John's 1972 "I Think I'm Gonna Kill Myself" speaks frankly to the notion of a teenager's desire to die by suicide, get some publicity, and see who cares afterward. In the 1976 Blue Öyster Cult song "Don't Fear the Reaper," about a proposed suicide pact, suicide is seen in a positive light. Several groups have recorded songs about suicide. These include the Doors' "Yes, the River Knows," Gravediggaz's "1-800-Suicide," Nine Inch Nails' "Something I Can Never Have," Suicidal Tendencies' "How Will I Laugh Tomorrow," "Feel Like Shit . . . Deja-Vu," and "Suicide's an Alternative," Life of Agony's "River Runs Red," the Cure's "Burn," Suicidal Failure's "When I Can't Even Smile Today," Filter's "Hey Man, Nice Shot," Suede's "Stay Together," and Pink Floyd's "The Postwar Dream," "The Final Cut," and "Comfortably Numb."

During the early 1980s, one song that became connected to the whole issue of imitation and suggestion by way of music was Ozzy Osbourne's "Suicide Solution." Ozzy, famous at the start of the twenty-first century as the star of MTV's *The Osbournes* reality program, was the former leader of the heavy metal group Black Sabbath who is remembered for such outlandish stunts as biting off the head of a bat onstage. In 1986 he was sued for causing the suicide of a teenager.

On the evening of October 27, 1984, 19-year-old Ozzy Osbourne fan John McCollum of Indio, California, went to his bedroom. While listening to Ozzy's music, he killed himself with his father's handgun. Allegedly he spent five hours listening to "Suicide Solution." The song contains the line "Suicide is the only way out." McCollum's mother claimed that the police photo of her son's death showed the headphones were still on her son's ears when he died.

McCollum's father filed suit against Ozzy Osbourne and CBS Records early in 1986 in Los Angeles Superior Court, charging in court records that the singer's "violent, morbid and inflammatory music . . . encouraged John McCollum to take his own life."

Tom Anderson, the McCollums' attorney, told the UPI's Catherine Gewertz: "They knew this record was going to encourage or promote suicide. I think we have in this case opposing forces: Satan and God."

Osbourne claimed he was misunderstood and that the song was really antisuicide, antidrug, and antialcohol. He picked a good lawyer to represent his case, Howard Weitzman, who represented John DeLorean, best known as the creator of the gullwinged sports car bearing his name, against the government case that charged DeLorean with drug trafficking and money laundering in an FBI sting. Weitzman told UPI that the lawsuit against Osbourne was "a slanderous assault on artistic freedom. On this premise, one might equally make a connection between teenage suicide and *Romeo and Juliet*. The logical extension of this type of suit is censorship."

On August 7, 1986, Superior Court Judge John Cole dismissed the suit against Osbourne. The judge said that although the music "may be totally objectionable and repulsive" to many, the McCollums' attorney had failed to show why Ozzy Osbourne's songs should be exempt from First Amendment protection. Judge Cole told the court, in an oft-quoted one-liner, that "trash can be given First Amendment protection, too."

Judas Priest Fans "Try Suicide"

Soon after the Osbourne case was dismissed, another music-suicide suit was filed. In December 1986 the British rock group

Judas Priest and CBS Records, Inc., were ordered to stand trial in a civil lawsuit that charged them with inducing two Reno, Nevada, teens to shoot themselves.

James Vance and Raymond Belknap allegedly formed a suicide pact and shot themselves with a shotgun after spending six hours listening to an album by the band. On December 23, 1985, Belknap and Vance drank beer, smoked marijuana and then listened to the album for six hours. Afterward they took a shotgun to a nearby school playground where Belknap shot and killed himself. Vance then blew away his jaw, mouth, and nose but lived for more than three years before dying of effects from the shooting.

Kenneth McKenna, Belknap's mother's attorney, said to the AP that "the suggestive lyrics combined with the continuous beat and rhythmic, nonchanging intonations of the music combined to induce, encourage, aid, abet, and otherwise mesmerize the plaintiff into believing the answer to life was death." Attorney Vivian Lynch, who represented Vance's family, told reporter Cy Ryan of UPI that the album the boys listened to, *Stained Class,* contained the hidden phrases "Try suicide," "Let's be dead," and "Do it, do it."

Meanwhile, lawyers for CBS Records and Judas Priest argued that the band was protected by constitutional guarantees of freedom of expression and insisted that there was no claim in the suit for which the band could be held liable for damages.

When the case finally went to trial in 1989, the judge ruled that the plaintiffs had failed to prove that Judas Priest had intentionally placed subliminal messages on the album or that the messages had indeed been the cause of the suicide and attempted suicide. The judge did rule, however, that while the First Amendment protects song lyrics, subliminal messages are not protected.

Celebrity Suicides and Copycatting

Youthful music fans will follow the lead of their idols not only in terms of hairstyle and everyday behavior but also, sometimes, in suicide. Rock stars' sudden and violent deaths sometimes are connected to later self-inflicted deaths. Herbert Hendin, in *Suicide in America,* wrote: "After John Lennon was murdered, several suicides linked their deaths to his." Today musicians' suicides and violent deaths have become major news because of the star's status. Media coverage of these events has a great impact on youth. In the past it was more a matter of "out of sight, out of mind." You can't imitate what you don't know about.

According to Dave Marsh and Kevin Stein, authors of *The Book of Rock Lists,* one of the first noteworthy rock musician suicides was that of Johnny Ace, who died on Christmas Eve 1954 while playing Russian roulette backstage at the Houston City Auditorium. Other modern musician suicides have included Paul Williams of the Temptations in 1973, Pete Ham of Badfinger in 1975, folksinger Phil Ochs in 1976, Donny Hathaway in 1979, and Ian Curtis of Joy Division in 1980. Marsh and Stein also noted the complex suicides of two other famous rockers. Rory Storm, onetime Mersey beat bandleader, was found dead in his home in 1974 with his head in the oven, the result of a suicide pact with his mother, whose body was found nearby. (Ringo Starr was playing with Storm and his group the Hurricanes when Starr joined the Beatles.) Terry Kath of the group Chicago died at the Los Angeles home of a friend in 1978 when the gun he was playing with, à la Russian roulette, went off as it was pointed at his head. This occurred in full view of his wife and one of the band's sound crew.

These suicides were not widely noted by the media and appear to have had little impact.

But the links to some suicide copycats are unmistakable.

Sid and Nancy

The prototypical hero of teen suicides is Sid Vicious. Sid, as a member of the Sex Pistols, foreshadowed much of the New Wave and punk rock movement now so well established in America and Europe. Sid Vicious and his girlfriend Nancy Spungen were sad and lonely characters. Late in the 1970s their pathetic punk love affair turned very dark, and, so the story goes, they made a murder-suicide pact. In October 1978, Sid stabbed Nancy, killing her. But he did not die by suicide himself until February 3, 1979. This twisted love story is still the source of much fascination and groupie interest, especially in New York City. In 1986 the play *Vicious,* the book *And I Don't Want to Live This Life,* and the movie *Sid and Nancy* were very popular with teen punk-rock followers. How much Sid Vicious's suicide influenced the suicides of young people in the metropolitan New York area may never be known, for the impact may be hidden in covert behaviors, such as drug abuse, that were and are so much a part of Sid's old Twenty-third Street underground scene.

Oddly, one of the actresses who almost played Nancy in the 1986 movie *Sid and Nancy* is Courtney Love, who later was to become Kurt Cobain's wife. During the early 1980s Love had met Alex Cox, who would direct *Sid and Nancy* and who received much praise for his earlier offbeat movie *Repo Man.* Cox invited her to try out for the part of Nancy opposite Gary Oldman's Sid. She didn't get that part but did land the role as Nancy's best friend in the movie. Meanwhile, according to the book *Who Killed Kurt Cobain?* (1998), rumors circulated that Cox and Love were lovers. The speculation appeared to be confirmed when Love turned up in the lead role of Cox's next film, *Straight to Hell,* a critical failure. Nevertheless, the movie opened the doors to Love's high-fashion groupie lifestyle among various rock stars (e.g., Elvis Costello and Joe Strummer) that lead to her days with Kurt Cobain (see the next chapter).

The Singing Idol Suicide Wave

On April 8, 1986, at noon, Japanese teen singing idol Yukiko Okada, 18, climbed to the top of the seven-story building that housed her recording studio and jumped to her death. According to William Weatherall in the *Far Eastern Economic Review,* Yukiko was despondent over an unhappy love affair with an actor who was "old enough to be her father." She had been hospitalized in the days before her leap. She had made previous suicidal attempts, once by slashing her wrists and another by filling her apartment with gas. But Yukiko Okada had not always been so sad. In 1983 she had won a national talent contest, which was followed in 1985 by an award as Japan's top new singer. She was extremely popular and had a large following.

This popularity became even more evident soon after Okada's death. The place that Okada's body hit, a busy downtown Tokyo street corner, became an impromptu shrine where many laid wreaths. Some fans could be seen standing at the corner, gazing upward at the building from which she jumped. The media broadcast several hours of reports on the Okada suicide, interviewing her family, her friends, even the boyfriend who jilted her. But no one knew how influenced her fans were by her suicide until they began killing themselves by the dozens.

The cluster began two days after Okada's suicide when two sisters, aged 12 and 18, jumped from the roof of their apartment house. In the days that followed, at least one young person a day killed him- or herself in apparent imitation of the Okada suicide. For example, on April 16, 16-year-old Korean-Japanese Pak Migi told her sister, "I want to become like Yukiko Okada," before plunging from the thirteenth floor of her building.

The newspapers and television stations spent an enormous amount of time analyzing Okada's and her followers' suicides. One 17-year-old high school student, Izumi Furukawa, noted, "I think [Yukiko Okada's] death triggered this. My friends, we all talked about it after that and said how we've felt like doing it too." The media attention was intense.

The rate of suicides increased dramatically. During the weekend of April 19–20, five young people under eighteen killed themselves, including one girl who was just 9 years old. The 9-year-old jumped from the roof of a department store west of Tokyo after having been scolded by her mother. The girl had told friends she was very affected by the Okada suicide. The same weekend three others in their twenties did the same thing. On Monday, April 21 six people under 20 killed themselves. On Tuesday, April 22, the total for the day was five; one was a 14-year-old boy who set himself afire. The next day a 15-year-old Fukuoka City boy hung himself at a construction site.

Thirty-three young people took their lives in the seventeen days following Okada's suicide. Number thirty-three, on April 24, was 12-year-old Tomoko Humaska. She jumped from the thirteenth floor of her suburban high-rise apartment building. She left a note to her parents saying, "I'm sorry it had to end this way." Family members said that the girl had repeatedly re-played and watched a video of a television program about Okada's suicide.

One of the last suicides in this cluster occurred on May 2, when 21-year-old Masanno Majima jumped from the same roof as Okada and landed where her makeshift shrine had been. Ma-jima had photographs of Okada in his pocket and had been seen loitering in front of the building for several days before his jump. Twenty-two of the thirty-four deaths were like Okada's: suicides by jumping from buildings. The others were by hang-ing, fire, or asphyxiation.

Midway through the wave of deaths, the article by William Weatherall in *Far Eastern Economic Review* quoted child psy-chologist Tsutomu Komazaki as saying, "This is definitely a trend. These kids see someone doing it, and they get the same idea. We're seeing a snowball effect here." By mid-April 1985, a total of 177 Japanese under 20 years of age had killed themselves. But by mid-1986, 213 youths had died by suicide, thirty-six more than for the same period the previous year.

Faced with a similar situation, Americans might have been unwilling to link one death to another, but there seemed little doubt in the minds of the Japanese that the wave of suicides were directly related to the young singer's death. As the National Police Agency spokesperson declared, "Since she died, we have indeed seen a lot more kids jumping off buildings or killing themselves by other means."

There is a long history of briefly noting the possible copycat effect in music and rushing away from it. The influence of music and the media are strong on the minds and actions of young people, and, despite denials to the contrary, the copycat effect played itself out in a massive fashion after the death of yet another musician, Kurt Cobain.

CHAPTER THIRTEEN

Cobain Copycats

K urt Donald Cobain was born on February 20, 1967, to a cocktail waitress and her mechanic husband in the small Washington town of Hoquiam. Cobain grew up in the poor logging town of Aberdeen. By the 1990s he was known as the creator and leader of Nirvana, the award-winning grunge rock band that defined the music of the times. Along the way he met groupie and later musician and actress Courtney Love of the group Hole. They married on February 24, 1992, in Waikiki, Hawaii, reportedly while wasted on heroin, according to Cobain friend Dylan Carlson, as reported in Ian Halperin and Max Wallace's *Who Killed Kurt Cobain?*

Cobain "Burns Out" with a Bang

Then, after years of depression, suicide attempts, and substance abuse, Cobain locked himself in his tiny dirty storage greenhouse behind 171 Lake Washington Boulevard, his Seattle mansion, and finalized his dance with death. The medical examiner believes Cobain killed himself on April 5, 1994. But April 8,

1994—three days later—has always been "celebrated" as Cobain's "death day," as it was the day when Cobain's body was found by an electrician visiting the house to install a security system. Gary Smith, an employee of Veca Electric, went around the back of the house when no one answered the front door and peered through various windows. This was about 8:56 A.M. Pacific Time. Smith was unclear what he saw when he first looked in the greenhouse window. He thought the body he saw was a mannequin until he observed what looked like blood oozing from the right ear and a shotgun on the chest. Smith knew whose house he was at and put two and two together.

Gary Smith first called in his report to the dispatcher at Veca Electric. At 9:40 A.M., Marty Reimer, the host of the morning show on KXRX-FM, an alternative rock station, received a call from the dispatcher informing him that Cobain was dead. The media had the news first. The dispatcher then called the police.

At 10:15 A.M., the Seattle police arrived and found the greenhouse locked. Finally a firefighter smashed in a window, allowing the police in, and they discovered the rock star dead on the floor, a Remington twenty-gauge still pointed at his chin. Nearby they found a red-inked suicide note addressed to Love and Cobain and Love's then 19-month-old daughter, Frances Bean. It ended with the words *I love you, I love you.*

By eleven A.M. the media had surrounded the house, and the three King County coroners quickly told the press that Kurt Cobain had died of a self-inflicted gunshot wound. News of the Cobain suicide instantly spread around the world via such outlets as CNN and MTV News. Cobain was just 27 and joined an eerie exclusive club of other rock stars (Jimi Hendrix, Janis Joplin, Jim Morrison) who had died when they were just 27 years old.

Cobain had an enormous fan base. Two days after Kurt Cobain's body was found, approximately five thousand people gathered in the little park near Seattle's Space Needle for a memorial candlelight vigil. It would turn into a mild disturbance as distraught fans yelled profane chants, burned their flannel shirts (a symbol of the grunge movement), and fought with police. Although Courtney Love promised to appear, she only sent a tape in which she read from Cobain's suicide note as she interjected curses to him. For example, Cobain had used a line from the song "My My, Hey Hey" (noted by some as "Hey Hey, My My") by rockers Neil Young and Jeff Blackburn to end his suicide note: "It's better to burn out than to fade away." Love introduced the line by saying: "And *don't* remember this, 'cause it's a fuckin' lie!" After she read the note, she decided to frame it with her editorial: "God, you asshole!" Courtney's anger was apparent throughout her curses on the tape. The crowd was stirred up.

Only One Cobain Copycat?

Attending the Seattle gathering on April 10, 1994, were several very upset followers of Kurt Cobain. According to the literature on the Cobain suicide, only one person in that crowd would kill himself in imitation of Kurt Cobain. Within hours of the candlelight vigil, 28-year-old Daniel Kasper returned to his Maple Valley, Washington, residence and used a gun to end his life. Authors Halperin and Wallace noted that neighbors said Kasper was despondent over the death of Cobain.

The standard suicide prevention books and journal articles believe that among all the supposed copycats that have followed a well-publicized celebrity suicide, what followed the 1994 suicide of grunge band leader Kurt Cobain is a story of successful deterrence. The myth of "no Cobain copycats" goes deep in American culture and is nicely summarized by routine governmental stamps of approval of this piece of folklore.

In 1999, Surgeon General David Satcher called for greater suicide awareness and intervention in the United States, and a national strategy to improve suicide prevention was launched in 2001. The federal publication *U.S. Medicine* detailed the recommendations, noting studies conducted during the last thirty years showed that there is an increase in suicide by readers or viewers of media programs when the number of stories about individual suicides increases. This government periodical then went on to note the one existing exception to this rule: *U.S. Medicine* published that Madelyn Gould, professor of psychiatry and public health at Columbia University, had noted that after the celebrity suicide of Kurt Cobain "there was no increase in suicide because of a combination of sensible reporting and a strong anti-suicide message from his wife, Courtney Love."

In November 1996 the journal *Suicide and Life-Threatening Behavior* began the drumbeat that still continues today. "We were truly shocked by what didn't happen," wrote David A. Jobes in an article on the impact of Cobain's suicide on impressionable young Nirvana fans after researchers found only a small number of copycat suicides modeled on Cobain's. Jobes, a Catholic University psychology professor in Washington, D.C., and the study's chief author, was at a conference of suicide prevention specialists when Cobain's body was discovered at the Nirvana singer's home on April 8, 1994.

"We just looked at each other and said, 'This is going to be a disaster.' We were convinced," Jobes told AP reporter Tim Klass.

As Jobe informed the Senate Subcommittee on Children and Families' Hearing on Teen and Young Adult Suicide on September 7, 2001: "Along with colleagues at the Centers for Disease Control, I was part of an effort to fax media guidelines and other suicide prevention information to the Seattle Mayor's office and to other community leaders in King County, Washington. Bottom line, the coordinated leadership of the Seattle/King County community orchestrated a thoughtful and measured response to this crisis and along with a great deal of responsible journalism the copycat suicide crisis that we all anticipated never actually happened. In research that we conducted in King County there was no discernible increase in completed suicides after Cobain's death. However, crisis calls to Seattle's suicide hotline reached record levels following the death. From a scientific standpoint we cannot interpret a direct causal relationship between the community-based interventions that were used in Seattle and the absence of an outbreak of suicides in this community. But the promise of the Seattle example is the intuitive virtue of a community-based suicide prevention response that coordinates roles played by federal agencies, state and local governments, suicide prevention experts, journalists, and community-based crisis center services."

In the four weeks following Cobain's death, eighteen suicides were recorded in Seattle and the rest of King County, including the grunge megastar and the obvious and one acknowledged copycat, Daniel Kasper. Or so we were led to believe.

David P. Phillips, a leading expert on suicide, cautioned that more research should have been done to determine whether Jobes's finding held on a nationwide basis. Phillips believed that the local sample was too small to yield meaningful results. "I would say [Jobes's study is] inconclusive, and it will remain inconclusive until the same study can be done on a national or at least a larger scale," Phillips told reporter Klass in 1996. Jobes countered that he lacked the resources for a nationwide study but suggested that if any place had experienced a sizable ripple effect it would have been Seattle, where grunge music originated and Nirvana had its strongest following.

As recently as 2003, when professor of sociology Steven Stack won the famed Dublin Award for suicide prevention for his paper, "Suicide: Media Effects, a Meta Analysis," the study contained only Jobes's conclusion that no copycats followed publicity from Cobain's suicide. But in a private correspondence with me on this subject, Stack wrote that "the impact of Cobain's suicide has never been fully tested, as far as I know, nationwide in any rigorous statistical sense."

What I have found, instead, in my years of researching the issue of the Cobain copycats is that the Kurt Cobain suicide did have an impact on suicides, but these were mostly *outside* the Seattle area. In Australia, Canada, and France, suicides related to Cobain's death are detailed in the popular literature; there are perhaps seventy copycat suicides directly linked to Cobain, and the list continues to grow.

The suicide prevention community seems unaware of this. The Cobain events are seen as a "success story" in which "negative reactions" and "faxed flyers" are promoted as the "reason" for the low Seattle suicide copycats. Perhaps the local interventions did work. But that doesn't seem to be the whole story. Looked at on a worldwide basis, the Cobain celebrity suicide did what other celebrity suicides have done before: created copycats.

A Worldwide Epidemic

The copycats occurred not long after Cobain's body was found on April 8, 1994. The only officially acknowledged copycat, Daniel Kasper, was *not* alone. Christopher Sandford's *Kurt Cobain* notes that in April, not only did Brian Lever, 22, from Melbourne, Australia, hang himself, after leaving behind a poem about Cobain, but an unnamed teen in southern Turkey also killed himself in imitation of Cobain.

On June 15, 1994, Kristen Pfaff, the bass player for Courtney Love's band Hole, shut herself in her bathroom and died of an alleged drug overdose. She was found in her bathtub, in a death scene eerily similar to that of rock star Jim Morrison, who was found dead in his Paris bathtub. Kristen was supposed to be returning to Minneapolis the morning of June 16. Some feel her death was a "hidden suicide." She was 27, the same age as Cobain and Morrison when they died.

Edmonton Journal reporter David Staples has linked the often-discussed suicide of Bobby Steele, 18, of Edmonton, Alberta, in July 1994 to Cobain. Steele became obsessed with Cobain when he first heard Nirvana's *Nevermind* album in 1992. He was often online, constantly "chatting" with others about the band's leader, and used the passwords *Cobain* and *NirvanaNirvana*. Steele admired Cobain because he supported "nerds," battered women, and gays. Steele reportedly was discovering he was gay. Upset by Cobain's suicide, Steele wrote many suicide notes and wills during the spring and early summer of 1994, relating his state of mind to Cobain's death. Writing a note the night he killed himself, Steele said, "It's been the most painful 84 days of my life." Kurt Cobain's body had been found eighty-four days earlier. Taking Polaroid pictures that he placed around his room, reclining on his bed with the Nirvana's *In Utero* CD above his head, and positioning his shotgun exactly as Cobain had, Steele killed himself on July 3. The Alberta teen had arranged his suicide so that when he was found, anyone would notice that the setting mirrored the famous photograph of Cobain's Seattle death scene. The Nirvana song "Endless Nameless" was playing on his stereo. Bobby's grieving father, Major Robert Steele, reportedly sought out at-risk youth to counsel and talked six other Cobain-obsessed youth out of suicide attempts in Edmonton by the end of 1994 alone.

Some suicides that occurred during this time are not described in as much detail as Steele's. For example, according to a survey article on the phenomena appearing in France's *Le Monde* three years later, two American teenage fans of Cobain, aged 14 and 15, died in July 1994 by shooting themselves with a sawed-off shotgun in a similar manner to Cobain.

In October 1994, Steve Dallaire of Labrador City, Newfoundland, and two young men, Stephane Langlois and Michael Cote of Fermont, Quebec, killed themselves in dramatic fashion. (Labrador City is near the Quebec border; hence this case has become known as "the three teenagers from Quebec.") The three youth took a cross-continental trip that ended in Langley, British Columbia, where they died by suicide in their car by carbon monoxide poisoning. They left a journal describing their actions and a pair of used denim jeans covered in handwritten ink with Cobain's lyrics. A cassette tape by Nirvana was found in the car's cassette deck. The Royal Canadian Mounted Police stated that the case of the death of these three teenagers was Cobain-related. A later suicide of one of their friends is also thought to be Cobain-related. The incident attracted major Canadian and international news coverage, including a feature cover story in *MacLean's Magazine* and a full one-hour television documentary by CBC-TV's award-winning investigative journalism program *The Fifth Estate*. The suicides startled many Canadians who had previously not thought about the wide-ranging influence of Cobain's death.

Soon after the "three Quebec teens" story broke, the Quebec provincial police reported that an unnamed 17-year-old Quebec youth, a male, leaped from the Jacques Cartier Bridge on October 15, 1994, while listening to a Walkman containing a Nirvana cassette tape.

In November 1994, two unnamed youths both died at Niagara Falls, Ontario, in what has been labeled as Cobain-related suicides. The first death was that of a 17-year-old who hung himself in his basement bedroom. The other death was the young man's 19-year-old friend, who hung himself from a tree in the park the day following his friend's funeral.

Meanwhile, other violence was being connected to Cobain. In November 1994, British teen Jamie Petrolini, 19, murdered a London taxi driver. Petrolini tried to explain to the rock music weekly *Melody Maker* why he did it: "I know how Kurt Cobain felt . . . Please understand . . . Please help. I don't want to end up like Kurt."

Also in November 1994, a 16-year-old girl killed herself with a shotgun in Dublin, Ireland. She left behind a suicide note that said she had "done it for Kurt."

In December 1994 a Vancouver woman named "Colleen" died by suicide apparently influenced by the Cobain-related suicides of the "three teenagers from Quebec."

The year 1994 ended with one of those all-too-frequent "suicide by accident" incidents. Twenty-year-old student Gaston Lyle Senac of Tracy, California, was fooling around with his friends, acting out the Cobain suicide with them during the first week of December. He took a twelve-gauge shotgun, propped it on the floor, and then knelt over it with his mouth over the barrel. He said to his friends: "Look, I'm just like Kurt Cobain." At that instant the gun went off, killing Senac immediately.

Quebec continued to be a focus of Cobain copycats in 1995. In Île d'Orléans, near Quebec City, Simon Nolin, 11, hung himself in the basement of his family home. At Simon's feet his father found a note that read "I'm killing myself for Kurt." On April 10, 1995, Lyndon Gagnon, a "devotee of the rock group Nirvana," died by suicide, followed by his girlfriend, Linda Goldsmith, on April 15. Both were 13 years old.

The international extent of the Cobain copycat suicides appears to have been completely overlooked by United States suicidologists. Besides Canadians, many young people in other countries from Australia to Turkey were affected. In May 1995 a 16-year-old boy in Lebanon shot himself in the head. On the walls of his bedroom, covered with posters of Kurt Cobain, he had scrawled slogans encouraging suicide. Eight other Lebanese youth had done the same. Shortly afterward the Lebanese authorities stopped a concert from the British hard rock band Iron Maiden, saying their music encouraged suicide, according to *Le Monde*.

In January 1996, Rich Truman, 18, from Leduc, Alberta, hung himself in an alleged Cobain-related suicide, and soon after, a 16-year-old from the same area killed himself with a gun.

In October 1996 a 17-year-old male leapt from the eighth floor of a building in Italy. He left letters to his family in which he referred to Kurt Cobain and Cobain's suicide note.

Three years to the date after Cobain's body was found in 1994, another young follower took his own life. Angela Workman, the suicide victim's mother from Eureka, California, wrote the following statement, which has been distributed throughout cyberspace in an effort to prevent further Cobain copycats:

> My 15 year old son, Michael, took his own life with a single gunshot to the head on April 8, 1997. He was a wonderful person, straight A student, very smart, creative and now, we realize, very lonely and sad. He left a note that said he just didn't care anymore and this was the only way out for him. What I want to comment on is that he also was a fan of Kurt Cobain, from the band, Nirvana and Kurt also killed himself by gunshot on April 8th. This was a copycat suicide that in some ways I feel responsible for because I knew how much he liked the music and he identified with Kurt. I never thought that he would have followed his path; we even discussed what a loser he was to commit suicide. My son called me before he made his choice and he told me he loved me, so in some ways I also feel he had made up his mind regardless. I think about him constantly and I feel empty and without purpose. I keep busy but it's just going through the motions. In time I hope joy will return. I just wish I could hold him again. I love you, Michael! Mom.

On May 14, 1997, the deaths of two suicide victims rocked France. French schoolgirls Valentine, 12, and Aurelie, 13, from the town of Somain, near Lille, in northern France, killed themselves by shooting themselves in the head with a .22-caliber rifle. They were self-described Nirvana fanatics who professed their love for Kurt Cobain. "The girls had written notes which left no doubt about their intentions. School friends tried to talk them out of it without success," public prosecutor Jean-Marie Descamps told reporter Marcus Errico. "There seems to have been a sort of adoration, of veneration for members of Nirvana, and especially of the singer who committed suicide," he added.

In a bizarre extension of the influence of Cobain's suicide, Toby Andrew Amirault, webmaster of the controversial website *The Murder of Kurt Cobain,* apparently killed himself on March 13, 2001. Amirault, 35, of Woburn, Massachusetts, fought off at least three people trying to stop him from jumping out a Columbia, South Carolina, hospital window. He landed on a roof over the hospital's third floor. He had been at the hospital recovering from a head injury and a broken leg suffered in a previous suicide attempt in which he jumped in front of a moving car in Clarendon County.

On April 10, 2001, a 14-year-old girl killed herself "for Kurt" in Italy. That the date was so close to the Cobain "death date" has not been lost on observers. When the Internet Nirvana Fan Club reported this, the webmaster commented: "This is the 68th copycat suicide I have heard about. The news was only printed in Italy."

Pipe Bombers Too?

The impact of Kurt Cobain's suicide has continued in some unexpected ways. In May 2002, University of Wisconsin–Stout student Luke John Helder, 21, crossed the country, leaving pipe bombs in mailboxes. In a time of heightened terrorism awareness, Helder's acts seemed strange and weird. Later he came to be known as the "Smiley Face Pipe Bomber," because he said he was trying to make a smiley face on the map of the United States. Helder, of Pine Island, Minnesota, who had named his punk rock band Apathy, was obsessed with Kurt Cobain and, at the time of his arrest in Lovelock, Nevada, was wearing a black Kurt Cobain shirt. Charles R. Cross's book about Cobain, *Heavier Than Heaven*, was found among Helder's possessions, according to the FBI. Says Cross: "Kurt Cobain was apathetic— I'm sure he may have inspired the name of Helder's band—but there aren't any Nirvana songs that say, 'Blow up mailboxes,' or that urge action of any kind."

"With his neck-length blond-reddish hair and raw, understated-then-overinflated voice, Luke Helder was a dead ringer for Kurt Cobain," wrote Jonathan Linder (*Flak* magazine, 2002). While also influenced by the Bible to New Age (Ben Radford, *Skeptical Inquirer,* 2002), the Cobain obsession was real. Linder editorialized: "When the news media paint a gaudy, sensationalized portrait of a tragic event, attention seekers are always willing to keep the story going. Copycats may follow. If they do, will his or her own life merge readily into the now-established storyline?"

Nevertheless, the copycats of the copycat continued. After Helder's arrest, in May and June 2002 other mailboxes exploded in Tuttle, Oklahoma; Philadelphia, Pennsylvania; Spokane, Washington; Idaho Falls, Idaho; Olathe, Kansas; and Gray and Minot, Maine. As Helder awaited trial in an Iowa prison, a young man from Waseca, Minnesota, was arrested in November 2002 for having eleven pipe bombs in his University of Wisconsin–Stout dorm room, and in March 2003 another pipe bomb went off in nearby River Falls, Wisconsin.

The United States government may downplay the aftermath of Kurt Cobain's suicide and actually use it as a model of how to prevent suicides. But the reality is that a widespread copycat legacy is involved. The death of strong personalities, portrayed in the media as celebrity suicides and murders, influence the future—whether the person being discussed is a rock star or a sports figure or an actor.

CHAPTER FOURTEEN

Suicide Squeeze

opycats haunt the national pastime too.

It was a typical fall Thursday night at the ball game in Chicago. The date was September 19, 2002, and the crowd was excited to see the White Sox take on the out-of-towners, the Kansas City Royals. But then something happened in the game that would turn into a repeating copycat cycle, bringing a fear of "terrorism" to the very fields of dreams.

Royals first base coach Tom Gamboa was calmly watching home plate. During the ninth inning of a game that had no bearing on the play-offs, Gamboa took a short trip into hell. He didn't know what hit him. Two men, a father and his juvenile son, both shirtless, were on top of Gamboa, punching away at him and slamming him to the ground. The 54-year-old coach told ESPN he felt like a "football team" had hit him. Soon Gamboa's teammates, as well as the umpires and the White Sox team, piled on to get the attackers off. Security then quickly moved in. Royals first baseman Mike Sweeney told ESPN: "If it wasn't for them, we'd probably still be beating on those guys."

Gamboa walked off the field to a standing ovation from the crowd at Comiskey Park, where the Royals beat the Chicago

White Sox 2–1. Gamboa escaped with only a few cuts and a bruised cheek (though a year later he suffered partial hearing damage in his right ear and had to be moved to the bullpen), but the attack was a shock to Major League Baseball. A folded pocketknife was found on the ground near the scene, and White Sox outfielder Aaron Rowand said he saw it slip out of one of the attacker's pockets.

Attacks against sports figures by fans are rare. The most notorious came when tennis star Monica Seles was stabbed in the back by an obsessed fan in 1993 during a match in Hamburg, Germany. In 1995, at Wrigley Field, a 27-year-old bond trader who ran out of the stands charged Cubs reliever Randy Myers. Myers saw the man coming, dropped his glove, and knocked him down with his forearm. In 1999 a 23-year-old fan attacked Houston right fielder Bill Spiers at Milwaukee. Spiers ended up with a welt under his left eye, a bloody nose, and whiplash.

"It's sad and disturbing, very disturbing," said general manager Kenny Williams, who apologized to Tom Gamboa and the Royals after the game in which Gamboa had been attacked. "Words don't express the sorrow when you look at a man and he's got blood on his face. All he was doing was coaching first base."

Then less than a year later came the copycat incident. During the night of April 15, 2003, fans ran onto the field during a White Sox game with the Royals in Chicago. According to the Associated Press, the first fan came out before the top of the seventh inning, while the second one ran onto the field at the start of the bottom half of the inning before he was nailed in center field by security. Another fan raced toward the infield minutes later, following a strike fired by left-handed reliever Kelly Wunsch as he was facing Raul Ibanez with the bases loaded, two outs, and the White Sox leading by one run.

Then, in the ninth inning, a fan attacked first base umpire Laz Diaz, who stood near where Gamboa had been attacked in the ninth inning of that September 2002 game, also between the Royals and White Sox. The field has been renamed U.S. Cellular Field, but the location was the same. Soon, Royals and White Sox players, security, and umpires were wrestling the attacker to the ground, in an eerie repeat of the previous year.

"When the guy ran on the field and came after the umpire, it did bring back memories of last year [with Gamboa]," White Sox first baseman Paul Konerko told ESPN shortly after the second attack in two years. "I don't know how you prevent it, unless you have someone every inch of the way."

The reality of copycat behavior of this kind has hit baseball hard. Security has been increased and improved since the 2002 season, with sixty to seventy police officers at the stadium in Chicago, for example. But it is a well-known fact that the security force will always be outnumbered, even on nights of low attendance.

White Sox veteran Frank Thomas mentioned that the actions could have had something to do with the full moon. Billy Koch, who blew the save in the ninth with four runs, joked, tongue in cheek, about how the last fan should have waited a few batters to charge him. But more seriously, White Sox manager Jerry Manuel and Royals manager Tony Pena expressed concern and even some fear over the growing number of incidents. "It's kind of a sad commentary for Chicago, at least our ballpark," Manuel told reporter Scott Merkin at MLB.com. "I don't believe it reflects who we are as Chicago people. It's unfortunate that it happened, and unfortunate that it happened in Chicago when Kansas City comes to town."

Pena also commented to reporter Merkin: "There's no question I was concerned. That's what I told the umpire, 'How can I know my players will be safe or not?'"

Now Playing at Cellular Field

As 2003's major league baseball season opened, the craze of fans jumping on the fields to attack players and umpires was compounded by a new "fad" of throwing cell phones at players. The initial incident that year happened in California on April 19 and was followed too quickly by another, in Chicago, Illinois, on April 27.

Mike Cassidy of the San Jose *Mercury News* wrote on April 27, 2003: "This wireless wigginess broke onto the scene eight days ago at Oakland's Network Associates Coliseum when some clown tossed his phone at Texas Ranger Carl Everett. The phone hit Everett in the head . . . The latest phone chucking came at Wrigley Field, where drunken Cubs fans have grown tired of tossing home run balls back onto the field. In the eighth inning Thursday, some imbecile winged a cell phone instead and hit San Diego Padre Sean Burroughs in the foot. And no, that is not what Burroughs gets for playing home games at a stadium named Qualcomm." Of course, cell phone serial numbers make identifying the throwers relatively easy.

The media couldn't decide whether to take this bout of lunacy seriously or not. Elliot Harris, a columnist for the *Chicago Sun-Times* wrote on April 28: "If they're going to start tossing cell phones at Wrigley Field, shouldn't they start tossing sticks of gum at U.S. Cellular Field? OK, probably not. Surprising that Cubs brass says it doesn't want to ban cell phones. Well, maybe not until Tribune Co. can install pay phones at every seat in the park." Joe Hawk of the *Las Vegas Review-Journal* is clear about how he feels, as he sees it as a "rash of idiocy at baseball parks" that includes "the brain-dead hurling batteries and cell phones from the stands, [and] the liver-damaged running onto the field to assault base coaches and umpires."

Sadly, the game that symbolizes tradition and history is also high imitative and prone to the copycat effect. After all, this is the game that took "the wave"—invented during football games in the mid-1980s at the University of Washington—and made it its own. Baseball has a way of internalizing the copycat effect in ways both playful and deadly serious.

A Gathering Storm

Baseball researchers have an incredible affection for both statistics and stories. In a similar fashion, within the research field of suicidology, suicidologists know the value of stats and case studies in research surveys; their ultimate objective, of course, is suicide prevention. The metaphor and lessons from baseball suicides may prove informative, I thought, when in 1987–88 I undertook a study of baseball player suicides, which led to a significant statistical prediction. At the time I was a project director and principal investigator of a three-year, quarter-million-dollar federal project on suicides at the University of Southern Maine. And having had a passionate interest in baseball all my life, I wondered if the databases that existed for ballplayers could provide any clues, in terms of stories or statistics, that might inform the trends and patterns in baseball players' suicides and suicide clustering.

With the assistance of my fellow members of the Society for American Baseball Research (SABR), especially Bill Deane at the Baseball Hall of Fame in Cooperstown, New York, and SABR members Richard Topp and Frank Russo, I was able to determine the suicide rate among baseball players as of 1988.

We first identified a total of 13,160 players and 95 nonplaying managers active in the major leagues between 1871 and 1988. Of these, 6,374 were deceased, and for 578 of these deceased the cause of death was listed as unknown. The 68 known baseball suicides, as of 1988, yielded a suicide percentage (a little over 1 percent) that was lower than the percentage of deaths in males due to suicide (1.9 percent for deaths in the United States in the year 1980). Of course, the baseball individuals who killed themselves stretched over many age groups. Furthermore, by the time an individual gets to the major leagues, they have largely been prescreened for suicidal and psychiatric behavior by grueling schedules, bus rides, dingy hotels, and overall high stress levels experienced in the minor leagues or in their college baseball days. The number of suicides among major league alumni was thus rather surprising.

I found that the method of suicide in the major leagues from 1871 to 1988 followed the normal patterns among the general population: 50 percent used guns; 22 percent poisons/overdoses; 8 percent unknown methods; 5 percent jumping; 3 percent hanging; and 2 percent drowning. Their ages ranged between 26 and 83, with a little more than half of the players being in their late twenties through their forties. Active baseball players were most likely to die by suicide during the off-season; if the individual was a recent player, within three years of an active involvement in the majors; or after age 65, after a "retirement" from a postbaseball career. For some former players the end of March to the April opening days seemed to be a specific temporal black hole.

Analyzing the players by position, I found 45.3 percent of the players dying by suicides were pitchers or had done some pitching. Even though the number of pitchers who are left-handed outnumbered the percentage found in the general population by a factor of three, not one baseball player who died by suicide who was a pitcher between 1900 and the time of my initial survey in 1988 was left-handed. All the pitcher suicides were right-handed.

The Winter of Their Discontent

The reality and metaphor of the "winter" has a special meaning in the micro-studies of ballplayers' suicides. Players rarely die by suicide during the regular baseball season. Baseball players either kill themselves off-season if they are active players, or soon after their playing years—during the actual winter—or in the "winter" of their years.

Searching through the archives, only one active player, Willard Hershberger, a Cincinnati Reds catcher, completed his suicide during the actual season in which he was an active player. He used a razor in a scenario that in many ways mirrored his father's suicide. On September 3, 1940, in a Boston hotel, Hershberger spread towels on the floor so others would not have to clean up a bloody mess as he had to do after his father killed himself. Hershberger, 30 years old, held himself responsible for a bad call on a pitch he felt lost an important game near the end of the season.

Psychologist David Lester and SABR member Richard Topp published a baseball player suicide paper in 1988 discussing how they found that seven players "killed themselves within one year of the last season they played, three within two years of that date, and six within three years." Besides Hershberger, they mentioned four suicides that were directly baseball-related: "Marty Bergen had broken [his] hip in a close play at home plate which ended his career, Tony Brottem was depressed after his release from a minor league club, Pea Ridge Day was depressed after an operation failed to restore his pitching arm, and Benny Frey had just retired rather than face being sent to the minor leagues." (Day's mother had also died by suicide.)

These were all dramatic early baseball era suicides. Marty Bergen, 28, a Red Sox catcher up through the 1899 season, took an ax to his two children and his wife on the morning of January 19, 1900, then cut his own throat with a razor. Tony Brottem, 37, saw the end of the road and used a gun on August 5, 1929. Pea Ridge Day, 34, slit his throat with a hunting knife on May 21, 1934. Benny Frey, 31, died on November 1, 1937, when he ran a hose from his car's exhaust to the vehicle's interior.

Examples of young baseball players who took their lives soon after their playing time ended continue on into the modern era. Don Wilson, 29, is an example from 1975. A Houston Astros pitcher, Wilson enjoyed a no-hitter on May 2, 1969, and then experienced a rapid decline (15–10 in 1972, 11–16 in 1973, and 11–13 in 1974). Tragically, when he decided to kill himself on January 5, 1975, the carbon monoxide from his car seeped into his home and took the life of his 5-year-old son as well. Danny Thomas, 29, who killed himself by hanging on June 12, 1980, was an outfielder for the Brewers. He had refused to play on Sundays because of his religious beliefs and only lasted one season in the majors. He seemed to have never recovered from his rejection. Francisco Barrios, 28, a pitcher who killed himself with a drug overdose on April 9, 1982, played through the 1981 season with the White Sox. His career had taken a sudden turn for the worse after an 8–3 year in 1979.

Some individual suicides were obviously timed to Opening Day. Francisco Barrios was one. Another was Carlos Bernier on April 5, 1989. Frank Ringo died by suicide on April 12, 1889, a few days before Opening Day. One of the other more memorable "near-Opening-Day" suicides is that of Boston Red Sox manager-player Chick Stahl on March 28, 1907, and the strange death of his young bride soon afterward. Stahl killed himself by drinking carbolic acid. He was having an affair and the stress was too much. His wife was found dead mysteriously in a doorway shortly after Stahl's death. Emmett McCann killed himself on April 15, 1937.

The "end" can be very symbolic in terms of the temporal clues.

Copycats in Time

Some clustering of baseball players suicides have occurred—mainly in 1927, 1934, 1945, 1962, and 1989—illustrating the impact of behavior contagion, celebrity models, and imitation. But the year 1950 stands out above all the rest as it occurred during a time of an overall low suicide rate nationally; six individuals either actively or formerly connected to major or minor league baseball died by suicide during the season between March 11 and September 3.

Based on the clustering and copycat effect, I hoped that my research into this subject would enable me to predict and prevent future suicides and to increase awareness within a vulnerable population. The data indicated that a bubble was ready to burst, as statistics, over the long term, can be very reliable.

At the end of the baseball season in 1988, I predicted that, as the decade ended, a major league baseball player would die by suicide. I wrote a letter dated October 4, 1988, to then commissioner Peter Ueberroth and every team owner noting that a baseball player suicide was statistically likely in 1989 or 1990 and asking that a study be undertaken to see if a retirement counseling program for ballplayers would be justified.

As *Sports Illustrated* detailed in the July 31, 1989 issue:

Sadly, Coleman's prediction came true last week. On July 18, at his home in Anaheim, Calif., former All-Star relief pitcher Donnie Moore drew a gun, shot and critically wounded his wife, Tonya, with whom police say he had been arguing, and then shot and killed himself. Moore, 35, had been released on June 12 by the Kansas City Royals' minor league affiliate in Omaha. Friends say that Moore was haunted by memories of the two-strike, two-out, ninth-inning home run he gave up to Dave Henderson of the Boston Red Sox while pitching for the Angels

in Game 5 of the 1986 American League Championship
Series. If Moore had retired Henderson, California would
have won the series four games to one. Instead, Boston
won Game 5 in extra innings and then triumphed in
Games 6 and 7 to advance to the World Series against the
Mets.

In 2001, ESPN Classics noted that Moore had told reporters
in 1988, "I'll think about that [pitch] until the day I die."

My earlier findings showed that Moore's death fit the typical
pattern for baseball player suicides. A shining star among African-
American relief pitchers, Moore, like half the players who took
their lives, had used a gun. He was, like more than half of baseball
player suicide victims, between his late twenties and late forties.
And, like 15 percent of the victims, he died within two years after
his major league career had ended. Moore's final big league season
was 1988. But perhaps most notable of all, Moore, as with all pitchers before him in the twentieth century who had killed themselves,
was a right-handed pitcher. Curiously, teammates had given Moore
the nickname "Lefty" because he seemed perhaps a little unpredictable, just as the mythic left-handed pitcher is said to be. One
wonders if it is the left-handed pitchers' flexible style that produces
an acceptable coping mechanism for their stresses and serves as a
protective factor against suicides.

While the media tend to always discuss the Moore suicide, it
was only one of many in 1989. It was only after Moore's suicide
that we learned that three other major leaguers and one college
player had killed themselves earlier that year. Dan Haycock, 19,
a sophomore pitcher for Virginia's James Madison University's
baseball team, shot himself on February 12, 1989. He had been
charged with drunk driving at two A.M. the morning of his death.
His body was found near home plate with the twelve-gauge
shotgun he had used. He had left a note. On April 5, the day
after the Pittsburgh Pirates' opening day, Carlos Bernier, an out-

fielder for the Pittsburgh Pirates in 1953, hung himself in Puerto Rico. Mike Reinbach, 39, a Baltimore Orioles outfielder for one year in 1974, drove his car off a San Diego cliff in a suicide on May 20. On May 30, 1989, Virgil Stallcup, a pitcher with the Cincinnati Reds in the late 1940s and early 1950s, shot himself.

Then, within a week of the Moore suicide, a rising African-American college basketball star, Ricky Barry, 24, of the Sacramento Kings killed himself using a gun in August 1989. How many other young African-American ballplayers died by suicide after the Moore death is unknown, because no one in major league baseball was tracking what was going on in 1989. The baseball establishment and the sports media circled their wagons, and little was heard of Donnie Moore or other suicidal players for years.

While Barry's suicide may have been modeled on Moore's suicide, those that preceded Moore's suicide clearly were not. But was Donnie Moore's death a copycat itself? Certainly those prior suicides would have been well known within the small fraternity of baseball players.

In any case, the suicides have continued. On May 31, 1990, almost a year exactly to the day of Stallcup's suicide, Charlie Shoemaker, a Kansas City second baseman in 1961–62 and 1964, shot himself.

The Baseball Hall of Fame's Bill Deane has noted in private correspondence that some less-well-known suicides also need to be added to the recent list, a list he says today contains the names of over eighty baseball players. Don Bessent, 59, a right-handed pitcher with the Dodgers from 1955 to 1958, died of alcohol poisoning on July 7, 1990, in Jacksonville, Florida. Even a left-handed pitcher would join the ranks of those who died by suicide. Jim Magnuson, 44, with the White Sox in 1970–71 and the Yankees in 1973, died by alcohol poisoning on May 30, 1991, in Green Bay, Wisconsin. Eric Show, right-handed pitcher with the Padres from 1981 to 1990 and the Oakland A's in 1991, died of a drug overdose on March 16, 1994 in Dulzura, California.

But talk of suicide within the ranks of baseball did not arise in the media again until 1995, when former American League umpire Ron Luciano died by self-inflicted carbon monoxide poisoning. Only 57, Luciano had made a name for himself with his over-the-top style of umpiring. He was one of the few umpires whose face was known, mostly through his five mid-1980s books (with Ron Fisher) on his life behind the mask. So when *The New York Times* obituary for January 20, 1995, noted that Luciano "was found yesterday in the garage of his home in Endicott, NY," baseball fans knew whom the *Times* was talking about. Luciano was very aware of others and "arranged his end carefully," noted *People Weekly* in its February 6, 1995 issue. Luciano had placed his dog in a kennel and he had arranged for a friend to come over to visit, thus discovering the body first, before his family returned home. But no apparent wave of copycats followed Luciano's suicide. Why? Perhaps because no one identifies with an umpire, no matter how famous.

Curses Can End

During 2002, ESPN Classics rebroadcast their documentary on the tragedy of the Donnie Moore suicide at the same time his Angels were on their way to winning the World Series. For the Angels there was open talk that the "Donnie Moore curse" had been lifted. Finally.

Today, major league baseball is quite aware of the need for professional counseling and other supports for those players who leave the field, both in the off-season and in the winter of their years. The safety net must not be ignored. The boys of summer grow into men who face all the stress and risks of life like the rest of us but have the added burden of perceived failure that is magnified by the celebrity of being a major league baseball player. The loss of status can be crushing, a real suicide squeeze.

CHAPTER FIFTEEN

Celebrity Deaths and Motion Picture Madness

The process is the same, although the celebrities and their fields may be different: baseball players, rock stars, movie actors and actresses. The graphic, unrefined coverage of celebrity deaths is glamorized, which then prompts imitation suicides, murder-suicides, and murders based on the real-life actions of these megastars. This simple fact has been known since the 1970s and has been confirmed repeatedly in contemporary studies. It should come as no surprise, then, that people will deliberately choose to copy the behaviors of strong characters in the movies as well.

Celebrity Suicides

Sociologist David Phillips found that after Marilyn Monroe's 1962 suicide, the suicide rate in the United States increased briefly by 12 percent. It was not a situation in which the actual number of suicides first increased and then decreased because all of the vulnerable people had died. What happens in this process is that a number of individuals—over and above the routine suicidal population—are added to the real numbers. In this case, after Monroe's highly publicized suicide, 197 people more than normally would have killed themselves in the month after Monroe's suicide did so. Kurt Cobain's suicide, as well as other examples reviewed, such as those of baseball players, would create models of similar behavior in others.

Steven Stack, the chair of the criminal justice department at Wayne State University, found that highly publicized celebrity deaths, such as that of Freddie Prinze, who at 22 died by shooting himself in the head on January 28, 1977, produce higher suicide rates among individuals who are about the same age, ethnicity, and gender as the celebrity suicide. After Prinze's death, several young Latino males took their own lives using guns. These suicidological studies indicate that suicide stories were not and are not precipitating suicides that would have occurred anyway, but are actually creating additional suicides that would not have occurred without the media accounts.

Celebrity suicides definitely activate the copycat effect, according to Stack's analyses, published in 2000 in the *Journal of Epidemiology and Community Health,* and his subsequent talks in 2003. Stack found that imitation was a confirmed factor as media reports about celebrity suicides are fourteen times more likely to prompt copycat suicides than other types of stories. Stack confirmed past findings that the celebrity suicide is likely to spark a much greater degree of identification than stories about the suicides of other people. Stack found that, in general, the greater the media coverage of a suicide, the greater the chances of a copycat effect. But there are differences, depending on the medium. His research showed that televised news coverage of suicides—many of which predated the current wall-to-wall cable coverage of the last five years—was 82 percent less likely than newspaper coverage to produce a copycat effect. The reason for the difference, Stack suggested, was that while (pre-24/7 cable news) television coverage typically lasted less than twenty seconds, newspaper reports contained more detail and could be saved, reread, or displayed, allowing the content to be memorized.

The copycat effect even affects celebrity families. Learned behavior and the modeling power of the copycat effect may be a stronger link than even biological predeterminism. The so-called Hemingway curse is one such example. Pulitzer and Nobel prizewinner Ernest Hemingway wrote literary masterpieces. His father and two siblings died by suicide, and the rumors of a Hemingway curse have become an urban legend. One allegorical story is told of Hemingway's mother baking a cake for him on his twenty-first birthday and putting the gun his father used to kill himself in the middle of the cake. The story was repeated in *Time* magazine. But other sources note that Hemingway's father died by suicide by gunshot when Hemingway was 26, and it was Hemingway who had asked his brother for the gun their father had used. Hemingway, nevertheless, decided to use the same basic method, death by shotgun, and killed himself on July 2, 1961. His granddaughter actress and singer Margaux Hemingway was only 41 years old when she died by suicide near the anniversary of her grandfather's suicide thirty-five years earlier. She was found on July 1, 1996, after overdosing on prescription drugs. Ernest and Margaux Hemingway are both interred in Ketchum Cemetery at Ketchum, Idaho. Mariel Hemingway, Margaux's sister, was interviewed by CNN News reporter Connie Chung on January 17, 2003. When Chung asked Mariel Hemingway about the "Hemingway curse," she responded: "I just think that it's an easy way for the media to go—it's just such a hook, the Hemingway curse and suicide and this, that, and the other thing. That's not my life."

The copycat effect may even play a role in the so-called Paradise syndrome. Reuters reporter Rachel Noeman explained the term in a 1996 news story: "They inherit celebrity names, appear to have it all and live apparently gilded lives, but what may at first seem like paradise can end in pain or even tragedy." Noeman was reporting on the suicide death of Amschel Rothschild, 41-year-old chairman of Rothschild Asset Management and great-great-great-grandson of Nathan Meyer Rothschild, who established in 1804 the merchant bank in the city of London that still bears his name. Amschel Rothschild hanged himself in a Paris hotel room ten days after Margaux Hemingway, who also was 41, was found dead. Noeman was making the link between the two in terms of the "Paradise syndrome." While the modeling of a suicide on those most like the suicide victim is most often discussed in terms of people basing their suicide on that of a celebrity, descendants of celebrities may actually be the most vulnerable for the copycat effect. Amschel Rothschild's widow, Anita Rothschild, repeated what is often said in the wake of such deaths: that it was "totally unexpected" and that the family was "shocked and devastated."

The fact that learned behavior, rather than genetics, may lie behind the "suicides running in families" is clearest if one compares the Fonda and Hemingway family situations. Among the Hemingways, alcoholism and depression are clearly an issue, but in the Fonda family the coping and modeling is oriented toward being the survivors of suicide. Henry Fonda was married to four women. His first wife, Margaret Sullivan, died of a drug overdose that many believe was a hidden suicide. His second wife, Frances Seymour Brokaw, was an actress and died by suicide on October 14, 1950, when she slit her own throat while in a mental health facility.

Peter Fonda, son of Henry and Frances Seymour Fonda, was never told how his mother died. He learned it by accident when he was 20 while doing summer stock in Fishkill, New York. In strange twists of fate, both Peter and Jane Fonda, like their father, found themselves surrounded by suicide. Peter's best friend Stormy killed himself. Peter's daughter is part of the legacy too. Bridget Jane Fonda (born January 27, 1964), the eldest daughter of Peter Fonda and Susan Brewer, is named after Bridget Hayward. Hayward was Peter's stepsister and the daughter of Henry Fonda's first wife, Margaret Sullivan. Like her mother, Bridget Hayward died by suicide in 1960. (Jane Fonda, incidentally, ended up being married for ten years to Ted Turner, whose father died by suicide.)

The Fonda family has embraced and understood that suicide is pervasive, and their copycat behavior has come as survivors, not victims. The act of completing a suicide is one form of the copycat effect, but making the choice to live and nourish others who are survivors of suicide can be a copied behavior also. Unfortunately, that sort of positive copycat effect is not what we see from the imitation of characters in the movies and other electronic media.

Copycatting the Movies

We see behaviors copied from the electronic media in teens imitating stunts from *Jackass* and in instances where kids have committed random crimes based on video games. But, as the levels of violence have intensified in fictional films, reality itself seems to have taken a cue from the visual media. More and more we see real-life events mirroring those on the screen.

Examples abound. Stanley Kubrick's movie *A Clockwork Orange* was linked to various copycat crimes so often in the early 1970s that the director personally had the film taken out of circulation. Another example is the case of George Hennard and the Luby's Cafeteria massacre. The band Missing Link's drummer was seen as a not-so-easy person to work with; he may have been one of the reasons the band broke up. Nevertheless, on

October 16, 1991, George Hennard drove a 1987 Ford Ranger pickup truck into Luby's Cafeteria in Killeen, Texas. He jumped out and screamed, "This is what Bell County has done to me!" while opening fire with a Glock 17 and then a Ruger P89, shooting to death twenty-two people, and finally killing himself with a shot to his head. At the time, this was the worst mass murder in U.S. history. On Hennard's dead body police found a ticket for *The Fisher King*, a 1991 Robin Williams movie in which Jeff Bridges is a shock-radio DJ, Jack Lucas, one of whose fans takes Lucas's rants literally and goes to a fancy restaurant with a gun, murdering guiltless diners. The movie's massacre resembles the one carried out by Hennard.

In 1993 a scene in the macho football movie *The Program* was deleted after copycats reenacted a dangerous scene. The film showed football players lying in the middle of a busy road. Soon after the movie's release, high school football players were placing themselves in harm's way on the centerlines of highways. Several children and teenagers were injured trying to re-create this stunt.

Trench-coat–clad Leonardo DiCaprio's use of a shotgun to slaughter his classmates in a scene in *The Basketball Diaries* and Keanu Reeves's (also in black trench coat) use of high-powered firepower in *The Matrix* have both been directly linked to the school shootings in Paducah, Kentucky, and at Columbine, in Littleton, Colorado. In Kentucky, 14-year-old Michael Carneal's murderous rampage was modeled on *The Basketball Diaries* and Stephen King's *Rage*. The black-trench-coat–wearing, heavily armed Eric Harris and Dylan Klebold walked into Columbine High School twenty days after *The Matrix* opened and killed thirteen before turning the guns on themselves. "It was a scene right out of the movie *Matrix*," Josh Nielsen, a junior at Columbine and a witness to the attack, told reporters.

The Matrix also was a favorite of John Lee Malvo, 18, who was arrested with John Allen Muhammad, 42, in connection with their cross-country shooting spree that left fifteen people dead, including the ten attributed to them as the "Beltway Snipers." Police confiscated several of Malvo's jail cell writings. "Free Your Mind! The Body Will Follow!" one writing said, quoting a line from Laurence Fishburne's character Morpheus in *The Matrix*. Another note read: "You are a slave to the *Matrix* 'control.' " During a six-hour interview with police on November 7, 2002, Malvo reportedly referred to the movie and its theories several times.

"The movie's violence is so fantastic, so surreal, that it appears no one is actually getting hurt," Los Angeles psychologist Henry Nguyen told *USA Today*. "It's like being in the middle of a video game. For an unstable individual with a predilection toward violence, those images may resonate."

Josh Stenger, who uses *The Matrix* as part of his film courses at Wheaton College in Norton, Massachusetts, told *USA Today* why the movie resonates with people: "*The Matrix* was a touchstone moment for a lot of people. It combines a compelling story, drawn from a folklore and mythological base of Christianity and Buddhism and Greek mythology."

Lawyer and author Julie Hilden noted in 2003 the links between *The Matrix* and mayhem. Writing in *Findlaw's Writ*, Hilden found that in addition to Beltway Sniper Malvo, "two defendants in criminal cases, by incorporating their strange beliefs about *The Matrix* as evidence of a mental disorder, have successfully asserted pleas of not guilty by reason of insanity. In each case, the *Matrix*-based plea was accepted by the judge." In one, in 2000, San Franciscan Vadim Mieseges dismembered his landlady and reported to authorities that he had been "sucked into *The Matrix*." In the other case, Ohioan Tonda Lynn shot her landlady, then told police it wasn't real but a dream, like all the crimes in *The Matrix*. But Hilden felt it would be "too simplistic" to see these movies as manuals for copycat crimes, and felt that movies "never can amount to direct advocacy of violence in the way that a political speech can."

Some would disagree with Hilden's position, however. In an article entitled "Natural Born Copycats," reporter Xan Brooks of the British paper *The Guardian* wrote that several killings have been blamed on Oliver Stone's 1995 film *Natural Born Killers*. Soon after the movie opened, on March 6, adolescent lovers Ben Darras and Sarah Edmondson set out on an Oklahoma to Mississippi to Louisiana killing spree that mirrored the characters in the film. Brooks wrote that after the couple's arrest, "it was revealed that they had prepared for the trip by dropping acid and screening *Natural Born Killers* on a continuous loop throughout the night. In the eight years since its release, Stone's picture has been confidently linked to at least eight murders— from Barras and Edmondson's wild ride, through the Texan kid who decapitated a classmate because he 'wanted to be famous, like the natural born killers,' to the pair of Paris students who killed three cops and a taxi driver and were later discovered to have the film's poster on their bedroom wall."

On March 8, 1999, the U.S. Supreme Court ruled that the family of a shooting victim in a crime, allegedly inspired by the film *Natural Born Killers,* could sue distributors Warner Bros., Time Warner, Inc., and director Oliver Stone for "negligence." The family charged that the group should have known *Natural Born Killers* would inspire copycat crimes. Author John Grisham, who had been a friend of one of the murdered victims, felt there was a direct "causal link" between the movie and the murders. Therefore, "the artist should be required to share responsibility along with the nutcase who pulled the trigger," he told *The Guardian.*

The court action against the movie was finally thrown out in March 2001 and reaffirmed as invalid by the courts in 2002. After the court action was over, Oliver Stone reflected on the similarities between *A Clockwork Orange* and *Natural Born Killers* and felt no responsibility for any copycats. Brooks asked Stone about Stanley Kubrick pulling his movie from distribution: "I think Kubrick was wrong to do that," Stone argued. "If it wasn't an admission of guilt, it was at least an admission of embarrassment."

"What I was doing was pointing the finger at the system that feeds off that violence, and at the media that package it for mass consumption. The film came out of a time when that seemed to have reached an unprecedented level. It seemed to me that America was getting crazier," Stone reflected.

And so it continues. In May 2003, a Potzlow, Germany, teenager described in court how he reenacted a scene from the 1998 movie *American History X,* about the brutal subculture of American neo-Nazis. The youth in 2002 forced a schoolmate with a speech impediment to bite a stone, "admit" he was Jewish, and then bludgeoned him to death with a concrete block. The German media called it a "copycat crime."

The Deer Hunter

While recent movies have been linked to individual copycat events, few movies have produced as much documented, direct evidence of emulation as the 1978 movie *The Deer Hunter,* directed by Michael Cimino. Initially released on December 12, 1978 (to qualify for the Academy Awards for that year), the motion picture was placed in wider release in February 1979, to critical acclaim. The film won the Best Picture prize from the New York Film Critics' Circle as well as various Golden Globes, and got nine Academy Award nominations as it went into national release, including Best Picture, Best Director, and acting recommendations for Robert De Niro, Christopher Walken, and Meryl Streep. The movie won Best Picture and Best Director and also picked up Oscars for Walken's performance, Sound, and Editing for 1978.

In one of the movie's most graphically violent scenes, the characters played by Robert De Niro, Christopher Walken, and John Savage are forced by Vietnamese Communists to play

Russian roulette. (Russian roulette is "played" by placing one bullet in a revolver's chamber; the chamber is then spun and the person holding the gun points it at his or her own head and squeezes the trigger. An individual "wins" if they don't die by suicide.) Later, Walken's character becomes so distraught by his memories of the war that he plays the "game" willingly and ultimately kills himself.

What kind of effect would such a movie have on people? Psychologist Tom Williams, who completed two tours of duty in Vietnam, wrote of his personal reactions to viewing *The Deer Hunter* in the book *Post-Traumatic Stress Disorders of the Vietnam Veteran*:

[In] 1979, I was overcome by a wave of poor judgment and saw the movie, *The Deer Hunter*. It was hard to watch the movie, but I white-knuckled it through. The sound of helicopters and the realistic battle scenes were disturbing, but not as disturbing as the metaphor of Russian roulette used to symbolize the constant stresses of combat in Vietnam. I was reminded of the guerrilla nature of the war, especially of the continued and heavy use of booby traps by the enemy. The movie brought up more memories and overwhelming emotions than I could handle. At the end of the movie, I was unable to talk. As I walked out, I hoped that someone would jostle me or some kid usher would tell me to go out a different exit than I intended so I could express my rage at him.

When my wife and I arrived at the car, I got in the passenger side, knowing full well I couldn't drive, and cried deeply and uncontrollably. All I could say was "those poor fucking kids" over and over again between my sobs. My wife made an excellent therapeutic intervention by taking me to a loud bar and buying me a taco and a beer. We talked. It helped, but I remained confused about being so completely overwhelmed by such a multitude of emotions.

Regardless of the debates over the authenticity of the Russian roulette scenes in the movie, they created an indelible metaphor for warfare and its atmosphere of sudden, random violence. And they also have served as one of the clearest models for direct copycatting from a movie.

Scores of suicides followed in the wake of seeing *The Deer Hunter,* according to researchers Thomas Radecki and Alan Berman. Dr. Radecki, an Illinois psychiatrist who at one time taught at the University of Illinois School of Medicine, and Dr. Berman, also a psychiatrist and former president of the American Association of Suicidology, followed the deaths allegedly caused by the showing of *The Deer Hunter* between 1979 and 1986. The evidence pointed to a strong correlation between the screening of *The Deer Hunter* in theaters, followed by the rental of the videotape and its airplay on television, and the records of viewers who were dying by suicide by playing the deadly game.

What follows is a brief review of Berman and Radecki's cases, as well as a few I have located myself.

Danny Turowski, 12, of Detroit, Michigan, died playing Russian roulette with his father's revolver at Lady Queen of Angels School, imitating a scene from *The Deer Hunter,* according to the *Philadelphia Bulletin*–UPI on May 11, 1979. Bruce K. Genke, 27, of St. Louis, Missouri, killed himself while reenacting *The Deer Hunter* in his car in the presence of a friend, reported the *St. Louis Post-Dispatch*–UPI on June 10, 1979. Dominick Didonato, 17, of Elizabeth, New Jersey, killed himself playing Russian roulette after having seen *The Deer Hunter* on September 3, 1979. In 1979, *The New York Times* noted that Oklahoma City policeman William Dillon Gates, apparently inspired by *The Deer Hunter,* shot himself to death in a game of Russian roulette with two other men.

A 16-year-old Helsinki, Finland, youth fatally shot himself playing Russian roulette after seeing *The Deer Hunter*, noted Reuters on January 18, 1980. Philip J. Hinshaw, 22, of Boulder Colorado, killed himself acting out a scene from *The Deer Hunter* with a .38-caliber automatic in front of his cousin, noted the *Rocky Mountain News* on February 9, 1980. He died five months later. James R. Groeneveld, 16, of La Grange, Illinois, killed himself reenacting *The Deer Hunter*'s Russian roulette scene with a .38-caliber revolver belonging to his father, according to a UPI dispatch in the San Francisco *Examiner* on March 21, 1980.

Adolfo Flores Madrigal, 30, of Covina, California, killed himself while demonstrating Russian roulette with a .38-caliber revolver to two friends shortly after he had seen *The Deer Hunter*, according to the *San Gabriel Valley Tribune* on May 15, 1980. Ten days later, the *Oklahoma City Journal-Record* of May 25, 1980, reported that Timothy Wayne Grubbs, 21, of Midwest City, Oklahoma, killed himself with a .357 pistol shortly after watching *The Deer Hunter* on HBO. Four days later the *Coachella Valley Sun* noted that Edward Eugene McClure, 17, of Indio, California, killed himself after watching *The Deer Hunter* on pay cable TV and playing Russian roulette with a .22-caliber revolver in front of his friends. The next day, on May 30, 1980, the New Orleans *Times-Picayune* reported that Mickey Culpepper, 23, of Metairie, Louisiana, had killed himself playing Russian roulette with a .38-caliber revolver; a friend quoted him as saying, "Look. I'm going to play *Deer Hunter.*"

On June 16, 1980, the *Atlanta Journal-Constitution* noted that Timothy Rowe, 13, of Augusta, Georgia, killed himself with his aunt's .38-caliber revolver after watching *The Deer Hunter* on television. The same day, the *Mesa Tribune* reported that John Phillip Triste, 8, of Mesa, Arizona, was killed by a 13-year-old friend with a .38-caliber revolver after the friend had watched *The Deer Hunter* on HBO. Two days later, *The Hart-*

ford Courant–AP said that Robin Koontz, 26, of Ohioville, Pennsylvania, killed himself while discussing *The Deer Hunter* with friends and imitating the Russian roulette scene with a .357 Magnum revolver.

On October 8, 1980, *The Baltimore Sun* reported that John C. Williams, 25, of New York City had been kidnapped near the World Trade Center. He was robbed, and the thieves tortured him by forcing him to play Russian roulette, borrowing the terror technique from *The Deer Hunter,* the *Sun* reported. Richard Mendoza, 24, of San Antonio, Texas, killed himself while watching *The Deer Hunter* with a friend by shooting himself with a .22-caliber revolver, saying, "I'm going to do it," according to *The Washington Post* of October 15, 1980. A mere eight days later an unidentified youth killed himself in the Philippines while playing Russian roulette in imitation of *The Deer Hunter,* according to the San Francisco *Examiner.* The same day, October, 23, 1980, Anthony Totten, 16, died by suicide in San Ramon, California, with a .38-caliber revolver the day after watching *The Deer Hunter* on cable television, reported the San Francisco *Examiner.*

Radecki noted that on November 9, 1980, William R. Vinck, 21, of Elgin, South Carolina, killed himself playing Russian roulette with a revolver after watching *The Deer Hunter* on November 9, 1980. The *Asbury Park Press* of November 12, 1980, reported that Mark Anderson, 19, of Jackson Township, New Jersey, killed himself playing Russian roulette one week after watching *The Deer Hunter* on TV. Anderson was drinking whiskey with friends when he pulled out a revolver, spun the cylinder, placed the gun to his head, and fired. He was working for a cable TV station and apparently saw the program on WOR-TV, which had paid $400,000 for the rights to air the film. Six days later, the Trenton *Times* told of Godfrey Saganowski Jr., 13, of Trenton, New Jersey, who shot himself in the head while discussing *The Deer Hunter* with his brother.

They had seen it the night before, apparently on WOR-TV.

Around the same time, Craig Miller, 17, of Tucson, Arizona, saw *The Deer Hunter* on HBO and was demonstrating Russian roulette to his girlfriend when he shot himself in the head with a .357 Magnum one hour before his Flowing Wells High School graduation. Craig gradually recovered over an eighteen-month period. An unidentified White House Secret Service agent shot himself in the head after playing Russian roulette while several agents watched the White House HBO showing of *The Deer Hunter.* Secret Service spokesman Jack Warner refused to confirm the details but said that an agent was in a local hospital recovering from an accidental gunshot wound, according to the *Washington Star* of November 21, 1980.

In 1981, according to a news report from January 26, Brian Jackson, 28, an Army veteran of South Holland, Illinois, killed himself with a .357-caliber revolver while demonstrating Russian roulette to his brother Craig. Jackson had bought a videotape of *The Deer Hunter* two weeks earlier.

Joseph Avalos, 29, of San Antonio, Texas, killed himself playing Russian roulette after watching *The Deer Hunter,* according to news accounts of February 5, 1981. The next day, reports told of Charles J. Koerth III, 15, of San Antonio, Texas, killing himself playing Russian roulette after watching *The Deer Hunter.* John W. Dorko, 23, of Piscataway, New Jersey, killed himself with a .38-caliber revolver while playing Russian roulette with his cousin after they had seen *The Deer Hunter* on television, said *The Review* of Edison, New Jersey, on February 19, 1981.

Joseph Murray, 19, of Olney, Pennsylvania, killed himself with a .38-caliber revolver playing Russian roulette with friends who had seen *The Deer Hunter* together the week before, according to the May 17, 1981, issue of *The Philadelphia Inquirer.* The following month, Donald Bouley, 23, of Andover, Minnesota, shot himself in the head during a game of Russian roulette inspired by watching the movie *The Deer Hunter* on television, according to the Anoka County Sheriff's Department. Witnesses reported that Bouley had been drinking the night of June 13, 1981, at a party at his apartment. He and several of his friends viewed an uncut version of the movie. Bouley then put a pistol to his head, pulled the trigger once, and killed himself with the gun's only .38-caliber slug. Then, on the twenty-fourth of the same month, UPI detailed how David Bouley, 23, of Andover, Minnesota, had killed himself playing Russian roulette with a .38-caliber revolver at a party while drinking the day after seeing *The Deer Hunter* on television. He shouted, "Want to play a game?" then spun the barrel, put the gun to his head, and pulled the trigger.

Bobby Joe Truelove, 22, of Oklahoma City, Oklahoma, died of a pistol bullet in his head after playing Russian roulette with a friend, reported the city's *Times* on September 1, 1981; *The Deer Hunter* had inspired him. Three days later, Matt Cianciulli III of Philadelphia, Pennsylvania, killed himself playing Russian roulette after watching *The Deer Hunter.*

Early in November 1981, researcher Thomas Radecki had asked Chicago station WFLD-TV to edit the Russian roulette scene before they showed *The Deer Hunter.* Radecki told the station that, up to that time, twenty-eight shootings and twenty-five confirmed Russian roulette deaths in the United States involved people watching the movie on videotapes or television. The movie was broadcast uncut despite his warnings. On Saturday, November 21, 1981, two male viewers shot themselves to death after watching the film. In separate incidents, David Radnis, 28, and Ted Tolwinski, 26, both of the Chicago area, sat down at their kitchen tables, held partially loaded guns to their heads, and pulled the triggers.

Radecki's warning went unheeded and the carnage continued across the country and around the world. According to a January 20, 1982, news report on KMGH-TV, Paul Whittaker, 17, of Denver, Colorado, killed himself with a .22-caliber revolver while playing Russian roulette with his brother and two girls the day after *The Deer Hunter* was shown on broadcast television. Four other Russian roulette deaths (Nicholas Wendt, Aripeka, Florida, January 14, 1982, according to the Lakeland *Ledger*; Matthew Stone, Santa Clara, California, January 14, 1982, according to the San Jose *Mercury News*; Lawrence Kelly, Deerfield Beach, Florida, January 19, 1982, according to the *Ft. Lauderdale News*; and Alfonso Munoz, Bexar County, Texas, January 24, 1982) occurred within six days of this, but newspaper reports do not mention whether the victims had seen the film. *The Deer Hunter* was being shown widely around the country during January 1982.

Two days before Christmas 1982, the *Indianapolis News* reported that Bryan Petro, 14, of Indianapolis, Indiana, fatally shot himself in the head with his father's .38-caliber revolver after watching *The Deer Hunter* on videotape at his father's TV store.

Robert Call, 13, of Kansas City, Kansas, shot himself in the head with his father's .357 Magnum at a friend's home, in imitation of the Russian roulette scene in *The Deer Hunter,* said the Associated Press on January 19, 1983.

On March 2, 1984, the Associated Press noted that Christopher Mahan, 17, of Fairport, New York, killed himself playing Russian roulette at a suburban high school party in his home while his parents were away. He had been drinking and had used his father's .38 revolver. The student had been very interested in violent movies and music videos and had been discussing these and *The Deer Hunter* before the shooting. His friends fled the scene without reporting it to the police.

In July 1984, Steven R. McGill, 28, a prison guard in Providence, Rhode Island, was arraigned for murder in the death of a prisoner whom he killed with a bullet in the head while talking about *The Deer Hunter* and after unsuccessfully taunting other guards to play Russian roulette with him, noted the *Providence Journal.*

Peter Richards, 14, of Trenton, New Jersey, according to local papers of February 23, 1985, killed himself with his father's revolver while playing Russian roulette. He had watched *The Deer Hunter* on TV with his father, a police officer.

Andrea Scanzi, 14, of Como, Italy, killed himself on April 15, 1985 with a Magnum revolver after watching *The Deer Hunter* on broadcast television, reported the *Milan Corriere.*

The Dallas Morning News of August 31, 1985, reported another death inspired by the Russian roulette scene in *The Deer Hunter* in Dallas, Texas, where a 26-year-old man shot himself in the head while watching the program on television. The movie had been shown on WGN cable television out of Chicago, which is owned by the *Chicago Tribune.* In 1985, three other Russian roulette deaths were reported in *Newsweek* magazine from Lebanon, where *The Deer Hunter* had set off a wave of young Lebanese playing fatalistic games of Russian roulette. In 1985, two other Russian roulette deaths in Miami were reported to have occurred within thirty minutes of each other in widely separated parts of town.

The copycat effect of *The Deer Hunter* left a spate of incidents in its wake during the ten-year period after the film's release. By March 1986, Berman and Radecki had documented forty-three Russian roulette deaths worldwide since 1978 that could be attributed to imitations of the Russian roulette scenes in *The Deer Hunter.* Radecki's campaign to have the movie edited continued to fall on deaf ears, and his research declined at the beginning of the 1990s.

But by end of the twentieth century, showings of *The Deer Hunter* were usually accompanied with advisories. When TNT cable television screened it, they ran "six advisories with the film, which would prepare any viewer for the violent content, but this film would still need some editing to air on the broadcast networks," wrote Mark Gado in *Criminal Motivation* (2003). The violence in *The Deer Hunter* is "lengthy and very intense," noted Gado, and when, late in the movie, the Walken character shoots himself in his head, it creates "a gut wrenching end to the film."

The imitation inspired by the film continued nevertheless. On March 9, 2000, two teens were reenacting a scene from the movie *The Deer Hunter* when one of them shot himself in the head, according to the *Milwaukee Journal Sentinel.* Brandon Accardi, 16, was pronounced dead at Beloit Memorial Hospital early Saturday after a shooting on Friday. Accardi and a 16-year-old friend were at Accardi's home alone. Connie Gerth, Accardi's mother, had bought him a semiautomatic handgun for protection while she was working and had him take a hunter safety course. She told detectives she last saw the gun under some clothing in her dresser drawer. But Accardi's friend told detectives he had been at the Gerth home both on the weekend of the shooting and the weekend before, and the gun was stowed under the mattress in Accardi's bedroom.

The *Milwaukee Journal Sentinel* reporter wrote: "The friend told detectives that on the weekend before last, the two were playing with the unloaded gun and taking pictures of one another. The two tied orange bands around their heads and reenacted a scene from *The Deer Hunter.* In that 1978 movie, Robert De Niro and costar Christopher Walken play Russian roulette at a Vietnamese gambling den. Patrons bet on who will survive."

Accardi's friend admitted the two had played with an unloaded gun the weekend before but had left it loaded on the day of Accardi's death. The shooting was considered accidental and the case was closed without charges.

The cable channel American Movie Classics rebroadcast *The Deer Hunter* during the first week of June 2002. When *The Deer Hunter* is screened, some Russian roulette shootings usually occur, and this time was no exception. On June 6, 2002, a 12-year-old Detroit boy was hospitalized after allegedly shooting himself while playing Russian roulette. The boy had knocked out a tooth and was listed in serious condition at Detroit's Sinai-Grace Hospital until he recovered.

And now the movies have even imitated life imitating the movies. Toward the end of the 1997 film *187* (the code for *murder*) is a scene in which *The Deer Hunter* is being watched by the lead character, Trevor Garfield (played by Samuel L. Jackson) and a gang of young people. The clip shown from *The Deer Hunter* is of De Niro and Walken playing Russian roulette. Then the *187*'s Trevor character imitates the movie, playing Russian roulette to prove to the youths he is not afraid. He ends up killing himself. And so we have the copycat effect itself fictionalized.

In 2002, *The Deer Hunter* was released on DVD. What effect this release has had we may never know. No one is tracking *Deer Hunter*–inspired deaths by Russian roulette any longer. The situation is now taken too much for granted.

CHAPTER SIXTEEN

The Magnetism of Milieu and Moment

opycat behavior in the realm of suicide and murder can manifest itself in many ways. The method of suicide or murder may be replicated, the reflected image of the individual performing the act—in reality (e.g., the nightly news) as well as fiction (e.g., the movies)—can be reproduced, and the event in its entirety can be imitated minutely. Much of this attention to detail is entirely lost on media observers.

We are unaware of most of what happens around us. Human rationalization and denial allow us to walk through our lives ignoring the hidden messages that abound in the more traumatic day-to-day episodes of our lives. But many subtle themes and motifs run through such events, which only culminate and are realized in terms of the end event. But in decoding a chain of outcomes, it is a summary of incidents that contains the essence of many themes. The motifs are sometimes so subtle, we may not realize that understanding them may merely take an opening of our consciousness to these symbolic images.

The message can invoke familiar constructs from the subconscious, which could generate an internal dialogue between the human conscious and subconscious. This element must be understood and deciphered if preventative efforts, investigative interventions, and psychological autopsies are to be successful. A useful tool to employ is to bear an ability to read the "twilight language" of these events before they happen as well as after the fact.

"Twilight language" concerns, from psychology, the hidden significance of locations, dates, and other signs; from religious studies, the hidden symbolism that lies in the texture of the incidents; and, from criminology, the profiling insights that have revealed the ritualistic nature of certain crimes and violent incidents.

Others have been this way before. Buddhism's tantras are thousands of years old and yet never publicly revealed, never written down. Gradually it became necessary to write the secrets down so they would not be completely lost. But when they were written, they were written in a "twilight language," that is, in allegory, symbolism, code, so they could not be misinterpreted and misused by unworthy seekers. For this reason, if we do not have a proper guide, the ancient texts may be confusing or even misleading to us today.

For all of us who wish to decipher the sites, dates, symbols, and twilight language behind suicides, murder-suicides, and violent "random" acts and attempt to prevent or understand these acts, the content may be as difficult to read as that of the ancient Buddhists' stories full of underlying meanings.

But two elements of this "twilight language" are becoming rather clearer as we examine this whole arena. The copycat effect can work through the power and pull over vulnerable and angry human beings through the specific locations where these incidents happen as well as the timing of them. Place and time, location and dates, milieu and moment are hiding in plain sight.

"This Is Where I Get Off"

Bridges have always been natural magnets for suicide, but not all bridges qualify. Of course, the number one bridge in the world for suicides is the Golden Gate Bridge, sitting astride San Francisco Bay between San Francisco and Marin County. The appeal of the Golden Gate Bridge cannot be understated.

"It's what I like to call an aura of grandeur . . . It's a magnificent setting," University of California–San Francisco professor of psychiatry Jerome Motto told the Associated Press in 1996 when campaigning to get a suicide barrier built on the bridge. "Some persons are very, very sensitive to appearance, style, and so on. With the certainty, the sort of aesthetic appeal, along with the quickness, and [alleged] painlessness, I think that is one important reason why the Golden Gate Bridge is used . . . I talked to one person who went to the bridge to shoot himself, and when I asked why did he go to the bridge, his reply was 'what a beautiful place to die.'"

The Golden Gate Bridge opened in May of 1937, and only three months passed before the first jumper disappeared over its side. Harold Wobber, 47, was a World War I veteran. He was walking across the bridge, stopped suddenly, and said to a stranger, "This is as far as I go." He jumped over the rail and his body was never recovered. Since Wobber, many have followed. Some are famous, such at Victoria's Secret founder Roy Raymond, in 1993, and Democratic bigwig and Al Gore's friend Duane Garrett in 1995. Most are ordinary Janes and Joes.

More people leap from the bridge than are known to have jumped. An individual may only have been known to leap because his or her body was found later in the water or on the rocks. A suicide victim who was seen to have gone off the bridge may never be found. Because of the large gaps in the loss of bodies and some people slipping over the rails in the dark, the unofficial yearly average of fifty suicides is difficult to confirm.

Law enforcement numbers are much smaller. Between 1937 and 1973, five hundred people "officially" died by suicide from jumping off the Golden Gate Bridge; that's a rate of fourteen a year. Between 1974 and 1995, when the next five hundred victims died, the rate had increased to about twenty-four a year. When the actual number of suicides neared a thousand, local media madness tried to document who would be number 1000. Tad Friend, writing in *The New Yorker* in 2003 about the approach of this milestone in 1995, recalled that a "local disk jockey went so far as to promise a case of Snapple to the family of the victim. That June, trying to stop the countdown fever, the California Highway Patrol halted its official count at 997. In early July, Eric Atkinson, age twenty-five, became the unofficial thousandth; he was seen jumping, but his body was never found."

By 2003, upward of 1,300 people were said to have died from throwing themselves off the Golden Gate Bridge, a yearly rate of nearly forty-three people a year. But one Coast Guard coxswain who works closely with others on the bridge recently told the media that the yearly average is, incredibly, closer to three hundred.

These deaths are not painless. The four-second falls end in fatalities that the local coroner reports are caused by "multiple blunt-force injuries," which *The New Yorker's* Tad Friend writes, "euphemizes the devastation. Many people don't look down first, and so those who jump from the north end of the bridge hit the land instead of the water they saw farther out. Jumpers who hit the water do so at about seventy-five miles an hour and with a force of fifteen thousand pounds per square inch. Eighty-five percent of them suffer broken ribs, which rip inward and tear through the spleen, the lungs, and the heart. Vertebrae snap, and the liver often ruptures."

Does this keep people from coming to the bridge to kill themselves? No. The Bay Area's suicide prevention specialists long ago discovered that the majority of East Bay residents who jump from the Golden Gate Bridge have to drive across the San Francisco–Oakland Bay Bridge, an unattractive double-deck bridge, to reach their goal, the beautiful Golden Gate Bridge with its wonderful vistas. Only local residents jump off the Bay Bridge. People come from all over the world to leap off the Golden Gate. A college student in Williamsburg, Virginia, was seen riding his bike before jumping off the Golden Gate Bridge twelve hours later. Friend wrote in his article about Marissa Imrie, 14, who on December 17, 2001, left her second-period class at Santa Rosa High School and caught a $250 taxi ride to her date with destiny from the Golden Gate Bridge. People fly in from around the world to the Golden Gate to die.

There are many suicide prevention efforts on the great San Francisco span. Cameras, as well as police officers on bikes, patrols, and others survey visitors for suicidal tendencies—like staring off in the distance too long, crying, agitation, leaving notes, or telling people that they are going to jump. Pressures to erect suicide barriers in the late 1970s and mid-1990s never gained favor. In one strange twist of fate, none other that Jim Jones of the People's Temple called for suicide barriers while addressing a crowd of six hundred in 1977. Most object to barriers because they would get in the way of the view.

The other argument against putting up a barrier is the myth that says, "Oh, people would just find another way to kill themselves." But this does not seem to be the case. The magnetic attraction of the place is the key to understanding this situation. Psychologist and suicidologist Richard Seiden tracked five hundred people who had been prevented from jumping. Of these, 94 percent were still alive twenty-five years after their attempts, or had died of natural causes. "Only 6 percent over twenty-five years killed themselves," Seiden told ABC News in 2001. "The whole linchpin of suicide prevention is that a person's not suicidal their entire life. It's related to crisis. And if we can get them through that crisis, there's a good chance they can have a decent life."

Other Suicide Bridges

If the Golden Gate Bridge is the number one suicide bridge in North America, the title of second now goes to Montreal's Jacques Cartier Bridge. The bridge, like San Francisco's marvel, is a beautiful wonder and sits high over the St. Lawrence River, outlining the city's skyline. An average of forty-five people try to kill themselves by jumping off the Jacques Cartier Bridge each year, of which ten die by suicide.

Other "suicide" bridges around the world include:

Bloor Street Viaduct, Toronto, Canada
Clifton Suspension Bridge, Bristol, United Kingdom
Menai Bridge, Wales, United Kingdom
Archway Bridge, London, United Kingdom
Duke Ellington Bridge, Washington, D.C.
Brooklyn Bridge and Mid-Hudson Bridge, New York
Glen Street Bridge, Glen Falls, New York
Cape Cod Canal Bridge, Cape Cod, Massachusetts
Citizens Bridge, Kittanning, Pennsylvania
Skyway Bridge, St. Petersburg, Florida
Arroyo Seco Bridge, California
Aurora Bridge, Seattle, Washington State
Story and Gateway Bridges, Brisbane, Australia
Sydney Harbor Bridge, Australia
Van Staden's River Bridge, South Africa

Four Bridges, Odense, Denmark
Franz Josef Bridge, Budapest, Hungary.

Aware of the magnetic draw these bridges have on suicidal individuals, some municipalities have added suicide barriers to their bridges. These include the Bloor Street Viaduct, the Arroyo Seco Bridge, the Cape Cod Bridge, the Sydney Harbor Bridge, the Duke Ellington Bridge, and the Glen Street Bridge.

A Centers for Disease Control study of the Duke Ellington Bridge in Washington, D.C., showed that the building of a barrier there in 1986 did not cause a corresponding increase in suicides at the nearby Taft Bridge, underlining the fact that potential suicide jumpers are drawn to specific sites. Given a barrier, those considering suicide are forced to pause, giving them an opportunity to rethink their predicament and seek help. "If you thwart jumpers from an immediately accessible site," said Alan L. Berman, executive director of the Washington-based American Association of Suicidology, "you will save some lives."

Cliffs of Peril

According to the British media, the Golden Gate Bridge is not the number one suicide spot in the world. This unique position is supposedly reserved for the 530-foot-tall cliffs named Beachy Head in the United Kingdom. Since the 1600s, about twenty suicides a year have taken place here. The beautiful East Sussex spot is where the popular television series *EastEnders* character Mark Fowler (played by actor David Scarboro) threw himself off in 1988. But more than suicides happen here. The local council had trenches dug by the cliff edge to prevent motorists from driving over to their doom. People accidentally fall over the cliffs too. And murder happens here as well.

In July 2002, police reported that a woman in her thirties

plunged to her death in an apparent double suicide, when in reality she had been bound and gagged. Her body was found with that of another woman, in her fifties, on a ledge three hundred feet down the cliffs. And in another suicide pact story involving Beachy Head, in April 2003, Louis Gillies, 36, who was due to stand trial for assisting the suicide of Michael Gooden, 35—who flung himself to his death from Beachy Head—was found hanged. They had met online and, after exchanging messages, the two met in a pub near Beachy Head to share a "last supper." Gooden jumped but Gillies did not. When Gillies failed to appear in court, Glasgow police on April 22, 2003, visited his home, where they found him hanged. A suicide note was found at the scene, according to reports by the Glasgow *Evening Times*. Judge Anthony Scott-Gall, who was due to preside over the trial, said: "It's a very bleak ending to a very bleak case."

Beachy Head is the most famous set of suicide cliffs, but there are others around the world, including Southerndown Cliffs near Ogmore in the Vale of Glamorgan, Wales; the Great and Little Orme in North Wales, United Kingdom; the cliffs of Lefcas and Lesbos in the Greek islands; the falls of Howick, South Africa; the Gap, South Africa; Lookout Point, Paradise, California; Niagara Falls, Niagara, Ontario/New York; and the sea bluffs of Cape Ashizuri, Japan (known to have suicide leapers and murders since the 900s).

During the 1930s, hundreds of Japanese threw themselves into a volcanic crater on the small island of Miharayama. This copycat phenomena occurred after a 19-year-old girl took a boat out to the island, climbed the mountain to the crater's edge, and jumped. In 1935 the government was able to stop the deaths by screening boat passengers to the island.

A thousand Japanese soldiers and civilians, both adults and children, threw themselves from two cliffs on Saipan in the Northern Mariana Islands when U.S. troops took control of the island in 1944, rather than face the feared humiliation of capture as well as rumored murder, torture, and rape at the hands of the Americans. As whole families jumped into the foaming seas, Americans in small boats offshore broadcast pleas to the Japanese not to die by suicide and tried to save the few who had not yet drowned. Today these sites, named Banzai and Suicide, are frequent stops for Japanese tourists who wish to honor the dead.

The Suicide Forest

One of the most significant copycat spots for suicides in Japan reverberates with the influence and imitation of location. The lush and sprawling forest called the Aokigahara woods is nestled at the foot of Mount Fuji and has long been one of the most popular places in Japan for suicides. At the end of every year there is an annual sweep of the Aokigahara woods. In 2002 the corpses of seventy-eight suspected suicide victims were found hanging in the vicinity of what has now become known in the media as the "suicide forest." The 2002 figure was an all-time high, eclipsing the previous 1998 record of seventy-three cases. In 1997 the police recovered just fifty-five bodies. Aokigahara became famous in the 1990s after a notorious suicide guidebook named it as an ideal place to complete one's own death. A total of eighty-three people were taken into custody in 2002 as they attempted suicide in the woods. In an effort to discourage copycat suicides, local Japanese authorities have posted signboards along paths in the Aokigahara forest that proclaim: "Please consult the police if possible before you (decide to) die."

Barring Suicide Magnets

The tragic magic of suicide locations is pervasive. The Hennepin County Government Center in Twin Cities, Minnesota, was a popular suicide spot before they glassed in the upper balconies. New York University's Bobst Library tenth-floor atrium was the site of suicides exactly a month apart in September and October 2003, before armed guards were placed on the balconies. The Chuo-sen is one of Tokyo's most popular train lines, and the city's premier suicide spot.

The construction of suicide barriers have also stopped people from killing themselves in many former "suicide spots," including Seattle's Space Needle, the Eiffel Tower, the Empire State Building, and the Basilica of St. Peter.

"Almost all the other dangerous places in the world have put up barriers," said Brian Mishara, a suicide authority at the University of Quebec at Montreal and vice president of the International Association for Suicide Prevention.

Well, almost all. The Golden Gate Bridge remains the most dangerous place in the world for suicides.

In Your Face

Sometimes the "twilight language" really could not be more obvious.

The Manic Street Preachers are a rock band from Wales who become increasingly successful in the 1990s. The Manics, as they came to be called, released their first single, "Suicide Alley," in mid-1989. Although not a full member of the band yet, rhythm guitarist Richey James Edwards designed the sleeve for this single and came up with the band's name. Edwards would become a moving force in the Manics in the early 1990s, once answering a reporter's question about how long the band would last by cutting *4 Ever* in his arm in front of the newsman. In 1992 the band's first top-ten hit was a cover recording of the theme song "Suicide Is Painless," from the television show *M*A*S*H*.

In 1995 the Manics were scheduled to leave for a tour in the United States, where they had established a large fan base. But on February 14, Valentine's Day, Edwards's car, a Vauxhall Cavalier, was found at an Aust service station, three hundred yards from the first Severn Bridge, which the press called a "notorious suicide spot." No body was ever found, and it was as if Edwards had simply vanished into thin air. In 2001 the United Kingdom courts officially declared Edwards dead, although most officials had felt for years he had taken his own life with a leap from the bridge.

Significance of Dates

Dates are important, and anniversary events especially so. Suicides, murder-suicides, and murders tend to clump around dates of loss for at-risk victims.

One such date is one that most people assume should be associated with happy feelings but it is not. That is Valentine's Day. For many people it's a day that speaks more to emptiness and loss than to joy and love. One cultural event seems to point to this feeling: the "St. Valentine's Day Massacre" of February 14, 1929, in Chicago. On this day the alleged henchman of gangster "Scarface" Al Capone murdered seven members of the George "Bugs" Moran gang in a North Clark Street garage. Colorful names, a memorable day, the windy city, a grand crime, and huge headlines have made this event enormously infamous in history. Books and movies have fueled the copycat effect of this date. A year after the St. Valentine's Day Massacre, Ben Hecht, well known for his many screenplays, authored *Scarface* (1930), which was made into a 1932 movie about the North Clark Street killings that was produced by Howard Hughes and directed by Howard Hawks. Hughes supposedly asked that *Scarface* be "realistic, as exciting, as grisly as possible." Censors blocked *Scarface* for two years before Hawks got it to the theaters.

How does culture make a 1929 event into currency for a future generation? Through the movies and other media, of course. *Some Like It Hot* (1959) had Jack Lemmon and Tony Curtis playing two Chicago musicians who witnessed the St. Valentine's Day Massacre and are forced to cross-dress as women in order to hide from Al Capone. *The St. Valentine's Day Massacre* (1967), starring Jason Robards, portrays the event in docudrama style.

But beyond fiction, real murders and murder-suicides have also been linked to the specific Valentine's Day 1929 gangland murders. The gangland and other ripples from the St. Valentine's Day Massacre certainly demonstrate an awareness of the twilight language of the event. The individual most often identified as the organizer of the Moran gang killings was Jack "Machine Gun" McGurn, one of Capone's most trusted men. McGurn (whose real name was James DeMora), an expert with the tommy gun who had an "eye for the ladies," especially for blond women, was killed on the eve of Valentine's Day, 1936. A nickel was put in McGurn's right hand, and next to his body the killers left a humorous valentine card. Sometimes personal histories reinforce the negative Valentine's Day link. My grandmother was killed by her second husband on Valentine's Day, 1940, in Illinois, in a murder-suicide as my future mother, a 12-year-old girl, looked on in horror. The copycat effect sometimes hits close to home. During the 1980s, Valentine's Day was a focus of teen suicide clusters around the United States, and many families felt the impact of the day.

Copycats pick out other personally significant dates and numbers also. The city of Mankota, Minnesota, had a youth pact that called itself "The 11th of the Month Club" when teens died by suicides on January 11, February 11, and other dates in 1986. The Bergenfield mass suicide also occurred on March 11, 1986. On September 11, 1992, Randy Earl Matthews, 17, pulled out a gun at Palo Duro High School in Amarillo, Texas, and shot six students. Another student was trampled by the fleeing mob. No one died.

Needless to say, the *11* in 9/11, as in September 11, 2001, has been pondered by many scholars, intelligence services, politicians, and others trying to find some meaning in the choosing of this date. Is there some special significance to the date? Perhaps there is none, but some items seem to go beyond mere coincidence. On September 11, 1922, the British mandate of Palestine began, and on September 11, 1939, Iraq and Saudi Arabia declared war on Nazi Germany. The origins of Black September began with Arafat's clashes with Jordan over hijacked planes. On September 6–12, 1970, four TWA, Swissair, and BOAC planes were hijacked and destroyed (an attempted El Al hijacking failed), and this was directly tied to Palestine civil uprisings and the resulting suppression that was to be called Jordan's "Black September." We must note that on September 11, 1972, the Munich Summer Olympics ended. Of course, it was at this Olympics that the Black September terrorists killed eleven Israeli athletes, on the fifth.

September 11 was the start date of that assault by a plane on the White House, in 1994. Pakistani Ramzi Ahmed Yousef, the alleged al-Qaida mastermind behind the first WTC bombing, who was quoted as saying after the failed 1993 attempt that they would do it right the second time, was also the brains behind the elaborate *Bojinka,* translated as the "explosion." This was a plot to place bombs on eleven American jetliners and have them all explode on the same day over the Pacific Ocean. Yousef carried out a test run for *Bojinka* by planting a bomb that detonated on Philippines Airlines Flight 434 on December 11, 1994. One tourist was killed, ten injured. Yousef called the Associated Press after this bombing to give credit to Abu Sayyaf. His friend Khalid Sheik Mohammed would launch the September 11 terrorist attacks, which were built from parts of *Bojinka.* It is clear a lot of elevens are involved in *Bojinka.* This twilight attention to this special number continued with the design of the Bali night-club explosion of October 12, 2002, in which 202 died. The Bali operation, originally scheduled for the first anniversary of 9/11, commenced instead while it was still October 11, 2002, in New York City, using 110 pounds of explosives at eleven o'clock local Bali time. The Madrid commuter train attacks (with a death toll of nearly 200) involved eleven knapsacks full of dynamite and occurred on March 11, 2004, exactly 911 days after the 9/11 assault on the Pentagon and the destruction of New York's Twin Towers ("11") through the use of Flight 11 and other aircraft.

Other locations have had their special dates. For Plano, Texas, it was February. The spark that led to a suicide cluster began with a violent car crash on February 19, 1983, and the suicide of a young man named Eric Harris on February 23, 1983. Plano's suicides continued over and over again throughout every February during the 1980s. Special attention should always be given to decode the anniversaries that are symbolic in an area, remembering that all age groups hold their own specific temporal memories.

During the 1990s, the focus shifted to March and April. Today, not a school system or law enforcement agency in this country is unaware of the "dangerous" significance of April 19–20. Patriots' Day (April 19), the date the Revolutionary War began, now has links to a date holding symbolic importance around the nation. April 19 is historically significant. In 1943, the Nazis entered the Warsaw Ghetto, in 1993, the Waco raid occurred, and then in 1995, the Alfred P. Murrah Federal Building in Oklahoma City was bombed.

This last event has also been tied to April 19, 1985, when two hundred lawmen surrounded the Arkansas compound of the paramilitary Covenant, the Sword and the Arm. When the CSA surrendered four days later, authorities discovered that several members of The Order, the group accused of assassinating Denver radio talk-show host Alan Berg, were hiding at the CSA compound. Kerry Noble, who was second-in-command for the CSA, told *The Denver Post,* "Dates are so important in the movement. Everything has to have some kind of significance, either with the dates or numbers or something." One of the people who found particular significance in the April 19 date was white supremacist Richard Wayne Snell, who had been associated with the CSA. A decade earlier he allegedly plotted to blow up the Murrah Building in Oklahoma City. At three minutes past noon on April 19, 1995—three hours after the Oklahoma City blast—Snell turned to a prison official as they watched live coverage of the tragedy. According to the minute-by-minute log of Snell's last days on death row, Snell told the prison lieutenant that "today is a very significant day for various reasons." On April 19, 1995, Snell was executed in Arkansas.

The significance of Adolf Hitler's birthday on April 20 has already been mentioned, as have the key dates of Rudolf Hess's birthday (April 26) and suicide (August 17). Neo-Nazis' foci on specific death anniversaries, birth dates, and hidden suicidal language appear to be underlying more of the violence than originally thought. Should we be surprised if neo-Nazi demonstrations and anti-Jewish violence occur on August 17? If future homegrown troubles in America focus on April 19 and 20? Or on the elevenths of upcoming months?

More notice should be taken of the special dates being chosen for these so-called random acts of violence and suicides, as there may be more of a link to the "twilight meanings" underlying them than originally envisioned.

Sometimes the setting, the surrounding, and the site serve as that special little push that beguiles the copycat's soul. Sometimes it's the date. Usually it is a combination of the two.

CHAPTER SEVENTEEN

Coming to Grips

I t should be obvious at this point that countless illustrations and examples of the copycat effect exist. The validity of the copycat effect is undeniable. This human phenomenon, which is hundreds if not thousands of years old, is being accelerated by our brave new world of in-your-face, wall-to-wall news coverage. The media's graphic coverage of rampage shootings, celebrity suicides, bridge jumpers, school shootings, and the like is triggering vulnerable and angry people to take their own lives and that of others.

This is not a statement the media wants to hear. Instead of facing up to their role in these events, the media, after a shooting rampage, a school shooting, or a famous suicide, engages in the "blame game." Are guns to blame? Is it Satan? Are parents, friends, schools, and drugs to blame? Or is the general public itself, conditioned now on a high protein diet of increasingly violent fare, to blame for wanting more and more? Of course, asking the question *Who is responsible?* deflects the attention away from the major socially reinforcing element in the mix: the media itself. Denying the clear evidence, as presented in these pages, that the copycat effect exists, is foolhardy.

But, as Harry Truman once said, "The buck stops here." The copycat effect has caught up to its purveyors. The media's part in the mechanism of the spread of this violence can no longer be ignored, and it is time for our modern electronic culture to take a deep, hard look at the harm it has wrought upon our society and future generations.

From Persuasion to Tipping Points and Memes

The copycat effect became a reality for me in 1987 when I wrote *Suicide Clusters.* Now, as we move into the twenty-first century, following the pioneering studies of Steven Stack and David Phillips, suicidologists have finally acknowledged the role of the media in suicide propagation. As Columbia University psychologist Madelyn S. Gould summarized in *Suicide Prevention: Clinical and Scientific Aspects* in 2001: "Since 1990, the effect of media coverage on suicide rates has been documented in many other countries besides the U.S.—Western countries, including Austria, Germany, Hungary, Australia, and East Asian countries, such as Japan. . . . The evidence to date suggests that suicide contagion is a real effect." We are now beyond the stage of denying that the copycat effect has a persuasive impact on our society.

Not surprisingly, perhaps, the marketing profession has been the quickest to accept—and capitalize—on the phenomenon. Why? Because it works to sell.

Long ago the seeds for understanding what we now call the copycat effect were being planted in the modern society. The ideas were most formally conceptualized by William MacPherson in *The Psychology of Persuasion,* published in 1920, and in Robert K. Merton's 1946 book *Mass Persuasion: The Social Psychology of a War Bond Drive.* The marriage of these early social psychology principles with the market-driven economy coming out of World War II led to a whole field, entitled "customer psychology," that utilized the copycat effect. After sociologist David Phillips and others had shown the seductive power of the copycat effect, psychologists in the 1980s were quick to follow up on the idea with such works as *Influence: The Psychology of Persuasion* by Robert B. Cialdini and *The Psychology of Persuasion* by Kevin Hogan.

The marketing profession took up the call in 2000. That year Malcolm Galdwell successfully overviewed such things as fashion trends, smoking, children's television, direct mail, and the early days of the American Revolution for clues about how ideas become infectious in a bestselling book called *The Tipping Point.* In true copycat fashion, a whole epidemic of similar books have since appeared in the bookstores: Emanuel Rosen's *The Anatomy of Buzz: How to Create Word of Mouth Marketing* (2000); Seth Godin's *Unleashing the Ideavirus* (2001); George Silverman's *The Secrets of Word-of-Mouth Marketing: How to Trigger Exponential Sales Through Runaway Word of Mouth* (2001); Ed Keller, Jon Berry, and Doug Reeves's *The Influentials: One American in Ten Tells the Other Nine How to Vote, Where to Eat, and What to Buy* (2003); and Seth Godin's *Purple Cow: Transform Your Business by Being Remarkable* (2003). Godin, the guru of the field, coined "purple cows" to mean you have to toss out everything you know and do something "remarkable" (the way a purple cow in a field of Guernseys would be remarkable) to have any effect at all.

Attempts to understand the tidal wave that is the copycat effect have also been undertaken by the protoscience of the meme or "idea virus." In terms of the history of the acceptance of the copycat effect, this is significant because the concept has moved from acceptance to explanation.

While the concept had been in the air since 1976, Richard Dawkins formalized the notion of memes in his 1990 book *The*

Selfish Gene. A meme (pronounced *meem*) is a contagious idea that replicates like a virus, passing from mind to mind. "Memes function the same way genes and viruses do, propagating through communication networks and face-to-face contact between people," noted David S. Bennahum, editor and founder of the newsletter *MEME* in 1995. "'Memetics,' a field of study, postulates that the meme is the basic unit of cultural evolution. Examples of memes include melodies, icons, fashion statements and phrases."

Some would say that an ad creates an audience, while others would note that a meme creates a network. In books like Aaron Lynch's *Thought Contagion: How Belief Spreads through Society* (1996), ideas about memes are spreading. Susan Blackmore wrote *The Meme Machine* (1999) because, she says, she had caught the "meme meme."

Memes are applied to suicides and murders via the Werther effect, of course, the concept coined by David Phillips. One of Phillips's first associates, Paul Marsden, has been working on a book called *Contagion: The Science of Infectious Ideas,* which essentially reworks his psychology doctorate thesis. The subjects he covers illustrate how widespread the memetics people think memes are: reflex contagion (e.g., yawning and laughter), emotional contagion (e.g., fear, anxiety, sadness, and depression), crowd contagion (e.g., aggression and panic), hysterical contagion (e.g., psychogenic disorders such as anorexia, deliberate self-harm, and chronic fatigue syndrome), suicide contagion (e.g., suicidal thoughts and acts), financial contagion (e.g., speculative trading) and consumer contagion (e.g., fads, fashions, and crazes).

Marsden has become a firm convert to the meme. He feels that "mind viruses spread through a Darwinian process of imitation. We know for example that if a suicide is reported in the mass media, the suicide rate will rise in the following month. A few people with poor immunity to this mind virus will become infected and display similar symptoms to the original victim—they will commit suicide." Furthermore, writes Marsden, "the amount of violence seen on US television screens correlates positively with US homicides. We know as well that suicide victims following a publicized suicide story will more likely than not resemble the reported victim."

The point is that the copycat effect is real. Social scientists know it exists and are working hard at conceptualizing it in the framework of new theories about its rise and spread. Advertisers know that it works and use it as an accepted way to market their products. And the media knows it is real, too, using it to focus on the next epidemic, the next death story, or the next threat—and unconsciously triggering the next event they will be reporting on.

Time for the Media to Wake Up

Until recently the media has kept its head buried in the sand on the subject. News executives only began to pay attention to their role in the copycat effect in September of 1986, when David Phillips and colleague Lundie L. Carstensen published their study "Clustering of Teenage Suicides After Television News Stories About Suicide," in *The New England Journal of Medicine*. Their study concluded that the television news stories actually "triggered" additional suicides among teens. In an editorial in the same issue of *The New England Journal of Medicine,* Dr. Leon Eisenberg said: "It is timely to ask whether there are measures that should be undertaken to limit media coverage of suicide."

Interviewed soon after the article was published, David Phillips observed: "It is really up to the news media themselves to decide where it leaves us. Only the media should be involved in the debate. As a native of South Africa, a country without freedom of the press as we know it, I value freedom of the press very highly. I would be very upset if people used my findings in order to suppress news media coverage. But I do think it would be responsible for the news media themselves to bear in mind results of studies like these."

No one is asking the media to stop reporting the news. This is not about censorship. It is not about the right or left, conservative or liberal. It is about looking at how the stories are being presented, how the current approach has backfired and triggered the copycat effect. In essence, the media has to stop using rampage shootings, celebrity suicides, bridge jumpers, and school shootings the way it uses tornadoes, hurricanes, and earthquakes to get people to watch their programs. Human behavior reporting impacts future human behaviors. Copycats are a consequence of a thoughtless, sensational media, and denial and ignorance of the problem will not make it go away.

Recommendations

The media remain undereducated or uninformed about the copycat effect and what they can do to prevent it. As clinical psychologist Madelyn Gould noted in the *American Behavioral Scientist* in 2003, while discussing a recent survey of journalists, "Many reporters did not appreciate the potential for suicidal contagion as a result of newspaper stories. Those who had heard about the phenomenon expressed doubts about its validity."

Despite the atmosphere of media denial and skepticism, attempts have been made to get a handle on the media's propagation of copycats. In 1989 groups of prevention experts gathered to make recommendations to the Centers for Disease Control, beginning with the media guidelines that might help diminish the contagion when reporting suicides. Many of the strategies they proposed apply just as well to all the violent acts of the copycat effect. From those early meetings (of which I was a part), in 1994, Patrick W. O'Carroll, M.D., director of the Office of Program Support of the Centers for Disease Control (CDC) formalized a series of copyright-free government recommendations ("Suicide Contagion and the Reporting of Suicide") that were published and reproduced widely so that members of the media would be aware of them and hopefully follow them. These recommendations pointed out, for example, that certain types of coverage (graphic, photographic, sensational) stimulated copycat suicides, and that responsible mass media might do well to minimize such representations. The guidelines indicated that it was undesirable for the media to present and report how-to descriptions of suicides or describe technical details about the method of suicide. Glorifying suicide or persons who commit suicide, the CDC concluded, often leads to more suicides.

Out of these findings, in 1995 the CDC, the American Foundation for Suicide Prevention, the American Association of Suicidology, and other prevention organizations issued more specific recommendations for the media, noting, for instance, that the language the media used to describe suicides could contribute to "suicide contagion" or copycat suicides. The World Health Organization then adapted many of the recommendations of the CDC, Gould, and others, and came out in the late 1990s with further guidelines aimed at the media. They felt the media could play a proactive role in helping to prevent suicide by acting on many of these recommendations, in addition to listing help-line phone numbers and focusing on messages of sympathy for the grieving survivors.

Despite hopes that these media guidelines would be rapidly implemented, the reality was otherwise. Suicides are still sensationalized by the media, and suicide clusters continued to occur in this new century from California to Connecticut, and from Maine to Florida. Yet, the worth of such guidelines has been confirmed, unintentionally, by "accidental censorship" events like news strikes. Several studies conducted by suicidologists in the 1980s and 1990s found that age- and gender-linked suicides do decrease during "suicide blackout" periods caused by newspaper strikes. Strict implementation of media guidelines, in a case that verges on censorship, works also. Finding itself in the middle of an "epidemic" of subway suicides in Vienna, Austria implemented media guidelines for suicide news reporting developed by the Austrian Association for Suicide Prevention in 1987. During the first year an immediate significant decline (7 percent) in suicide rates occurred. In the four-year period following the forced removal of suicide stories from the newspapers, the overall suicide rate decreased nearly 20 percent, with an even sharper decline (75 percent) in subway suicides, the specific focus of the media guidelines.

For a while in the wake of the terrorist events of September 11, 2001, when a virtual media moratorium occurred with regard to reporting school shootings and workplace rampages because the mass media concentrated mostly on terrorism and war, the number of copycat incidents of these kinds of rampage shootings dropped to almost zero in the United States. By 2003, however, the media had returned to reporting sensational stories of local violence, again feeding the copycat effect frenzies of the recent past.

Suicides, murder-suicides, and murders—the events that are at the core of the most negative projections of the copycat effect—will remain newsworthy in the eyes of the media in the foreseeable future and will continue to be reported. So what, short of self-censorship, should the media do to halt the contagion of the copycat effect? While the recommendations of prevention experts during the last two decades have applied specifically to suicides, I have generalized them so that they also apply to all forms of violence that fall under the media-driven propagation of the copycat effect.

Here, then, are my seven recommendations:

(1) The media must be more aware of the power of their words. Using language like "successful" sniper attacks, suicides, and bridge jumpers, and "failed" murder-suicides, for example, clearly suggest to viewers and readers that someone should keep trying again until they "succeed." We may wish to "succeed" in relationships, sports, and jobs, but we do not want rampage or serial killers, architects of murder-suicide, and suicide bombers to make further attempts after "failing." Words are important. Even the use of *suicide* or *rampage* in headlines, news alerts, and breaking bulletins should be reconsidered.

(2) The media must drop their clichéd stories about the "nice boy next door" or the "lone nut." The copycat violent individual is neither mysterious nor healthy, or usually an overachiever. They are often a fatal combination of despondency, depression, and mental illness. School shooters are suicidal youth that slipped through the cracks, but it is a complex issue, nevertheless. People are not simple. The formulaic stories are too often too simplistic.

(3) The media must cease its graphic and sensationalized wall-to-wall commentary and coverage of violent acts and the details of the actual methods and places where they occur. Photographs of murder victims, tapes of people jumping off bridges, and live shots of things like car chases ending in deadly crashes, for example, merely glamorize these deaths, and create models for others— down to the method, the place, the timing, and the type of individual involved. Even fictional entertainment, such as the screening of *The Deer Hunter,* provides vivid copycatting stimuli for vulnerable, unstable, angry, and depressed individuals.

(4) The media should show more details about the grief of the survivors and victims (without glorifying the death), highlight the alternatives to the violent acts, and mention the relevant background traits that may have brought this event to this deathly end. They should also avoid setting up the incident as a logical or reasonable way to solve a problem.

(5) The media must avoid ethnic, racial, religious, and cultural stereotypes in portraying the victims or the perpetrators. Why set up situations that like-minded individuals (e.g., neo-Nazis) can use as a road map for future rampages against similar victims?

(6) The media should never publish a report on suicide or murder-suicide without adding the protective factors, such as the contact information for hotlines, help lines, soft lines, and other available community resources, including e-mail addresses, websites, and phone numbers. To run a story on suicide or a gangland murder without thinking about the damage the story can do is simply not responsible. It's like giving a child a loaded gun. The media should try to balance such stories with some concern and consideration for those who may use it to imitate the act described.

(7) And finally, the media should reflect more on their role in creating our increasingly perceived violent society. Honest reporting on the positive nature of being alive in the twenty-first century may actually decrease the negative outcomes of the copycat effect, and create a wave of self-awareness that this life is rather good after all. Most of our lives are mundane, safe, and uneventful. This is something that an alien watching television news from outer space, as they say, would never know. The media should "get real" and try to use their influence and the copycat effect to spread a little peace rather than mayhem.

What About This Book?

I had to ask myself as I was writing this book: Could my book it-self cause copycat crimes, suicides, and other violent acts? Would exposing the media's responsibility in the copycat effect trigger some reader into copycatting? Frankly, I don't think so. Why? Because I know that the copycat effect does not propa-gate well in an environment in which the hidden is made mani-fest. Now that we understand and know there is a problem, the protective factor is the realization that there are things that can be done to stop it.

My hope, of course, is that this book will stir up a much-needed debate on the subject and hopefully lead to social change, to a change in how the media handles these stories, to put the brakes on the copycat effect. Our future—our children's future—is at stake.

It is not too late to change what is going on. In the end, the point of the copycat effect does not lie in the details of the indi-vidual incidents but in its spread. This book has to become a virus itself to counter the violence that is out there. Fighting the copycat effect can only happen if the contagion factor can be utilized for a positive good.

The time has come for someone to say, *Stop it. Stop sensa-tionalizing the violence. Stop triggering violent behaviors now.*

A Comparative List of Events

This partial list of copycat events does not include baseball suicides, suicides by burning, plane crashes, most sniper events, and Cobain copycats, in order to better view the ebb and flow of the more routine, noncelebrity copycat events in time and place. Violent, and usually deadly, human events, initially of only a local nature (e.g., suicide clusters and rampages of all kinds) are often turned into national breaking-news items by the media. This list illustrates the shifts in media attention over time, the gradual swing from teen suicide clusters and nonstudent school rampages to student-involved school shootings, and from postal-only focused rampages to generalized workplace violence. The occasional lacunae, caused by the media's coverage of the O. J. Simpson trial 1994 and the September 11 terrorist event, are also evident. Apparent also is an increase in the tempo of violent copycat events in recent years. This is the sad history of the influence of the media-mediated copycat effect on the history of violence in America.

Key = **SC** (suicide cluster event), **GP** ("going postal" situation), **WV** (workplace violence incident), **SN** (school rampage by non-student), **SS** (school shooting), **FR** (other fatal rampage), **SBC** ("suicide by cop"), **W** (total others wounded). Please note the "Total Dead" figures include those who have died by suicide by their own hand or by the police in the cumulative number. Descriptions may appear by generic locations (e.g., "post office," "high school") or are listed by specific identifying proper names (e.g., "Luby's Cafeteria," "Columbine High School"), as these names have become tied to research data collection on these events.

TYPE OF EVENT	DATE	LOCATION	TOTAL DEAD (# SUICIDE) OTHERS WOUNDED
SN	August 1, 1966	University of Texas Tower, Austin, Texas	19 (1) W 31
SN	January 29, 1979	Cleveland Elementary School, San Diego, California	2 (0) W 7
FR	May 8, 1981	Oregon Museum Tavern, Salem, Oregon	4 (0) W 19
SC	February 23, 1983	Plano, Texas	1 (1)
SC	February 29, 1983	Plano, Texas	1 (1)
SC	April 18, 1983	Plano, Texas	1 (1)
SC	August 17, 1983	Plano, Texas	2 (2)
GP	August 19, 1983	post office, Johnston, South Carolina	1 (0) W 3
SC	August 22, 1983	Plano, Texas	1 (1)
GP	December 2, 1983	post office, Anniston, Alabama	1 (0) W 1
SC	February 4, 1984	Peekskill, New York	1 (1)
SC	February 13, 1984	Plano, Texas	1 (1)
SC	February 14, 1984	Putnam, Valley, New York	1 (1)
SC	February 16, 1984	Tarrytown, New York	1 (1)
SC	February 21, 1984	Pelham Village, New York	1 (1)
SC	February 24, 1984	Fordham, New York	1 (1)
SC	March 14, 1984	Mount Kisco, New York	1 (1)
SC	May 12, 1984	Plano, Texas	1 (1)
FR	July 18, 1984	McDonald's Restaurant, San Ysidro, California	23 (1 SBC) W 19
SC	July 25, 1984	Yorktown, New York	1 (1)

TYPE OF EVENT	DATE	LOCATION	TOTAL DEAD (# SUICIDE) OTHERS WOUNDED
SC	August 9, 1984	Clear Lake, Texas	1 (1)
SC	September 11, 1984	Mahopac, New York	1 (1)
SC	September 17, 1984	Clear Lake, Texas	1 (1)
SC	October 4, 1984	Lattingtown, New York	1 (1)
SC	October 4, 1984	Clear Lake, Texas	1 (1)
SC	October 6, 1984	Clear Lake, Texas	1 (1)
SC	October 9, 1984	Clear Lake, Texas	1 (1)
SC	October 11, 1984	Clear Lake, Texas	1 (1)
SC	October 17, 1984	New Rochelle, New York	1 (1)
SC	November 1, 1984	Leominster, Massachusetts	2 (2)
SC	December 20, 1984	Haverstraw, New York	1 (1)
SC	December 22, 1984	Mahopac, New York	1 (1)
SC	February 12, 1985	Tarrytown, New York	1 (1)
SC	February 18, 1985	Jefferson County, Colorado	1 (1)
GP	March 6, 1985	post office, Hapeville, Atlanta, Georgia	2 (0) W 1
GP	May 31, 1985	post office, New York City, New York	0 (0) W 1
SC	August 12, 1985	Wind River, Wyoming	1 (1)
SC	August 16, 1985	Wind River, Wyoming	1 (1)
SC	August 20, 1985	Wind River, Wyoming	1 (1)
SC	September 13, 1985	Wind River, Wyoming	1 (1)

SC	September 14, 1985	Wind River, Wyoming	1 (1)
SC	September 15, 1985	Wind River, Wyoming	2 (2)
SC	September 28, 1985	Wind River, Wyoming	1 (1)
SC	October 31, 1985	Leominster, Massachusetts	1 (1)
SC	December 25, 1985	Helena, Montana	1 (1)
SC	December 31, 1985	Leominster, Massachusetts	1 (1)
SC	January 11, 1986	Mankato, Minnesota	1 (1)
SC	February 3, 1986	Omaha, Nebraska	1 (1)
SC	February 4, 1986	Omaha, Nebraska	1 (1)
SC	February 7, 1986	Omaha, Nebraska	1 (1)
SC	February 10, 1986	Spencer, Massachusetts	1 (1)
SC	February 11, 1986	Mankato, Minnesota	1 (1)
SC	February 18, 1986	North Sioux City, South Dakota	2 (2)
SC	February 19, 1986	Mankato, Minnesota	1 (1)
SC	February 23, 1986	Plano, Texas	1 (1)
SC	March 18, 1986	Wind River, Wyoming	1 (1)
SC	March 20–22, 1986	Fort Lauderdale, Florida	4 (4)
SC	March 26, 1986	Leominster, Massachusetts	1 (1)
SC	April 26, 1986	Mankato, Minnesota	1 (1)
SC	June 18, 1986	Leominster, Massachusetts	1 (1)
GP	August 20, 1986	post office, Edmond, Oklahoma	15 (1) W 6
FR	August 9, 1987	street, Melbourne, Australia	7 (0) W 10
GP	December 8, 1987	post office, Melbourne, Australia	9 (1) W 17

TYPE OF EVENT	DATE	LOCATION	TOTAL DEAD (# SUICIDE) OTHERS WOUNDED
WP	February 16, 1988	ESL Corporation, Sunnyvale, California	7 (1)
SC	February 18, 1987	Kansas City, Missouri	1 (1)
SC	February 24, 1987	Kansas City, Missouri	1 (1)
SC	March 11, 1987	Bergenfield, New Jersey	4 (4)
SC	March 12, 1987	Alsip, Illinois	2 (2)
SN	May 20, 1988	elementary school, Winnetka, Illinois	2 (1) W 6
GP	June 29, 1988	post office, Chelsea, Massachusetts	2 (1) W 0
SN	September 26, 1988	elementary school, Greenwood, South Carolina	2 (0) W 7
GP	December 14, 1988	post office, New Orleans, Louisiana	0 (0) W 4
SN	January 17, 1989	Cleveland Elementary School, Stockton, California	6 (1) W 30
GP	March 25, 1989	post office, Poway, California	1 (1) W 0
GP	May 9, 1989	post office, Boston, Massachusetts	1 (0) W 0
GP	August 10, 1989	post office, Escondido, California	4 (1) W 2
WP	September 14, 1989	Standard Gravure Corp., Louisville, Kentucky	9 (1) W 12
FR	June 18, 1990	General Motors Acceptance Corp., Jacksonville, Florida	10 (1) W 4
FR	August 17, 1991	shopping mall, Strathfield, NSW, Australia	8 (1)
GP	October 10, 1991	post office, Ridgewood, New Jersey	4 (0) W 0
FR	October 16, 1991	Luby's Cafeteria, Killeen, Texas	23 (1) W 20
GP	November 14, 1991	Royal Oak Post Office, Royal Oak, Michigan	5 (1) W 5
SN	May 1, 1992	high school, Olivehurst, California	4 (0) W 10

GP	June 3, 1992	post office, Citrus Heights, California	1 (1) W 0
SS	September 11, 1992	Palo Duro High School, Amarillo, Texas	0 (0) W 7
FR	October 27, 1992	Sydney, Australia	6 (0) W 0
SS	January 18, 1993	East Carter High School, Grayson, Kentucky	2 (0) W 0
GP	May 6, 1993	post office, Dearborn, Michigan	2 (1) W 2
GP	May 6, 1993	post office, Dana Point, California	2 (0) W 4
FR	July 1, 1993	Pettit and Martin Law Offices, San Francisco, California	9 (1) W 6
WP	December 2, 1993	unemployment office, Oxnard, California	5 (1 SBC) W 4
FR	December 7, 1993	Long Island Railroad, Long Island, New York	6 (0) W 19
FR	February 25, 1994	holy site, Hebron, Israel	30 (1 SBC) W 100+
WP	March 14, 1994	electronics factory, Santa Fe Springs, California	4 (1) W 0

The murders of O. J. Simpson's wife, Nicole Brown and her friend, Ron Golden, on June 13, 1994, along with the 133 days of the first televised courtroom trial ending on October 3, 1995, transfixed the mass media and drew its attention away from postal and workplace rampages for a time.

GP	March 21, 1995	post office, Montclair, New Jersey	4 (0) W 1
WP	April 3, 1995	refinery inspection station, Corpus Christi, Texas	6 (1) W 0
WP	July 19, 1995	C. Erwin Piper Technical Center, Los Angeles, California	4 (0)
GP	July 10, 1995	post office, City of Industry, California	1 (0) W 1
GP	August 17, 1995	postal worker's home, Portland, Maine	1 (1) W 0
GP	August 29, 1995	post office, Palatine, Illinois	0 (0) W 2
WP	December 15, 1995	trucking company, Evendale, Ohio	3 (0) W 0

TYPE OF EVENT	DATE	LOCATION	TOTAL DEAD (# SUICIDE) OTHERS WOUNDED
SS	February 2, 1996	junior high school, Moses Lake, Washington	3 (0) W 1
SN	March 13, 1996	elementary school, Dunblane, Scotland	18 (1) W 11
WP	April 24, 1996	firehouse, Jackson, Mississippi	5 (0) W 0
FR	April 28, 1996	Broad Arrow Café, Port Arthur, Tasmania	35 (0) W 11
GP	August 15, 1996	post office, Paterson, New Jersey	0 (0) W 2
GP	December 19, 1996	post office, Las Vegas	1 (0) W 0
SS	February 19, 1997	high school, Bethel, Alaska	2 (0) W 2
FR	February 23, 1997	Empire State Building, New York, New York	1 (0) W 7
SN	March 30, 1997	two schools, Sanaa, Yemen	8 (1) W 0
WP	June 5, 1997	plastics factory, Santa Fe Springs, California	3 (1) W 4
WP	June 9, 1997	military logistical support center, Seaside, California	1 (0) W 1
WP	June 11, 1997	police station, Bangkok, Thailand	6 (1) W 5
WP	June 13, 1997	embroidery plant, Santa Fe Springs, California	2 (1) W 1
FR	August 19, 1997	offices, Colebrook, New Hampshire	5 (1 SBC) W 4
GP	September 2, 1997	post office, Miami Beach, Florida	3 (1) W 0
WP	September 15, 1997	parts plant, Aiken, South Carolina	4 (0) W 3
SS	October 1, 1997	Pearl High School, Pearl City, Mississippi	3 (0) W 7
WP	October 7, 1997	paging company, San Antonio, Texas	3 (1) W 0
SS	December 1, 1997	Heath High School, West Paducah, Kentucky	3 (0) W 5
SS	December 15, 1997	high school, Stamps, Arkansas	0 (0) W 2

GP	December 18, 1997	post office, Milwaukee, Wisconsin	2 (1) W 3
WP	December 18, 1997	maintenance yard, Orange, California	5 (1 SBC) W 0
GP	December 24, 1997	General Mail Facility, Denver, Colorado	0 (0) W 7
SS	March 24, 1998	Westside Middle School, Jonesboro, Arkansas	5 (0) W 10
GP	April 17, 1998	Northaven post office, Dallas, Texas	1 (0) W 0
SS	April 24, 1998	Parker Middle School, Edinboro, Pennsylvania	1 (0) W 3
SS	April 28, 1998	school, Pomona, California	2 (0) W 1
WP	March 6, 1998	Connecticut Lottery Corp., Newington, Connecticut	5 (1) W 0
SS	May 19, 1998	Lincoln County High School, Fayetteville, Tennessee	1 (0) W 0
SS	May 21, 1998	cafeteria, Thurston High School, Springfield, Oregon	4 (0) W 26
SS	May 21, 1998	high school bus, Onalaska, Washington	1 (1) W 0
SS	May 21, 1998	high school, suburban Houston, Texas	0 (0) W 1
SS	June 15, 1998	high school, Richmond, Virginia	0 (0) W 2
GP	July 4, 1998	Alameda County Fair, Alameda, California	0 (0) W 8
FR	July 24, 1998	Capitol, Washington, D.C.	2 (0) W 0
GP	September 4, 1998	postal worker's home, Hartford, Connecticut	0 (0) W 3
GP	October 6, 1998	city council, Riverside, California	0 (0) W 5
FR	January 14, 1999	office building, Salt Lake City, Utah	1 (0) W 1
FR	March 18, 1999	attorney's office, Johnson City, Tennessee	2 (0) 0
WP	April 7, 1999	bus terminal, Ottawa, Canada	5 (1) W 2
FR	April 15, 1999	Mormon Family History Library, Salt Lake City, Utah	3 (1 SBC) W 4
SS	April 16, 1999	high school, Notus, Ohio	0 (0) W 0
SS	April 20, 1999	Columbine High School, Littleton, Colorado	15 (2) W 24

TYPE OF EVENT	DATE	LOCATION	TOTAL DEAD (# SUICIDE) OTHERS WOUNDED
SS	April 28, 1999	Myers High School, Taber, Alberta, Canada	1 (0) W 1
SS	May 20, 1999	Heritage High School, Conyers, Georgia	0 (0) W 6
FR	June 11, 1999	clinic, Southfield, Michigan	3 (1) W 4
WP	July 29, 1999	two brokerage offices, Atlanta, Georgia	13 (1) W 13
WP	August 5, 1999	two offices, Pelham, Alabama	3 (0) W 0
FR	August 10, 1999	Jewish Community Center, postal route, Granada Hills, California	1 (0) W 5
WP	August 30, 1999	auto parts store, Garden Grove, California	2 (0) W 4
FR	September 14, 1999	hospital, Anaheim, California	3 (0) W 0
FR	September 15, 1999	Wedgewood Baptist Church, Fort Worth, Texas	9 (1) W 7
FR	November 1, 1999	Bad Reichenhall, Germany	4 (0) W 6
WP	November 2, 1999	Xerox Corporation, Honolulu, Hawaii	7 (0) W 0
WP	November 3, 1999	shipyard, Seattle, Washington	2 (0) W 2
SS	November 19, 1999	middle school, Deming, New Mexico	1 (0) W 0
SS	December 6, 1999	Ft. Gibson Middle School, Fort Gibson, Oklahoma	0 (0) W 5
SS	December 7, 1999	high school, Veghel, Netherlands	0 (0) W 5
WP	December 30, 1999	Radisson Bay Harbor Inn, Tampa, Florida	5 (0) W 3
SS	February 29, 2000	Buell Elementary School, Mt. Morris Township, Michigan	1 (0) W 0
FR	March 1, 2000	Burger King, McDonald's, Wilkinsburg, Pennsylvania	3 (0) W 2
SS	March 5, 2000	school, Savannah, Georgia	2 (0) W 0

SS	March 10, 2000	Beach High School, Savannah, Georgia	2 (0) W 0
WP	March 20, 2000	Mi-T-Fine Car Wash, Irving, Texas	5 (0) W 1
FR	April 24, 2000	National Zoo, Washington, D.C.	1 (0) W 4
FR	April 28, 2000	Indian grocery, Chinese restaurant, karate school, suburban Pittsburgh, Pennsylvania	5 (0) W 1
FR	May 24, 2000	Wendy's Restaurant, Queens, New York	5 (0) W 2
SS	May 26, 2000	Lake Worth Middle School, Lake Worth, Florida	1 (0) W 0
WP	June 21, 2000	sausage factory, Santos Linguisa, California	3 (0) W 0
WP	December 26, 2000	Edgewater Technology, Wakefield, Massachusetts	7 (0) W 0
SS	January 17, 2001	school, Baltimore, Maryland	1 (0) W 0
SS	January 18, 2001	school, Jan, Sweden	1 (0) W 0
WP	February 5, 2001	Navistar International plant, Melrose Park, Illinois	5 (1) W 4
SS	March 5, 2001	Santana High School, Santee, California	2 (0) W 13
SS	March 7, 2001	Neumann Junior–Senior High School, Williamsport, Pennsylvania	0 (0) W 1
SS	March 22, 2001	Granite Hills High School, El Cajon, California	0 (0) W 6
SS	March 30, 2001	school, Gary, Indiana	1 (0) W 0
GP	April 10, 2001	post office, Kearny, New Jersey	1 (1 SBC) W 3
SN	June 8, 2001	Ikeda Elementary School, Osaka, Japan	8 (0) W 13

The September 11, 2001, terrorist events immediately took the media's focus away from American school and workplace rampages. None are reported nationally for over a year, with only infrequent media reports of suicides and international school shootings that end in suicides during 2002.

TYPE OF EVENT	DATE	LOCATION	TOTAL DEAD (# SUICIDE) OTHERS WOUNDED
WP/SS	February 19, 2002	company, high school, Munich, Germany	3 (1) W 2
SS	April 26, 2002	Johann Gutenberg High School, Erfurt, Germany	17 (1)
SS	April 29, 2002	high school, Vlasenica, Bosnia-Herzegovina	2 (1) W 1
FR	January 20, 2003	Burger King, Pomona, California	2 (1 SBC) W 0
SS	January 28, 2003	high school, Taiuva, Brazil	1 (1) W 8
WP	February 25, 2003	Labor Ready, Inc., Huntsville, Alabama	4 (0) W 1
SS	April 7, 2003	technical college, Natchitoches, Louisiana	1 (0) W 1
SS	April 24, 2003	middle school, Red Lion, Pennsylvania	2 (1) W 0
FR	May 13, 2003	Case Western Reserve University, Cleveland, Ohio	1 (0) W 1
WP	July 2, 2003	Modine Manufacturing, Jefferson City, Missouri	4 (1) W 3
WP	July 8, 2003	Lockheed Martin parts plant, Meridian, Mississippi	7 (1) W 8
SS	July 9, 2003	school, Coburg, Germany	1 (1) W 1
SN	July 17, 2003	school, Charleston, West Virginia	0 (0) W 3
FR	July 23, 2003	real estate office, San Antonio, Texas	3 (1) W 1
WP	July 23, 2003	City Hall, New York, New York	2 (1 SBC) W 0
WP	August 19, 2003	Andover Industries car plant, Andover, Ohio	2 (1) W 0
WP	August 27, 2003	Windy City Core Supply, Chicago, Illinois	7 (1 SBC) W 1
WP	August 29, 2003	Electric Picture, Nashville, Tennessee	2 (1) W 0
SS	September 18, 2003	community college, Dyersburg, Tennessee	1 (1 SBC) W 4

SS	September 24, 2003	Rocori High School, Cold Spring, Minnesota	2 (0) W 0
SS	September 25, 2003	school, Lawndale, North Carolina	0 (0) W 2
SS	October 1, 2003	school, Sacramento, California	0 (0) W 1
FR	October 5, 2003	church, Atlanta, Georgia	3 (1) W 0
WP	November 6, 2003	Watkins Motor Lines, West Chester, Ohio	2 (0) W 3
WP	December 9, 2003	printing plant, Visalia, California	2 (1) W 0
SS	January 12, 2004	college school, The Hague, Netherlands	1 (0) W 0

Bibliography

Other than the news stories cited in the text itself, the following sources have been consulted in the research and writing of this book.

"19th Indian Commits Suicide," *USA Today,* October 2, 1985.
"2 Die in Fiery Plane Crash on Atlantic City Road," *New York Times,* May 19, 1986.
"2 Found Dead in Car in Bronx; Murder-Suicide Is Suspected," *New York Times,* May 19, 1986.
"2 Men Torch Themselves in London as Iranian Protests Continue," AFP Press Service, June 21, 2003.
"2 More Buddhists Suicides by Burning in Vietnam Protest," *New York Times,* August 16, 1963.
"2 More French Fire Suicides," *New York Times,* January 31, 1970.
"2 More Persons in France Commit Suicide by Fire," *New York Times,* January 27, 1970.
"2 Suicides Reported," *Namibian,* April 19, 2002.
"2,500 Suicides Reported (in Nazi Poland)," *New York Times,* January 23, 1940.
"6th Teen Suicide in Mass. Town," Associated Press, March 27, 1986.
"8 Indian Suicides Stir Action," Associated Press, September 29, 1985.
"A Baffling Series of Suicides," *San Francisco Chronicle,* April 12, 1974.
"A Suicide Epidemic in a Psychiatric Hospital," *Diseases of the Nervous System* 38, 1977.
"Aircraft Crashes Nationwide Kill 19," Associated Press, May 19, 1986.

"Another Suicide Arouses Vietnam," *New York Times,* August 5, 1963.

"Anti-Suicide Efforts Stirring Resistance," Athol, MA, *Daily News,* April 14, 1986.

"Arapahoe Youth's Hanging Added to Suicide Toll," Associated Press, March 20, 1986.

"Arden Hills Teen Suicide," United Press International, April 21, 1986.

"Astronomer Links Comet to Floods," Portland, ME, *Press-Herald,* February 5, 1986.

"Boy, 14, Is Found Hanged on Tree," *New York Times,* February 16, 1984.

"Buddhist Monk Dies in Act of Self-Immolation," WSOC-TV, Columbia, South Carolina, December 24, 2003.

"Buddhists Gather, Remember Monk Who Burned Self," *Myrtle Beach Times,* January 1, 2004.

"Burned Student Still in Danger," *New York Times,* December 20, 1974.

"But for the Grace of God," *U.S. News and World Report,* February 24, 1986.

"CDC Official Not Concerned With Media Coverage," United Press International, May 9, 1986.

"CDC Official Not Concerned with Media Coverage," United Press International, May 9, 1986.

"Copycat Suicide Rumor Stops Broadcast," Portland, ME, *Press-Herald,* February 28, 1986.

"Counselor Cited For Work Following Six Suicides," Athol, MA, *Daily News,* June 6, 1986.

"Cripple a Suicide by Fire in Queens," *New York Times,* August 14, 1970.

"Czechs Agog Over Teen Immolations," CBS News, November 3, 2003.

"Death of Girl, 15, Ruled a Suicide," *New York Times,* September 22, 1984.

"Depression Over Suicides Lifting," United Press International, February 11, 1986.

"Did Song Lead to Teen Suicide," Associated Press, January 14, 1986.

"Dutch teacher seriously wounded in school shooting," *MCN International,* January 13, 2004.

"Frustration Vented at Meetings," United Press International, February 11, 1986.

"Girl Shot to Death; Suicide Suspected," *New York Times,* September 14, 1984.

"Girl, 15, Bums to Death on L.I.," *New York Times,* October 5, 1984.

"Grieving Students Rally Against Suicides," United Press International, February 10, 1986.

"Houston Suburb Institutes Anti-Suicide Plan," *New York Times,* October 14, 1984.

"Idol Leads Teens to Their Deaths," United Press International, April 23, 1986.

"Indian Elders Fight Teen Suicide," Associated Press, December 27, 1985.

"Indian Suicide Rate Worst," *Toronto Sun,* May 23, 1986.

"It's Time for a Hard Look at the Postal Service's Labor Costs," *Nation's Business,* August 1990, p. 67.

"Jan Palach: True to His Own Conscience," *Prague Times,* January 6, 2004.

"Killed Watching for Comet," *New York Times,* May 19, 1910.

"Ky. Man Dies After Setting Himself On Fire," Channel 5, Cincinnati, Ohio, December 31, 2003.

"Leominster Moment of Silence," United Press International, March 27, 1986.

"Man tries to set himself on fire," *Aftenposten,* December 26, 2003.

"Mankato School Has Fourth Suicide," *Minneapolis Star and Tribune,* November 27, 1986.

"Mankato Youth Commits Suicide," *Mankato Free Press,* April 28, 1986.

"Man's Death Ruled Suicide in Leominster," *Boston Globe,* June 19, 1986.

"Mass Killer Commits Suicide," United Press International, May 19, 1986.

"Minnesota Man, 23, Kills Himself Trying Russian Roulette at Party," *New York Times,* June 25, 1981.

"MKO supporters pursue fiery protests across Europe," AFP Press Service, June 20, 2003.

"Monk Suicide by Fire in Anti-Diem Protest," *New York Times,* June 11, 1963.

"Montana Kids: Help Us Combat Suicides," *Bismarck Tribune,* January 3, 1986.

"Montclair Student Sets Himself Afire," *New York Times,* December 24, 1974.

"More Death in the Mailroom," *Time,* November 25, 1991, p. 51.

"Mother Attempts Suicide by Burning," *New York Times,* November 12, 1965.

"Mother Finds Boy Hanged in Attic," *New York Times,* October 18, 1984.

"Motorist Suicide by Fire," *New York Times,* July 17, 1969.

"N.Y. Officer Kills Self After Arrest," Associated Press, September 9, 1986.

"New Bedford Police Close Book on Teen's Suicide," *Boston Herald,* March 18, 1986.

"Number of Teen-Age Suicides Alarms Parents in Texas City," *New York Times,* September 4, 1983.

"Officials Discuss Suicides," United Press International, February 12, 1986.

"Officials Meet on Indian Suicides," *Boston Globe,* October 3, 1985.

"Ozzy Osbourne Defends His Song," Associated Press, January 23, 1986.

"Parents Say Singer's Lyric Prompted Son's Suicide," Associated Press, January 15, 1986.

"Parents Upset Over Media Coverage," United Press International, February 14, 1986.

"Parents Warned of Suicide 'Clusters,' " Associated Press, February 14, 1986.

"Pilot Buzzes Boston Airport, Shooting Up the City," *New York Times,* May 11, 1989.

"Psychiatrist Fears Murder-Suicide Link," *Calgary Herald,* September 22, 1986.

"Putnam Man, 21, Is Found Hanged," *New York Times,* December 24, 1984.

"Puzzle of Nine Indian Suicides," United Press International, October 1, 1985.

"Reason for Suicides by Indians Disputed," *New York Times,* April 2, 1980.

"Rebel in Torch Horror (in Korea)," London *Sun,* May 23, 1986.

"Requiem Tomorrow for Pacifist Suicide," *New York Times,* November 12, 1965.

"Russian Roulette Fatal for Boy," *New York Times,* October 25, 1983.

"School Battles Suicide Threat," Associated Press, February 10, 1986.

"School Talks Over Suicide Wave," Associated Press, February 11, 1986.

"Seton Hall Student Kills Self by Fire," *New York Times,* October 6, 1970.

"Some Driven to Suicide," *New York Times,* May 19, 1910.

"String of Suicides Halted," *USA Today,* November 4, 1985.

"Students at High School Hit by 3 Suicides Urged to Choose Life/Comfort Classmates," *Boston Globe,* February 11, 1986.

"Suicide at Bear Mountain," *New York Times,* December 8, 1974.

"Suicide Crisis on Indian Reservation," *New York Times,* September 30, 1985.

"Suit Against Osbourne Suicide Song Dismissed," Associated Press, August 8, 1986.

"Team to Examine Teen-Age Suicides," *New York Times,* March 19, 1984.

"Teen Suicides: Is There a Pattern?" *Science News,* March 31, 1984.

"Teen-Age Suicides Stir Texas Prevention Drive," *New York Times,* April 12, 1984.

"Teenager Dies After Setting Himself Ablaze," Associated Press, March 6, 2003.

"Three Suicides Last Week Shatter School," *Portland Press Herald,* February 10, 1986.

"Times Square Suicide Was Ex-N.Y.U. Student," *New York Times,* July 20, 1970.

"Town Has Rash of Teen Suicides," Associated Press, November 4, 1985.

"Town Stunned by Deaths of Teen-Age Girls," Associated Press, November 4, 1984.

"TV Station Helps to Avert Possible Suicide," United Press International, February 12, 1986.

"Two Die After Plea Fails to Halt Showing of Film," *New York Times,* November 25, 1981.

"Two Women Set Afire," *New York Times,* November 11, 1972.

"Veteran in Danang Dies in Immolation by Fire," *New York Times,* August 25, 1971.

"Vietnamese Monk Dies in Fiery Protest in U.S.," Reuters, December 27, 2003.

"Vietnamese Woman Who Tried to Self Immolate Awaits Sentencing," Associated Press, January 29, 2003.

"Westchester Man, 20, Is Found Dead in Yard," *New York Times,* July 30, 1984.

"Wisconsin Student Burned," *New York Times,* February 19, 1972.

"Woman a Suicide by Fire," *New York Times,* August 29, 1972.

"Woman in Moscow Sets Herself Afire," *New York Times*, March 10, 1974.

"Youth Kills Himself Over Broken Romance," *New York Times*, August 25, 1983.

"Youth Suicide Wave in Japan," Associated Press, April 22, 1986.

"Youth's Immolation Said to Stir Rioting in a Lithuanian City," *New York Times*, May 22, 1972.

Alvarez, A. *The Savage God: A Study of Suicide*. New York: Random House, 1972.

Anderson, Brian and Scott Marshall. "Suspect in Meat Factory Shootings Charged With Four Counts of Homicide," *Contra Costa Times*, June 24, 2000.

Ashton, John R. and Donnan, Stuart. "Suicide by Burning as Epidemic Phenomenon: An Analysis of 82 Deaths and Inquests in England and Wales in 1978–9." *Psychological Medicine*, 11, 1981.

Barraclough, B. M.; Shephard, D.; and Jennings, C. "Do Newspaper Reports of Coroners' Inquests Incite People to Commit Suicide?" *British Journal of Psychiatry*, 131, 1977.

Berkowitz, L., and Rogers, K. H., (1986). "A priming effect analysis of media influence." In J. Bryant and D. Zillmann (eds.), *Perspectives on Media Effects*, pp. 57–81. Hillsdale, NJ: Lawrence Erlbaum Associates.

Berman, Alan L. "Fictional depiction of suicide in television films and imitation effects." *American Journal of Psychiatry*, 145, pp. 982–86, August 1988.

Berman, Alan L. "Mass Media and Youth Suicide Prevention," presented at the National Conference on Prevention and Interventions, Oakland, CA, June 11, 1986.

Berman, Alan. Personal communication, 1985–87, 2003–2004.

Binns, W.; Kerkinan, D.; and Schroeder, S. "Destructive Group Dynamics: An Account of Some Peculiar Interrelated Incidents of Suicide and Suicidal Attempts in a University Dormitory." *Journal of the American College Health Association*, 14, 1966.

Blackmore, Susan. *The Meme Machine*. Oxford University Press, Oxford, 1999.

Bollen, Kenneth A. "Temporal Variations in Mortality: A Comparison of U.S. Suicides and Motor Vehicle Fatalities, 1972–1976." *Demography*, 20: 45–59, 1983.

Bollen, Kenneth A., and Phillips, David P. "Imitative suicides in a national study of the effects of television news stories." *American Sociological Review,* 47, 1982, pp. 802–9.

Bollen, Kenneth A., and Phillips, David P. "Suicidal motor vehicle fatalities in Detroit: a replication." *American Journal of Sociology,* 87, 1981, pp. 404–12.

Brent, D. A.; Kerr, M. M.; Goldstein, C.; Bozigar, J.; Wartella, M.; Allan, M. J. "An outbreak of suicide and suicidal behavior in a high school." *American Academy of Child and Adolescent Psychiatry,* pp. 918–24, 1989.

Buckley, Thomas. "Man, 22, Immolates Himself in Antiwar Protest at U.N.," *New York Times,* November 10, 1965.

Bucknell, R. S., and Stuart-Fox, Martin, *The Twilight Language: Explorations in Buddhist Meditation and Symbolism.* Richmond: Curzon Press, 1993.

Bulwa, Demian, "Inspector's Tingle of Fear; Inspector Sought Cops' Aid," *San Francisco Examiner,* June 23, 2000.

Burgess, John. "Seven Japanese Women Kill Selves After Cult Leader Dies," *Huntsville Times,* November 3, 1986.

Burnam, Tom. *More Misinformation.* New York: Ballantine, 1980.

Calder, Nigel. *The Comet Is Coming!* New York: Viking, 1980.

Carlson, Margaret, "Mailroom Mayhem," *Time,* December 25, 1989, p. 30.

Centers for Disease Control and Prevention. "Suicide Contagion and the Reporting of Suicide: Recommendations for a National Workshop." *Morbidity and Mortality Weekly Review,* 43, (RR-6) 9–18, April 22, 1994.

Centers for Disease Control. "Adolescent suicide and suicide attempts—Santa Fe County, New Mexico, January 1985–May 1990." *Morbidity and Mortality Weekly Review,* 1991; 40:329–31.

Centers for Disease Control. "Cluster of suicides and suicide attempts—New Jersey." *Morbidity and Mortality Weekly Review,* 1988; 37:213–16.

Centers for Disease Control. *Youth Suicide in the United States, 1970–1980.* Atlanta; Centers for Disease Control, 1980.

Chapman, Robert D., and Brandt, John C. *The Comet Book.* Boston: Jones and Bartlett, 1984.

Choron, James. "Notes on Suicide Prevention in Antiquity," *Bulletin of Suicidology,* 4, July 1968.

Cialdini, R. B. *Influence: Science and Practice*. New York: Harper-Collins, 1984.

Clube, Victor, and Napier, Bill. *The Cosmic Serpent*. London: Faber and Faber, 1982.

Cohen, Susan and Daniel. *Teenage Stress*. New York: M. Evans, 1984.

Coleman, Loren, and David Lester. "Boys of Summer, Suicides of Winter." Paper presented at the 22nd Annual Conference of the American Association of Suicidology, San Diego, California, April 14, 1989.

Coleman, Loren. "Boys of Summer, Suicides of Winter: An Introduction to Baseball Suicide." In Edward J. Rielly (ed.), *Baseball and American Culture*. New York: Haworth Press, 2003.

Coleman, Loren. "Comets and Suicides: Astrosociological Folklore?" *Fortean Times*, 47, Autumn 1986.

Coleman, Loren. "Teen Suicide Clusters and the Werther Effect," University of Southern Maine: *The Network News*, 3, March 1986.

Coleman, Loren. *Suicide Clusters*. Boston and London: Faber and Faber, 1987.

Committee on Post Office and Civil Services. *A Post Office Tragedy: The Shooting at Royal Oak*. Washington, D.C.: Government Printing Office, 1992.

Corliss, Richard. "Sid and Nancy," *Time*, November 3, 1986.

Crosby, K.; Rhee, J.; and Holland, J. "Suicide by Fire: A Contemporary Method of Political Protest," *International Journal of Social Psychiatry*, 23 (1977).

Cruz, Barbara C. *School Shootings and School Violence*. Berkeley Heights, New Jersey: Enslow, 2002.

Danelski, David, "Effects of Riverside Rampage Remain," *Riverside Press-Enterprise*, October 3, 1999.

Davidson, L. E., and Gould, Madelyn. "Contagion as a risk factor for youth suicide." In *Alcohol, Drug Abuse, and Mental Health Administration. Report of the Secretary's Task Force on Youth Suicide, Vol 2: Risk factors for youth suicide*. Washington, D.C.: U.S. Department of Health and Human Services, Public Health Service, 1989:88–109; DHHS publication no. (ADM)89–1622.

Davidson, Lucy E.; Rosenberg, M. L.; Mercy, J. A.; Franklin, J.; and Simmons, J. T. "An epidemiologic study of risk factors in two teenage suicide clusters," *Journal of the American Medical Association*, 1989, 262:2687–92.

Davidson, Jean. "Epidemic of Teenage Suicides Has Experts Searching for Cure," *Chicago Tribune,* June 1, 1986.

Davidson, Lucy E. "Suicide clusters and youth." In C. R. Pfeffer, (ed.), *Suicide among Youth: Perspectives on Risk and Prevention,* pp. 83–89. Washington, D.C.: American Psychiatric Press, 1989.

Davidson, Lucy. "Contagion and Media." Paper presented at Department of Health and Human Services Task Force on Youth Suicide, May 1986.

Davis, B. R., and Hardy, R. J. "A suicide epidemic model." *Social Biology,* 33(3–4), (1986), pp. 291–300.

Davis, Patricia A. *Suicidal Adolescents.* Springfield, IL: Charles C. Thomas, 1983.

Dawkins, R. *The Extended Phenotype.* Oxford, Oxford University Press, 1982.

Dawkins, R. *The Selfish Gene.* Oxford, Oxford University Press, 1976.

Deane, Bill, Baseball Hall of Fame. Personal communications, 1985–2003.

deFiebre, Conrad. "Teen's Suicide Is Fourth in Mankato in 3½ Months," *Minneapolis Star and Tribune,* April 30, 1986.

Della Valle, Paul. "Leominster Leaders Unite on Youth's Problems," Worcester, MA, *Telegram,* April 23, 1986.

DeVore, Brain. "2 Teen-Agers Commit Suicide," *Des Moines Register,* February 20, 1986.

Dionne, E.J. "Postal Workers Are Feeling Second Class," *Riverside Press-Enterprise,* October 20, 2001.

Doan, Michael, and Peterson, Sarah. "As Cluster Suicides Take Toll of Teenagers," *U.S. News and World Report,* November 12, 1984.

Doherty, Paul B. *The Arrival of Halley's Comet.* Woodbury, NY: Barron's, 1985.

Dublin, Louis I. *Suicide: A Sociological and Statistical Study.* New York: Ronald, 1963.

Durkheim, E. *Suicide: A Study in Sociology.* Translated by J. A. Spaulding and G. Simpson. London: Routledge & Kegan, 1951. (Originally published in French in 1897.)

Dwyer, Philip M. "An Inquiry into the Psychological Dimensions of Cult Suicide," *Suicide and Life-Threatening Behavior,* 9:2, Summer 1979.

Easteal, Patricia. *Killing the Beloved.* Washington, D.C.: Criminal Justice Press, 1993.

Editor, "Editorial [Snipers]." *The University Journal*, October 22, 2002.

Eisenberg, Leon. "Does Bad News About Suicide Beget Bad News?" *New England Journal of Medicine*, 1992; 327:502–3.

Ensslin, John C. "Indian Reservation Copes with Epidemic of Suicides," Scripps Howard News Service, October 7, 1985.

Errico, Marcus. "Two Cobain fans kill themselves," *Eonline*, May 15, 1997.

Etzersdorfer, E., and Sonneck, G. "Preventing suicide by influencing mass-media reporting: The Viennese experience, 1980–1996," *Archives of Suicide Research*, 4, 1998, pp. 67–74.

Farberow, Norman L. "Cultural History of Suicide." *Suicide and Attempted Suicide.* Stockholm: Nordiska Bokhandlens Forlag, 1972.

Fekete, S., and Schmidtke, A. "The impact of mass media reports on suicide and attitudes toward self-destruction: Previous studies and some new data from Hungary and Germany." In B. L. Mishara (ed.), *The impact of suicide.* New York: Springer, 1995, pp. 142–55.

Flaste, Richard, et al. *The New York Times Guide to the Return of Halley's Comet.* New York: Times Books, 1985.

Fort, Charles. *The Books of Charles Fort.* New York: Paraview, 2004.

Fox, James Alan, and Jack Levin. "Helping set the stage for copycat school shooting," *Boston Globe,* March 11, 2001.

Frankel, Bruce, and Johnson, Peter. "N.Y. Counties Stress Prevention in Response to Teen-age Suicides," *USA Today,* November 3, 1984.

Freud, Sigmund. "Zur Selbstmond Diskussion," *Diskussion des Weiner Psychoanalytisch en Vereins,* 1910.

Garland, Robert. "Death Without Dishonor: Suicide in the Ancient World," *History Today,* 33, January 1983.

Geen, R., and Thomas, S. "The immediate effects of media violence on behavior." *Journal of Social Issues,* 42, 1986, pp. 7–27.

Gelman, David, and Gangelhoff, B. K. "Teen-age Suicide in the Sun Belt," *Time,* August 15, 1983.

Gewertz, Catherine. "Osbourne Suited Over Suicide," United Press International, January 13, 1986.

Gibbon, Edward. *The Decline and Fall of the Roman Empire.* New York: Harcourt, Brace, 1960.

Goodavage, Joseph F. *The Comet Kohoutek.* New York: Pinnacle, 1973.

Gorman, Tom, and Richard Serrano. "Postal Employee Kills Wife, 2 Co-Workers," *Los Angeles Times,* August 11, 1989.

Gorman, Tom, and Richard Serrano. "Violent Death Not New to Postman," *Los Angeles Times,* August 12, 1989.

Gould, Madelyn S. "Suicide and the Media," *New York Academy Annals of Science,* 2001.

Gould, Madelyn S. "Risk Factors for Suicide Contagion." Paper presented at the Annual Meeting of the American Association of Suicidology, April 3, 1986.

Gould, Madelyn S. "Suicide and the Media." In H. Hendin and J. J. Mann (eds.), *The Clinical Science of Suicide Prevention.* New York: Annals of the New York Academy of Sciences, 2001, pp. 200–224.

Gould, Madelyn S., and Shaffer, D. "The impact of suicide in television movies: Evidence of imitation." *New England Journal of Medicine,* 315, 1986, pp. 690–94.

Gould, Madelyn S., and Davidson, Lucy. "Suicide contagion among adolescents." In Stiffman, A. R., Felman, R. A. (eds.), *Advances in Adolescent Mental Health, Vol. III: Depression and Suicide.* Greenwich, CT: JAI Press, 1988.

Gould, Madelyn S.; Shaffer, David; and Kleinman, M. "The impact of suicide in television movies. Evidence of imitation: Replication and commentary," *Suicide and Life-Threatening Behavior,* 18, September 11, 1988, pp. 90–99.

Gould, Madelyn S.; Petrie, K.; Kleinman, M.; and Wallenstein, S. "Clustering of attempted suicide: New Zealand national data." *International Journal of Epidemiology,* 23, 1994, pp. 1185–89.

Gould, Madelyn S.; Wallenstein, S.; and Davidson, Lucy. "Suicide clusters: A critical review," *Suicide and Life-Threatening Behavior,* 19, 1989, pp. 17–29.

Gould, Madelyn S.; Wallenstein, S.; Kleinman, M. H.; O'Carroll P. W.; and Mercy, J. A. "Suicide clusters: an examination of age-specific effects," *American Journal of Public Health,* 80 (1990), pp. 211–12.

Gould, Madelyn S.; Wallenstein, S.; and Kleinman, M. "Time-space clustering of teenage suicide," *American Journal of Epidemiology,* 131 (1990), pp. 71–78.

Gropman, Donald, with Mirvus, Kenneth. *Comet Fever.* New York: Fireside/Simon and Schuster, 1985.

Grosser, Helper. *The Causes and Effects of Anti-Semitism.* New York: Philosophical Library, 1978.

Gunter, B. "The question of media violence." In J. Bryant and D. Zillmann (eds.), *Media Effects: Advances in Theory and Research*. Hillsdale, NJ: Erlbaum, 1994.

Gutman, Dan. *Baseball Babylon*. New York: Penguin, 1992.

Hacker, J. F. C. *Epidemics of the Middle Ages*. London: Trubner, 1859.

Hafen, Brent Q., and Frandsen, Kathryn J. *Youth Suicide*. Provo, UT: Behavioral Health Associates, 1986.

Häfner, H., and Schmidke, A. "Do televised Fictional Suicide Models Produce Suicides?" In C. Pfeffer, (ed.), *Suicide among Youth: Perspectives on Risk and Prevention*, Washington, D.C.: American Psychiatric Press, 1989, pp. 117–41.

Halberstam, David. "Nun's Act a Surprise," *New York Times*, August 16, 1963.

Hall, John R. "Apocalypse at Jonestown," *Society*, 16:6, 1979.

Halperin, Ian, and Wallace, Max. *Who Killed Kurt Cobain?* New York: Citadel, 1998.

Handkoff, L. D. "An Epidemic of Attempted Suicide," *Comprehensive Psychiatry*, 2, 1967.

Hankoff, L. D. *Suicide: Theory and Clinical Aspects*. Littleton, MA: PSG, 1979.

Hanley, Robert, "4 Slain in 2 New Jersey Attacks," *New York Times*, October 11, 1991.

Hanley, Robert, "Suspect in Spree Refused to Fight Loss of His Job," *New York Times*, October 12, 1991.

Hart, Matthew. A *Viewer's Guide to Halley's Comet*. New York: Pocket Books, 1985.

Hassan, R. "Effects of newspaper stories on the incidence of suicide in Australia: A research note," *Australian and New Zealand Journal of Psychiatry*, 29, 1995, pp. 480–83.

Hecker, J. F. C. *Epidemics of the Middle Ages*. London: Trubner, 1859.

Hendin, Herbert. *Suicide in America*. New York: W. W. Norton, 1982.

Herbaugh, Sharon. "Suicides," Portland, ME, *Press-Herald*, October 17, 1984.

Herman, P. *Reporting of Suicide*. Sydney: Australian Press Council News, May 1996.

Hernon, Peter. A *Terrible Thunder: The Story of the New Orleans Sniper*. New York: Doubleday, 1978.

Hess, John L. "France Stirred by Immolations," *New York Times*, January 25, 1970.

Hill, Lisa O'Neill, "City Hall Suspect Claims Insanity," *Riverside Press-Enterprise,* October 30, 1999.

Jobes, D. A.; Berman, Alan; O'Carroll, Patrick; Eastgard, S.; and Knickmeyer, S. "The Kurt Cobain suicide crisis: Perspectives from research, public health, and the news media." *Suicide and Life-Threatening Behavior,* 26:3 (1996), pp. 260–69.

Jonas, K. "Modeling and suicide: A test of the Werther effect," *British Journal of Social Psychology,* 31 (1992), pp. 295–306.

Jones, David. "Woman, 82, Sets Herself Afire in Street as Protest on Vietnam," *New York Times,* March 18, 1965.

Juffner, Jane and Weller, Tim. "Teen Deaths 'Affect Psyche' of Omaha," *USA Today,* February 11, 1986.

Kataoka, Mike, "Trial Date Set in City Hall Shootings," Associated Press, May 5, 1999.

Kaull, Mary, "Teen Suicide: Many Links in Deadly Chain," *USA Today,* February 13, 1986.

Kessler, R. C.; Downey, G.; Stipp, H.; and Milavsky, R. "Network television news stories about suicide and short-term changes in total US suicides," *Journal of Nervous and Mental Disease* 177 (9) (1989), pp. 551—55.

Kevan, Simon M. *Perspectives on Season of Suicide.* London: Pergamon, 1980.

Kilian, Michael, "Postmaster Unseals Plan For Survival," Associated Press, April 6, 2002.

King, Stephen. "The Bogeyboys." Keynote address, Vermont Library Conference, VEMA Annual Meeting, May 26, 1999.

Kleinfield, N. R., "Death Invades a Tranquil Village, and Ridgewood Deals with Horror," *New York Times,* October 13, 1991, 40(1).

Kopvillem, Peeter, "In Cold Blood," *Maclean's,* September 1, 1986, p. 27.

Kuruvila, Matthai Chakko, "Friends Say Sausage Factory Owner Had Made Private Threats to Kill Inspectors," *San Jose Mercury News,* June 28, 2000.

Lasseter, Don. *Going Postal: Madness and Mass Murder in America's Post Offices.* New York: Pinnacle, 1997.

Lavergne, Gary M. *A Sniper in the Tower: The Charles Whitman Murders.* Denton, Texas: University of Texas Press, 1997.

Leftowitz, Mary R., and Fant, Maureen B. *Women in Greece and Rome.* Toronto: Samuel-Stevens, 1977.

Lehr, Dick. "Teen-age Suicides: How One City Coped," *Boston Globe,* March 29, 1985.

Lester, David and Aaron T. Beck. "'Suicide and National Holidays," *Psychological Reports,* 36 (1975).

Lester, David, and Topp, Richard. "Suicide in the Major Leagues," *Perceptual and Motor Skills,* 67:934 (1988).

Levenson, Alan. "Pushing the Envelope at the Post Office," *Business Week,* November 25, 1991, p. 56.

Makihara, Kumiko. "Teen Deaths Wrack Japan," Associated Press, April 24, 1986.

Malinowski, W. Zachary. "Rash of Suicides Puzzles Parents in Leominster," *Providence Sunday Journal,* May 25, 1986.

Marsden, Paul. "Memetics and Social Contagion: Two Sides of the Same Coin?" *Journal of Memetics—Evolutionary Models of Information Transmission,* 2 (1998).

Marsden, Paul. "Review of Thought Contagion: How Beliefs Spread through Society by A. Lynch," *Journal of Artificial Societies and Social Simulation* (1999).

Marsh, Dave. *Rock Book of Lists.* San Francisco: Rolling Stone, 1982.

Matthews, Tom, et al. "The Cult of Death," *Newsweek,* 112:23, December 4, 1978.

May, John. *Curious Facts.* New York: Holt, Rinehart and Winston, 1980.

McGill, Douglas C. "Fordham Student Hangs Himself at Parent's Home in Westchester," *New York Times,* February 26, 1984.

McGill, Peter. "Japan Upset at Copycat Suicides After Death of Pop Star," *London Observer,* April 21, 1986.

McIntosh, John L. *Research on Suicide: A Bibliography.* Westport, CT: Greenwood Press, 1985.

Meerloo, J. A. M. *Suicide and Mass Suicide.* New York: E. P. Dutton, 1962.

Menninger, Karl. *Man Against Himself.* New York: Harcourt, 1938.

Metz, Jerred. *Halley's Comet, 1910: Fire in the Sky.* St. Louis: Singing Bone Press, 1985.

Morrow, Lance. "The Lure of Doomsday," *Time,* 112:23, December 4, 1978.

Motto J. "Suicide and Suggestibility," *American Journal of Psychiatry,* 124 (1967), pp. 252–56.

Motto, J. A. "Newspaper Influences on Suicide," *Archives of General Psychiatry,* 23 (August 1970), pp. 143–48.

Nash, J. Madeleine, and Lamar, Jacob V., Jr. "Crazy Pat's Revenge," *Time,* September 1, 1986, p. 19.

Neff, Donald. "Nightmare in Jonestown," *Time,* 112:23, December 4, 1978.

Newton, Michael. *Cop Killers.* Port Townsend, WA: Loompanics Unlimited, 1998.

Nicoletti, John, and Spencer-Thomas, Sally. *Violence Goes to School: Lessons Learned.* Denver: Nicoletti-Flater Associates, 1999.

O'Carroll, Patrick W. "Suicide causation: pies, paths, and pointless polemics," *Suicide and Life-Threatening Behavior,* 23 (1993), pp. 27–36.

O'Carroll, Patrick W., and Potter, L. B. "Suicide Contagion and the Reporting of Suicide: Recommendations from a National Workshop," *Morbidity and Mortality Weekly News,* 43(RR-6) (1994), pp. 9–18.

O'Dea, James J. *Suicide: Studies on Its Philosophy, Causes, and Prevention.* New York: G. P. Putnam's, 1882.

Olson, Roberta J. M. *Fire and Ice: A History of Comets in Art.* New York: Walker, 1985.

O'Neill, Richard. *Suicide Squads.* New York: Ballantine, 1984.

Ostroff, Robert B., et al. "Adolescent Suicides Modeled After Television Movie," *American Journal of Psychiatry,* 142, August 1985.

O'Sullivan, Arieh. "Copycat Effect," *Jerusalem Post,* October 3, 2001.

Pankratz, Howard. "April 19: A Nervous Date," *Denver Post,* April 18, 1997.

Pape, Robert A. "The Strategic Logic of Suicide Terrorism," *American Political Science Review,* 97 (August 2003), pp. 343–61.

Pape, Robert A. Personal communication, 2003.

Peck, Michael L.; Farberow, Norman L.; and Litman, Robert E. *Youth Suicide.* New York: Springer, 1985.

Pederson, Daniel. "10 Minutes of Madness," *Newsweek,* September 1, 1986, pp. 18–19.

Phillips, David P., and Carstensen, L. L. "The effect of suicide stories on various demographic groups, 1968–1985," *Suicide and Life-Threatening Behavior,* 18 (1988), pp. 100–14.

Phillips, David P.; Lesyna, K.; and Paight, D. J. "Suicide and the media." In R. W. Maris, A. L. Berman, J. T. Maltsberger et al. (eds.), *Assessment and Prediction of Suicide.* New York: The Guilford Press, 1992, pp. 499–519.

Phillips, David P. "Airplane Accident Fatalities Increase Just After Newspaper Stories About Suicide and Murder," *Science,* 20, August 25, 1978.

Phillips, David P. "Airplane Accidents, Murder, and the Mass Media: Towards a Theory of Imitation and Suggestions," *Social Forces,* 58 (June 1980), p. 4.

Phillips, David P. "Media Attentions Helps Encourage Teen Suicide," *USA Today,* September 19, 1986.

Phillips, David P. "Motor Vehicle Fatalities Increase Just After Publicized Suicide Stories," *Science,* 196, June 24, 1977.

Phillips, David P. "Suicide, Motor Vehicle Fatalities, and the Mass Media: Evidence Toward a Theory of Suggestion," *American Journal of Sociology* 84 (1979), p. 5.

Phillips, David P. "The Impact of Fictional Television Stories on U.S. Adult Fatalities: New Evidence on the Effect of the Mass Media on Violence," *American Journal of Sociology* 87 (1982), p. 6.

Phillips, David P. "The Influence of Suggestion on Suicide: Substantive and Theoretical Implications of the Werther Effect," *American Sociological Review,* 39 (June 1974), p. 39.

Phillips, David P., and Carstensen, Lundie L. "Clustering of Teenage Suicides After Television News Stories About Suicide," *New England Journal of Medicine,* 315 (September 11, 1986), p. 11.

Phillips, David P., and Liu, Judith. "The Frequency of Suicides Around Major Holidays: Some Surprising Findings," *Suicide and Life-Threatening Behavior,* 10 (Spring 1980), p. 1.

Phillips, David P.; Lesnya, K.; and Paight, D. J. "Suicide and media." In R. W Maris, A. L. Berman, and J. T. Maltsberger (eds.). *Assessment and prediction of suicide.* New York: Guilford, 1992, pp. 499–519.

Phillips, David P. "The influence of suggestion on suicide: Substantive and theoretical implications of the Werther effect," *American Sociological Review,* 39 (June 1979), pp. 340–54.

Plutarch. *Plutarch's Lives.* A. H. Clough, ed. New York: Collier & Sons, 1909.

Poirier, Patricia. "Mounties Cite Suicide Rate in Drive to Obtain Union," Toronto *Globe and Mail,* September 30, 1986.

Prescod, Suzanne (ed.) "Omaha Reacts to Rash of Recent Teen Suicides," *Children & Teens Today,* 6 (April 1986), p. 6.

Quinn, John C. (ed.) "Teen Suicide: Fall's Hot Made-for-TV Topic," *USA Today,* August 27, 1984.

Quinn, John C. (ed.) "Teen Suicides," *USA Today*, February 27, 1984.

Quinn, John (ed.) "4th Houston-Area Youth Kills Self Since Saturday," *USA Today*, October 12, 1984.

Quinn, John (ed.) "Teen Suicide," *USA Today*, February 26, 1985.

Radecki, Thomas. "Deer Hunter Deaths Climb to 43," *National Coalition on Television Violence News*, 7 (January–March 1986), pp. 1–2.

Radecki, Thomas. Personal communications, 1986, 2003.

Randall, Kate. "One week in America: workplace shootings, murder-suicides, killing spree plot," World Socialist website, July 11, 2003.

Rapaport, Richard. "Jonestown and City Hall slayings eerily linked in time and memory," *San Francisco Chronicle*, November 16, 2003.

Reinhold, Robert. "Postmasters Seek Greater Authority," *New York Times*, August 22, 1986.

Resnik, H. L. P. "The Neglected Search for the Suicidoccus, Contagiosa," *Archives of Environmental Health*, 19 (September 1969).

Rickard, Robert J. M. "Diary of a Mad Planet: The 1985 Halley's Comet," *Fortean Times*, 47 (Autumn 1986).

Rielly, Edward J. *Baseball and American Culture: Accross the Diamond*. New York: Haworth, 2003.

Ritchie, David. *Comets: The Swords of Heaven*. New York: Signet 1985.

Robbins, David, and Conroy, Richard C. "A Cluster of Adolescent Suicide Attempts: Is Suicide Contagious?" *Journal of Adolescent Health Care*, 3 (January 1983).

Robbins, William. "The Loner: From Shy Football Player to 'Crazy Pat,' " *New York Times*, August 22, 1986.

Robbins, William. "3d Suicide Stuns Students in Omaha," *New York Times*, February 11, 1986.

Rosenberg, Mark. "Cluster Suicides." Paper presented at the National Conference on Youth Suicide, Washington, D.C., June 19, 1985.

Rounsaville, Bruce J., and Weissman, Myrna M. "A Note on Suicidal Behaviors among Intimates," *Suicide and Life-Threatening Behavior*, 1 (Spring 1980), p. 1.

Russo, Frank. "The Deadball Era. Suicides," www.thedeadballera.crosswinds.net, 2002.

Sagan, Carl, and Druyan, Ann. *Comet*. New York: Random House, 1985.

Schmidtke, A., and Häfner, H. "The Werther effect after television films: New evidence for an old hypothesis," *Psychological Medicine*, 18 (1988), pp. 665–76.

Sciacca, Joe, and Murphy, Shelley. "Probers Seek Answers to Tragic Triple Suicides," *Boston Herald,* March 16, 1985.

Sedano, David. "Escondido Post Office Worker Shoots Down Wife, Colleagues," Associated Press, August 11, 1989.

Seiden, R. H., and Spence, M. "A tale of 2 bridges: Comparative suicide incidence on the Golden Gate and San Francisco–Oakland Bay bridges," *Omega: Journal of Death and Dying,* 14(3) (1983), pp. 201–209.

Severo, Richard. "Man Immolates Himself in Times Sq." *New York Times,* July 19, 1970.

Shepherd, Daphne, and Barraclough, B. M. "Suicide Reporting: Information or Entertainment?" *British Journal of Psychiatry,* 132 (1978).

Shuster, Alvin. "Czech Immolates Himself by Fire," *New York Times,* January 17, 1969.

Shuster, Alvin. "Czech Protester Dies of His Burns," *New York Times,* January 20, 1969.

Singer, Margaret Thaler, and Lalich, Janja. *Cults in Our Midst.* San Francisco: Jossey-Bass, 1995.

Smock, Frederick A. "Group Forms in Wake of Suicide," Worcester, MA, *Telegram,* April 22, 1986.

Sonneck, G.; Etzersdorfer, E.; and Nagel-Kuess, S. "Imitative suicide on the Viennese subway," *Social Science and Medicine,* 38 (1994), pp. 453–57.

Spoonhour, Anne. "The First Few Days Are The Hardest," *People,* 23 (February 18, 1985), p. 7.

Stack, Steven. "The effect of the media on suicide: Evidence from Japan, 1955–1985," *Suicide and Life-Threatening Behavior,* 26(2) (1996), pp. 132–42.

Stack, Steven. "A reanalysis of the impact of non-celebrity suicides—a research note," *Social Psychiatry and Psychiatric Epidemiology,* 25(5) (1990a), pp. 269–73.

Stack, Steven. "Celebrities and suicide: A taxonomy and analysis, 1948–1983," *American Sociological Review,* 52 (June 1987), pp. 401–12.

Stack, Steven. "Divorce, suicide, and the mass-media—an analysis of differential identification, 1948–1980." *Journal of Marriage and The Family,* 52(2) (1990b), pp. 553–60.

Stack, Steven. "Media coverage as a risk factor in suicide," *Injury Prevention,* Suppl. 4 (December 2002), pp. 30–32.

Stack, Steven. "Social correlates of suicide by age: Media impacts." In A. Leenaars (ed.), *Life Span Perspectives of Suicide: Timelines in the Suicide Process*. New York: Plenum Press, 1991, pp. 187–213.

Stack, Steven. "The Effect of the Jonestown Suicides on American Suicide Rates," *Journal of Social Psychology*, 119 (1983).

Stack, Steven. "The effect of the media on suicide—the great-depression." *Suicide and Life-Threatening Behavior*, 22(2) (1992), pp. 255–67.

Stack, Steven. Personal communications, 1985, 1986, 2003.

Steiger, Brad, and Hewes. Hayden. *UFO Missionaries Extraordinary*. New York: Pocket Books, 1976.

Stewart, Sally Ann. "Did Andrew Chilstrom Have to Die?" *USA Today*, February 6, 1985.

Tabachnick, Norman. "The Psychology of Fatal Accident," in *Essays in Self-Destruction*. New York: Science House, 1967.

Taylor, Charles S. "Comets—Are They Linked to Suicides?" Minden, LA, *Press-Herald*, April 7, 1986.

Taylor, Paul. "Cluster Phenomenon of Young Suicides Raises 'Contagion' Theory," *Washington Post*, March 11, 1984.

Valente, M. "History of Suicide," in *Suicide: Assessment and Intervention*. Norwalk, CT: Appleton-Century-Crofts, 1984.

Vilas, Joseph. Personal communication, 2002.

Walden, Geoff. "Dad Blames Son's Death on TV Movie," *Gannett Westchester Newspaper*, February 21, 1985.

Wasserman, I. M. "Imitation and suicide: a reexamination of the Werther Effect," *American Sociological Review*, 49 (1984), pp. 427–36.

Wetherall, William. "Japanese Youth and the Yukiko Syndrome," *Far Eastern Economic Review*, July 17, 1986.

Whipple, Fred L. *The Mystery of Comets*. Washington, D.C.: Smithsonian, 1985.

Whited, Lana. "Covering the schoolhouse tragedies—after Columbine," *Roanoke Times*, March 16, 2001.

Whitson, W. (trans.) *The Works of Flavius Josephus*. New York: World Publishing House, 1875.

Williams, Lena. "The Life and Death of Justin, 14," *New York Times*, March 14, 1984.

Williams, Tom. *Post-Traumatic Stress Disorders of the Vietnam Veteran*. Washington, D.C.: Disabled American Veterans, 1980.

Wilson, Jeff. "Marilyn Monroe: She Would Have Been 60 Today," Nashua, NH, *Telegraph,* June 2, 1986.

Witcher, Gregory. "Spencer Wondering in Wake of Teen-ager's Suicide," *Boston Globe,* February 14, 1986.

Wolf, Rick, and Lester, David. "A Theoretical Basis for Counseling the Retired Professional Athlete." Unpublished paper, 1989.

Woodward, Kenneth L., et al. "How They Bend Minds," *Newsweek,* 112:23 (December 1978), p. 4.

Workman, Angela. Personal communication, 2003.

Woutat, Donald, and Harmon, Amy, "3 Killed, 8 Injured in Shooting Rampage," *Los Angeles Times,* November 15, 1991.

Acknowledgments

Many individuals assisted with the mountain of data and mainstream ideas for this book. My special thanks to my friend and editor, Patrick Huyghe, for his vision, patience, and support to see this book come to light, and to David Phillips for the first inspiration from his thoughts about the Werther effect. This was not an easy or pleasant book to write, so I appreciate the help I also received from: Steven Stack, Paul Marsden, Sue O'Halloran, Cheryl DiCara, Deb Stone, Bill Deane, David Lester, Lanny Berman, Daniel Cohen, Kenn Thomas, Maddy Gould, David Clark, Sally Brown, Marsha Stultz, Murray Straus, Joel Eichler, Frank Russo, Dick Topp, Glenn Stout, Frank Phelps, Rick Wolf, Jason Goodman, Ira Beckow, Tom Radecki, William Forstchen, Edward J. Rielly, Mark A. Hall, Karyl Chastain Beal, Russ Blatt, Richard Hendricks, Theo Paijmans, Paul Wendt, Gayton White, Steve Jones, Gordon Rutter, Tim Chapman, Michael G. McGough, Steve Miles Lewis, Jim Brandon, Jim Boyd, Michael Newton, Matt Drudge, Larry King, Stephen King, and you, the readers of my books. You and others like you are part of my World Wide Web of associates, some of whom have become friends, who have supplied me with the significant bits of the information I needed to build the case in this book. There is another dimension of encouragement too, of course. There are the publishing and personal friends and family who have been there with their emotional, fiscal, and friendly support, too, namely Michael Bershad, Josh Martino, David Chesanow, Bob Durant, Paul Herman, Roger Armstrong, and Rick Berger, and especially Malcolm, Caleb, Leslie, Libbet, Patrick, Philip, Peyton, Alex, Peter, Des, Sue, Anna, Jerry, Bill, and Dan.

And finally, I am grateful for the positive and helpful comments shared with me by the postal employees at Portland's Downtown Station, who gave me insight into the normal working conditions at the USPS.

My hope is that the evidence I have collected for *The Copycat Effect,* with the assistance of all these colleagues and friends, will cause a shift in the media's approach to these stories as they come to realize that their influence is much greater than they have ever realized.

> With appreciation and best wishes,
> Loren Coleman, M.S.W.
> Portland, Maine
> February 14, 2004

Index

Need Help?

If you are feeling suicidal and live in the United States, there are people you can talk to about it. Please call one of the following numbers. I also encourage the media to publish this contact information:

National Suicide Hotline
Trained volunteers and professional counselors
National Hopeline Network
1-800-SUICIDE
1-800-784-2433
Toll-free in the U.S.
24 hours / 7 days a week

ABOUT THE AUTHOR

Loren Coleman, M.S.W. (Simmons School of Social Work, 1978), has worked with children and families since 1967, and with the media since 1969. He has been a professor, consultant, project director, documentary filmmaker, and lecturer since 1980, at six New England universities and with the State of Maine Governor's Children's Cabinet, on suicide prevention, mass media, behavioral contagion, and school violence. Coleman's popular course, "The Documentary: Its Social, Political and Emotional Impact," was offered almost every semester, year-round, 1989–2003, at the University of Southern Maine. From 1983–1996, Coleman was a senior researcher at the Edmund S. Muskie School of Public Policy.

The author of twenty-seven books, Loren Coleman has written and lectured extensively on the impact of media, including in his book *Suicide Clusters* (Boston: Faber and Faber, 1987), which was a Psychology Book Club selection. He was widely interviewed about that book and appeared, for example, on *The Larry King Show* and *All Things Considered* to discuss it. His work on baseball player suicides was featured in *Sports Illustrated, The New York Times, The Sporting News,* in the Donnie Moore *ESPN Classics* documentary, and on scores of radio talk shows. He has been a guest interviewee on National Public Radio, major television networks, and other media forums, analyzing Bergenfield, Waco, Heaven's Gate, the Hemingway Curse, Columbine, and other related topics.

Today, Loren Coleman lives in Portland, Maine, while adjunct teaching at the university level and supporting positive educational and baseball experiences for his sons, Malcolm and Caleb.